"If you are in or entering the new world of digital filmmaking and you want to know everything about everything... read this book by Scott Billups. You'll be sorry if you don't."

David Lynch, director

"The seismic wave of change is collapsing on each of us. Unless we understand something of its nature, we will be swept away into a third intellectual world. This book has served as guide and mentor for me and has been a critical assist in helping me to understand the world of digital technology. For those who are bewildered and stumbling in their efforts to comprehend this new world of communication technology, this is the definitive manual."

Marlon Brando, actor

"Just what the doctor ordered for all the no-budget filmmakers raring to get their first feature down on digi-tape. Billups is low on filler and high on hard facts."

Film Ireland Magazine

"Don't be scared, just get out there and do it! Full of practical, down-to-earth advice and information, this primer reads easily and will help you avoid many common mistakes. A great one to get you going!"

Flatiron Magazine, article "*Make That Movie!*"

"An individualist in a town where conformity can be a Zen-like state of grace, Billups is not afraid to lock horns with mainstream studios as he seeks to invent 'the new Hollywood.' "

Paula Parisi, *Wired* Magazine

"Scott Billups is a 21st century revival tent evangelist, but the story he's preaching has nothing to do with pearly gates, fire or brimstone. Scott is pushing the gospel of Silicon."

Craig McGillivray, *RES* Magazine

"With this book Scott Billups has opened the Pandora's Box of moviemaking once and for all. He demystifies and simplifies the new digital paradigm as only a real expert can. Scott details with wit and passion how you can't be stopped if you really want to make a movie. Between the pixels, digicams, and cyberspace, herein lies real literature for a new millennium."

Philippe Mora, writer/director/producer

"A laid-back, self-taught maestro of digital production, Billups is out on the cutting edge."

Buzz Magazine, LA's Top 100 List

"Digital Moviemaking should be required reading for everyone from film-industry students to hardened movie moguls. It gives new perspective to the creative process of capturing the moving image, while focusing on aspiring filmmakers with 'credit-card budgets' who are challenging the status quo through digital technology."

Robert J. Estony, Director, Communications, Ikegami Electronics

"Billups has been on the cusp of some of the film and television industry's more revolutionary digital projects and techniques."

Ann Fisher, Post Magazine

"Clearly, Billups and some other directors, producers, and studios are edging closer to what all of filmdom is eyeing with amazement, apprehension, and, well, avarice: the dawning of the digital age of film. Scott Billups and others in the film industry are exploring the digital realm with the fervor of paleontologists on the dig of the century."

Peter Britton, Popular Science Magazine

"Billups conceived of the idea of modifying a video camera to plug directly into a computer's hard disk drive so that images can be digitally recorded."

Eric Taub, emmy Magazine

"One of the earliest evangelists of digital motion picture technology is Scott Billups. He offers the possibility that a new generation of true film auteurs will be able to mold their story with the same control as painters or novelists."

Steven D. Katz, best-selling author, Directing: Shot by Shot

MICHAEL WIESE PRODUCTIONS
www.mwp.com

Since 1981, Michael Wiese Productions has been dedicated to providing novice and seasoned filmmakers with vital information on all aspects of filmmaking and videomaking. We have published more than 60 books, used in over 500 film schools worldwide.

Our authors are successful industry professionals — they believe that the more knowledge and experience they share with others, the more high-quality films will be made. That's why they spend countless hours writing about the hard stuff: budgeting, financing, directing, marketing, and distribution. Many of our authors, including myself, are often invited to conduct filmmaking seminars around the world.

We truly hope that our publications, seminars, and consulting services will empower you to create enduring films that will last for generations to come.

We're here to help. Let us hear from you.

Sincerely,

Michael Wiese
Publisher, Filmmaker

THE FILMMAKER'S GUIDE TO THE 21ST CENTURY

DIGITAL MOVIEMAKING

SECOND EDITION

ALL THE SKILLS, TECHNIQUES, AND MOXIE YOU'LL
NEED TO TURN YOUR PASSION INTO A CAREER

SCOTT BILLUPS

vi

Published by Michael Wiese Productions
11288 Ventura Blvd., Suite 621
Studio City, CA 91604
tel. (818) 379-8799
fax (818) 986-3408
mw@mwp.com
www.mwp.com

Cover Design: Art Hotel
Book Layout: Gina Mansfield
Editor: Blake Snyder

Printed by McNaughton & Gunn, Inc., Saline, Michigan
Manufactured in the United States of America

ISBN 0-941188-80-9

Library of Congress Cataloging-in-Publication Data

Billups, Scott.
  Digital moviemaking : all the skills, techniques, and moxie you'll
need to turn your passion into a career / Scott Billups.-- 2nd ed.
      p. cm.
  ISBN 0-941188-80-9
  1. Digital cinematography. I. Title.
  TR860.B46 2003
  778.5'3--dc21
                                      2003000763

To

Warren Miller

For giving me my first paycheck in this industry
and for the example he has given us all as filmmakers

In Memory of

James Wong Howe

For teaching me to see light

TABLE OF CONTENTS

ACKNOWLEDGEMENTS

My first acknowledgment is to the readers of the first edition of this book because they have truly shaped this one. Some things that I thought were obvious weren't. Some things that I thought were self-explanatory weren't. But that which surprised me most of all was the enormous response from people who had taken their miniDV experience and successfully parleyed it into jobs and projects using much more professional crews and equipment.

In addition to her work as an editor for both *American Cinematographer* and *Editor's Guild Magazines*, Stephanie Argy is also an accomplished editor and visual effects artist. Her valiant attempt to shape my geek-ridden verbiage into some semblance of common vernacular is present on nearly every page. This book will be much easier to read because of her kind efforts.

I wrote the first edition of *Digital Moviemaking* while recovering from a serious ice climbing accident and must admit that the morphine drip in my arm accounted for a few errors. The most popular one occurred on page 43 where 2n should have been represented as 2 to the nth power. Nearly two hundred readers caught it. Many also noted the error on page 78 where I represented the D-1 data rate incorrectly. The person who caught the most errors was Glenn Estersohn who is a well-respected industry writer — so I made him my technical editor. Thanks, Glenn.

After delivering the Keynote address at the 2002 NAB convention, I was confronted by a number of people who wanted me to autograph their copies of *Digital Moviemaking*. Near the end of the line was a hulking young man named Kent Nichols who thrust his dog-eared, highlighted, and beat-up copy of *DM* out to me to sign. I've since used Kent on several projects including an HBO project and as a VF/X unit camera operator on a Discovery Channel show that I directed. I feel that people like Kent represent the future of this industry and, being a rather crusty curmudgeon myself, his personal observations and suggestions for this edition became a constant guide.

FOREWORD

BY ROGER CORMAN

Entertainment is entirely controlled by the populace. If it doesn't develop an audience it's gone. This is as true on the Net as it is with the big screen. Real talent is hard to fake. There are formulas and techniques that can help, but the really good stuff always shines through in the face of budgetary limitations.

The motion picture industry has always been an exclusionary affair. It takes lots of money to make a studio picture. Through the years Hollywood has created filters that let some people in and excludes others. Then along comes digital technology and the price point of entry becomes affordable to just about everyone. Hollywood reeled a bit but soon recovered by tightening up the filters. Then along comes the Internet and the doors are swung akimbo.

Virtually anyone with an idea and a few bucks can now create a motion picture. In most cases the movie itself won't really go anywhere, but the instantaneous presence that it generates within the industry is truly revolutionary. Sure there's a lot of bad cinema being made by this new cadre of digitally endowed moviemakers. What's new?

The future of cinema lies in the power of the pixel. The injection of fresh ideas and methodologies will only serve to mix up the metaphorical gene pool and empower a new generation of filmmakers.

With more channels of distribution there will be a greater demand for content, but less money to create it. The people who can create content the most cost-effectively will have a clear cut advantage. Heck, anyone can kick out a movie if you throw enough money around, but if you can tell a compelling story within the confines of a severely limited budget, then you're a true moviemaker and the future is yours to shape.

With more than 500 motion pictures to his credit Roger Corman is the hands-down, all-time, reigning king of moviemaking.

Noted for his keen ability to spot young talent, his most lasting legacy will undoubtedly be the legion of producers, directors, writers, and actors he has fostered, among them: Jack Nicholson, Francis Ford Coppola, Peter Bogdanovich, Martin Scorsese, Ron Howard, Joe Dante, James Cameron, and the author of this book.

INTRODUCTION

PIXELMONGER MANIFESTO

This is not another introductory, "How-To-Make-A-Movie" book. It is not intended to take someone who just got their first camcorder and a personal computer and walk them through the production process.

This book is geared to professional-minded people who have hopefully had prior experience in some aspect of production and who understand the fundamental difference between a hobby and a career. It is about how to be successful at making movies. Not the kind of movies that you have to bribe your friends to watch, but the kind of movies that 14-year-old boys, on their first date with the girl next door, line up for on a Saturday night.

MiniDV moviemaking is not about introducing content into the conventional motion picture distribution stream. It never was. It never will be. It is about an affordable, entry level acquisition and postproduction environment that gives people an opportunity to experiment and demonstrate their abilities. It is about people going out and self-starting a project, involving others who might or might not find that they have a flair or interest in making movies.

You get something good down on miniDV and then you show it around; festivals, private screenings, DVD, Internet — whatever. If someone likes it they might give you a crack at a commercial project that will then be shot on a professional acquisition format like film or HD.

There have been a handful of projects shot on miniDV that have gained a modicum of success, but even the few, established industry luminaries who have used miniDV cinematically seem to regret their "artistic" choices.

Just because you can, doesn't mean you should.

The aesthetics of integrity that once endowed emerging moviemakers has been corrupted by snake-oil-salesmen who promise to throw open the gates of Hollywood to anyone who buys their latest product. They offer hardware, software, cameras, and accessories, as though without the newest, latest, fastest, thinnest your chances of success are something less.

My goal is to kick your professionalism, your toolset, and your image quality up a notch so that you can compete in the real world of cinema. After getting your feet wet with miniDV I want you to consider moving up to DVCPRO-50 or DigiBeta. If you're thinking of working in NTSC, I want you to consider PAL.

After you've learned the methodology and made your mistakes, and it finally comes time for you to make your cinematic entree, the only formats you should consider using are Hi-Definition video or Film.

There are no simple solutions, secret tricks, instant remedies, or gizmos that will turn you into a moviemaker. The odds are against you for a number of reasons. Some we can do something about, some we can't. My only promise to you is that by the time you've finished this book, your odds of success will have improved.

CLICHÉS THAT KILL

The word "passion" gets thrown around a lot in this industry. "You've got to have a real passion for filmmaking" they'll tell you. It is an easy phrase to use and looks real good in print, but the rancid alleyways of Hollywood Boulevard are full of kids who came to this town with a belly full of passion. Passion blinds you, and it is only your unyielding death grip on reality that will guarantee any measure of success in this business.

There are other gratuitous clichés that get thrown around like, "Have faith in your abilities." As though with faith alone you can surmount all obstacles. Well, get off your knees unless you're going for my zipper 'cause there is no cosmic external force that will turn a bad script into gold or make the clock move slower so you can catch up with your production schedule. There are no new stories to tell, no angles to exploit, no trends to follow.

The path through Hollywood was worn smooth long ago by people wearing shoes much bigger than yours or mine. Craft is important in making a quality movie, but without a firm grasp of the realities of the market and industry, you're just another slab of meat spread out on the deli tray.

Jeff Dowd is a prominent and outspoken Hollywood producer who drags his long, unbroken string of successful movies around like toilet paper stuck to the bottom of his shoe. Here is a man who is hard to impress. Perhaps it is his unyielding devotion to the fundamentals that has allowed such a gregarious character to flourish in Hollywood. *"Last year in the United States alone there were thousands of movies shot on [miniDV],"* he told those in attendance at a recent IFP seminar. *"They all sucked!"*

This whole wave of independent moviemaking is about to collapse on itself like the truckload of rotten tomatoes that it is. With so much easy access and hype, it has festered into a vast amalgam of self-indulgent mediocrity.

The "Indie look" has become more of a marketing strategy than alternative methodology. The irresistible lure of instant "hip" has caused a growing number of directors who should know better, to prove they don't.

I recently attended the Cannes Film Festival orientation and it was quite an eye-opener. Of the thousands of applicants vying for the four American spaces in the festival, there were only a dozen of us sitting there. That's thousands of lives that were put on hold, houses mortgaged, life savings drained, marriages strained, and I'll bet every one of them thought they were a shoo-in for the Palme d'Or.

The assault of thousands of semi-literate people with their half-baked, get-rich-quick schemes has taken its toll on the motion picture industry. A few well-connected kids with famous parents might make a ripple here or there, but the odds are stacked against you and they are simply overwhelming.

To make a living as a moviemaker in the digital age, you need to have good communication skills, a good eye, and an above average understanding of the desktop production environment. You also need to understand what motivates and engages people, and how to push their buttons.

Next, you need balls of steel (or ovaries as the case may be), and skin as thick as old shoe leather. A strong persistence of vision that borders on "jackass stubborn" will also serve you well as you continually forge past those who feel the urgent need to add their *dos centavos* to your little gem of a project.

Above all, you'll need an inspired point of view as well as the will and determination to get your project made. Even IF you possess all of the previous
abilities, without consummate people skills you've only got another pathetic
sideshow looking to hitch a ride with the grandest circus of them all.

To quote the always acerbic Dennis Miller, "From Balinese shadow plays to
bullfighters in Madrid to the porn studios of the San Fernando Valley, the
only human desire more universal than the urge to put on a show is the
urge to get paid for it."

So welcome to the freak show, my friend. I sure hope you're wearing your
bullet proof, Eddie Bauer safari-slash-director's jacket because there's nothing
that this industry loves more than a well-dressed corpse.

1 ⋗ THE MYTH OF TECHNOLOGY

*"Our myths need to keep up with our
understanding of the universe."*
Joseph Campbell

This is perhaps the easiest time in history to be successful. There is no other period in the timeline of human endeavor when so many people had the tools to do so much damage to the status quo.

I'm sure there are those who will accuse this book of glossing over the technical details or spending too much time with peripheral politics. Truth is, you don't really need to know all the tweaky little nuances of this digital stuff. The beauty of technology is that success isn't dependent on whether or not you understand how it works, all you need to know is what it does.

And when you get to the end of your production, hopefully with the best looking movie that your budget will allow, you'll actually have a clue as to what to do with it. To do that you'll need to have a decent understanding of the various industries involved and why they act the way they do. I've seen far too many aspiring artists stopped dead in their tracks because they lacked the most fundamental understanding of the real-world workings of the industry they were aspiring to.

There are no brick walls, only seemingly impenetrable gaps in our understanding.

I've always found that Tokyo, Japan is perhaps the very best place to take the pulse of technology. Not so much the actual use of that technology, but rather the tempo of the bits and pieces that are marching towards us over the binary horizon. Like any large city, Tokyo is divided into numerous thematic regions that pander to the various aspects of the global human condition. My two favorite districts are Akihabara and Shinagawa.

Akihabara is the gizmo capital of the world. Imagine an electronics store from six years in the future that covers more than a square mile. Every storefront, every sidewalk, every alleyway, packed with a mind-numbing assortment of the guts of future technology.

I bought a 15" flat panel monitor from a street vendor, four years before they were even mentioned here in the U.S. My first ophthalmic quality virtual headset was purchased from a merchant I found deep within the bowels of a dark alleyway. Every square foot of this technological utopia is covered with stores and venders, both large and small, selling everything from bootleg chips to teleconference videophones.

Shinagawa on the other hand, is the button-down yin to the haphazard yang of Akihabara. There's technology here all right, but it's not in plain view. Shinagawa is the heart of the global technocracy of image and sound, and the blood that courses through its veins is the hard currency of the world.

I like to stay at a particular hotel there that looks out over a lovely pastoral park.

Across the street is a stately tearoom complete with shoji screens and an ambiance of elegant industrialism. Off to the side of this ersatz tearoom is a rather formal lady sitting at a plain desk. Behind her stands a nondescript doorway that leads directly into the bowels of Sony corporate headquarters.

>>>>> Day in the life of Melrose Ave.
Digital production hasn't always been convenient as
this "location" shoot from the late '80s illustrates.

The first time Sony invited me for a visit was just after finishing my fully digital show called *A Day In The Life Of Melrose Ave*. The idea was to shoot and edit a show entirely on the hard disk of a computer and then take the computer to the television station and broadcast it directly from the hard disk. An entire show created entirely within the digital domain and never touching videotape. Attempting that today is no big thing, a couple Fire Wire drives plugged into a laptop, but this was back in the early '90s, well before the era of affordable gigabyte drives.

Well, the show was fun but somewhat anti-climactic domestically because hardly anyone realized what had just been done. There was no reference or context, and as I've come to realize, technology without context is irrelevant. Not so with the Japanese. Within two weeks of wrapping production, I found myself sitting in the Sony tearoom. Upstairs, in this ultimate shrine to the next big thing, I discovered an endless procession of production environments that give a razor sharp oracle of what is around our collective corner.

Now keep in mind that I had been writing about digital film and video production technology for five of the leading industry magazines for over six years. If anyone should have a clue about this stuff it should be me. What I saw completely blew my mind. How could I have been so blind to what was in the pipes? What I began to realize was that what we perceive as the bleeding edge of technology, even those of us writing about it, is only a carefully orchestrated ballet of illusion.

Once back from Japan, the digital camera concept became an obsession, every iteration getting smaller, with greater capacity and more resolution. The first truly luggable (as opposed to portable) camera system came off the benches in mid-1993. It took the RGB signal directly off of the imaging

Photo: Eric Taub

chips and recorded it in compressed 8-bit; 4:1:1 to the hard drive using a prototype Video Explorer videographic board custom made by my good friend, and nerd savant, Brett Bilbrey (now head of Apple Video Systems).

Since we were going for quality as opposed to quantity, the drive could only hold 23 seconds of video at a time. Still, we used it on several jobs and kept on moving.

<<<<< The Porta-Cam was dubbed by my friends as the first "luggable" digital camcorder. The batteries alone weighed more than twenty pounds.

Yeah, I know it's dorky-looking, but hey, it worked. Who'd-a believed that in less than five years even better resolution would be available in a pocket sized form-factor. Well, a couple weeks after the initial unveiling I found myself back in Japan, walking the hallowed halls of the undisputed leader in digital cameras, Ikegami.

We basically talked about where we saw this whole thing going, me talking about a future of low-cost digital cameras with enough resolution to be blown up to film, while they talked of distribution mechanisms that allowed high-resolution video to be instantaneously shuttled around on a personal level. I tried not to smirk at their preposterous notions of global, broadband communications.

I must've done something right because they let me borrow a digital camera head with a prototype imaging unit. They even supplied the chip schematics and wiring diagrams. My old friend, Scott Achmoody, stepped up to bat and made an even smaller and more powerful ITU-601 videographic board, which we hot-wired into the camera's encoder, (Sorry, Ikegami) and created a working digital camcorder.

OK, it wasn't the prettiest thing you ever saw but my SMPTE (Society of Motion Picture and Television Engineers) friends went nuts. Being a long-time SMPTE guy myself, that was enough for me.

<<<<< The Digi-Cam wasn't very pretty but its images were. The first true 601 camcorder that wasn't under a cloak of corporate secrecy gave semi-dependable service for almost a year. It was used on several commercials and music videos, and an infomercial.

A few years later I got a call from someone at the Academy of Television Arts & Sciences, asking if I knew that Avid was campaigning for an Emmy. It seems they were under the impression that they had developed the digital camcorder. They'd taken the same camera head (now called the HL-76), updated the same basic design and called it the CamCutter. I reminded them that there was a very nice article in the August '93 issue of their own *emmy* Magazine, with a lovely picture of me standing there holding my homemade digital camcorder that predated the Avid claim by more than two years. Never really heard much about it after that.

But I did get invited back to Japan. This time to give a presentation on digital production techniques at Matsushita (Panasonic). So here I was, back in Shinagawa, and they've put me up at the same hotel I was staying at when I was visiting Sony — what a coincidence. I had sent a bunch of projects that I'd been working on over to them several months before so they could process them. I wasn't really sure what process meant, but I figured that whatever it was, it wasn't going to hurt the resolution. The car shows up, I hop in and a few seconds later they let me off in front of a rather nondescript building. From what I could tell, it was just around the block from Sony.

The total absence of technology was what hit me first, and the enormous pyramidal vault of the interior. Easily ten stories high, each floor concentrically smaller than the last. After a few seconds, you adjust to the sheer dynamics of the lobby's volume as you're hit with the soothing sounds of a babbling mountain stream.

There on the lobby floor, meandering through hundreds of tons of perfect granite rocks and boulders, is a perfect mountain stream. With trout! Gotta tell ya, I'm a pretty ardent fly fisherman and this place had me going. An enormous Sequoia was laying on its side, its topmost surface hewn and polished to the perfect definition of wood. Off to the left, the stream passed before the entrance to a cave, apparently created by the random collision of several house-sized boulders in some theoretical cataclysm.

A tiny wooden bridge gently arched over the stream, allowing access to the enigmatic cavern. As you set foot among the mighty boulders you were guided through a few twists and turns before entering the most hi-tech theater environment in the world.

They had up-converted everything that I had sent them into their Hi-Vision (Hi-Def) format and had handed me a little controller that would transmit my processed video images directly to their Hi-Vision satellite, along with the live camera shot of my presentation. The resultant multi-stream signal could then be mixed real-time at any of the six locations that were receiving it. At each location, it was being projected onto an eighteen-by-thirty-two-foot electronic theater screen. This was back in 1994.

I'm not invited to Japan because I'm such a smarmy good guy and they just love my company. They haul my shaggy butt over there and give me access to nifty new toys because I do non-conventional things with their technology and because I create content. The two commodities that the Japanese have the least of, and value most. It was a relationship of mutual carnality that continues to this day.

The point I'm trying to make is that whatever hype or digital palaver you've been buying into, well, just don't buy into it to deeply. The man behind the curtain is Japanese and personally I'm very, very glad.

It has been my experience that the Japanese are hard but ethical business-men who constantly exhibit strong moral character. Society can only absorb so much technology at a time without killing itself off or re-igniting the Luddite rebellion.

Just imagine if the snakes that slither through the gutters of Hollywood actu-ally had a say in matters. They'd glut the market, take their booty, and retire in a heartbeat. You know it, I know it, and they know it.

The flow of technology is strictly regulated. It is a good thing. Get used to it.

So, what does this mean to our timeline of broadband digital movies and film-resolution cameras? Silicon, the relentless equalizer, has empowered a new generation of filmmakers by releasing them from the shackles of bur-geoning budgets. The enviable result of this rampant technogogary is the reemergence of the professional generalist. One person, armed with the power of silicon, who can perform the job of many.

While budgets fall in the face of innovation, the craft of cinema unfortu-nately suffers, too. By simply allowing more people access to the tools of the trade, we are creating a vast glut of mediocrity. Not that the studios don't kick out the mindless piece of crap on a regular basis. Difference is, people still pay good money to see their big budget, mindless pieces of crap.

In almost direct opposition to the fundamentals of enfranchised production, the studios aren't really interested in saving money. On the contrary, the bigger the better. They are in the business of moving money around. They want sure bets and solid investments to take to their shareholders. As long as teenage boys need a place to take a date, Hollywood blockbusters are a safe and sound investment. Russell Crowe and Julia Roberts are quantifiable investments. Leading edge digital-production concepts are not.

FODDER

You, however, as an enfranchised (independent) filmmaker must deal with an extremely large mechanism that is deeply vested in propagating an endless stream of festival fare. Kinda like spreading manure on your strawberry field. Spread enough of it and pretty soon something sweet's going to start popping up.

The fact that there are a lot of bad movies getting made is kind of a good thing. It means that the tools are becoming more accessible. Look at any other form of expression — painting, sculpting, or writing, for example. Everyone has access to the tools of creation. Everyone has the ability to put some words to paper, or pixels to liquid crystal as the case may be. A lot of people give it a shot and nothing happens. Doesn't necessarily mean that their words are less valuable. As the tools become affordable, the craft becomes an art form.

While art is very democratic, there are very few moviemakers who are truly artists. For the most part, successful moviemakers are first and foremost, good businessmen.

DIGITAL UBIQUITY

Virtually any contemporary home computer has the capacity to create a movie. It is becoming as ubiquitous as the pencil. In a few years your personal movie will become the equivalent of a calling card, your statement of who you are and what you believe. People will drop in to your site, watch your movie, and get a pretty good idea of what you're up to.

Perhaps you've key-worded it so it shows up in a broad spectrum of search engines. People start migrating to your "MooV" and realize that you've actually got something different to say or the way you say something common finally makes sense to them. That's the trick, you know. Taking an aspect of someone's life and giving them a fresh perspective on it. You figure out how to do that on a dependable basis and you've got a fan for life.

Then one day some guy with a co-opted, time-share satellite feed sees your movie and links it to a friend in London who agrees that it has a certain commercial *je ne sais quoi*. They offer to set up a theatrical exhibition and you agree. The on-line hype machine starts churning out PR and sending even more clips of your movie out to the numerous venue sites. And finally, when your pixels hit the screen, the crowd goes wild. What's not to like?

On-line exhibition is already a popular alternative release mechanism for both low- and high-resolution moviemakers. Every studio, every network, every Tom, Dick, and Scotty has their own website dedicated to seriously denting the status quo, and it's only going to get faster.

THE WORM TURNS

Time was when film grain meant you were watching a quality story. Generations of kids grew up accepting the cinematic nuance of film as a qualitative Holy Grail. Today's market grew up on the luminous images of video and computer games. Grain doesn't hold as much subliminal impact for them.

We are currently witnessing the emergence of digital communication innovations that allow us to download movies and play them on handheld devices. As much as we might like to believe that the cinema screen represents the pinnacle of success, it is access, more than size, that will drive this industry into the future.

What we sacrifice for the crisp pictures and clear sound of the new generation of digital films is the subtle richness and full spectrum of emotion that the projected medium provides. It is simply harder to be swept away by a tiny image.

The question is, "Will the audience notice?" That's all that really matters. I've spent my life behind film cameras. I can field strip and clean a Mitchell MK II in a swamp at midnight and come away with a clean gate. If anyone's gonna give you a negative report, it'd be some crusty ole curmudgeon like me. But I can't. I'd actually like to, but I just can't.

Digital isn't film, it won't be for several more years, but what it does deliver is a far more efficient method to produce and distribute motion pictures. Movies like *The Blair Witch Project* stand as a testament that resolution isn't nearly as important as a good story line. If you keep the audience involved, they will forgive just about anything.

Bottom line, digital projections are generally better for everyone. The inherent resolution and image quality of a well-projected digital image in many instances surpasses a majority of film projections. Industry pundits will try to argue resolution and colorspace issues, and to a certain extent they have a point. Fact is, if you follow the basic tenants of this book, your project, even if it's an ultra-low budget affair, will have the potential to compete with studio productions. And this, my friend, is where the solid human waste hits the air re-circulation device.

THE GATE KEEPERS

The reason it is so damn hard to break into the film business is that it is a tightly-controlled industry. Always has been. To succeed you must understand how the industry works, and to do that we must step, ever-so-lightly, outside the bounds of political correctness.

A hundred years ago the film industry was dealing with a dramatic evolution in both technology and methodology. The structure that the movie industry adopted was based on the work of some of this country's most respected industrialists. Thomas Edison and Henry Ford created a production methodology of such efficiency that Hollywood has never again accomplished so much, with so few, for so little.

Problem was, their formula presumed that each person in the process was highly proficient at their profession and it further presumed that they possessed a civilized sense of ethics.

Gradually, as more and more nonessential personnel infiltrated the studio system, it began to buckle from inexperience and graft. Nepotism became standard practice, and with it came the inevitable decline in the cost-effectiveness of the production process itself.

The current need for adaptation to a new set of technologies has created the same dilemma that the studio system was faced with back in 1902. The problem lies in the fact that Hollywood has very little direction today. The outstanding leaders in the field of technology and innovation have all run off to Nicosia, California (home of ILM) where they rewrite the industry behind closed doors.

Hollywood has become a corporate village where original thinkers are absorbed into the contextual womb of the enterprise. Of course once inside, the gates are locked as the suspendered MBAs and lawyers surround the fresh meat like the picadors of Pamplona.

FILTERS

As the single most prolific producer in the history of the motion picture industry stated in the foreword to the first edition of this book, "*Through the years Hollywood has created filters that let some people in and excludes others. Then along comes digital technology and the price point of entry becomes affordable to just about everyone. Hollywood reeled a bit but soon recovered by tightening up the filters.*"

Since Roger Corman wrote those words in 1999, the assault on Hollywood has more than doubled, as have the filters that bar access. The days of the "One Hit Wonders" have faded away as acquisition executives realized that a filmmaker without a firm grasp of the realities of this industry is just another liability.

Theatrical moviemaking is not a hobby, it is a profession; one of the more sought-after professions in the world I would imagine. As professions go, it's probably easier to become a proficient moviemaker than a quantum mathematics engineer, yet harder than say, a championship race car driver.

Any major industry that is predicated on craft has a sophisticated set of filters that prevent unqualified persons from getting in and bugger'n the works. Just because you show up outside the pit gates of the Indianapolis Speedway with a brand new McLaren MP4, doesn't mean that they're going to let you race on Memorial Day. The important thing to realize here is the difference between empowerment and enablement.

Low-cost video production environments have been with us for a while, and the sophisticated up-conversion algorithms that allow us to turn the video image into a frame of film have been around since the '80s.

Video filmmakers have been enabled for some time; however it's only recently, due to technological leaps in the Internet and alternative channels of media distribution, that videographers have been empowered to become filmmakers.

On the Internet, everyone has an equal opportunity to succeed or fail based on the quality or commerciality of his or her project. The Internet offers an ingenious moviemaker an opportunity to skirt around the filters by accessing the market directly.

Innovative Internet campaigns have created numerous success stories out of projects that otherwise might not have seen any action outside of a limited festival run.

This gaping loophole in the channels of distribution is a dangerous thing to an industry so heavily vested in convention. As hard as they try, the people who run the media can't get a foothold on the Internet. It moves too fast for organizations that are so lumbering and slow.

NEW RULES

The name of the game is content. C. O. N.T. E. N.T. Anyone who has an urge to dive into the pixelated pool of digital production should have it tattooed to the inside of their eyelids. Anything that you create, regardless of whether you call it a digital movie or on-line entertainment, is content.

We've got an entirely new environment here, with new rules and new opportunities. The infertile mind sees this merely as a way to combine existing environments rather than the entirely new communications modality that it truly is.

The studios are all actively trying to get involved by re-releasing preexisting catalogues. Sorry guys, shovel-ware doesn't work. They talk of generating new revenue streams rather than of fostering new experiences; eyeballs rather than minds. If you approach the Internet as just a way to make some money, all you'll end up doing is making money.

If, however, you approach it as a way to enrich people's lives by creating content that speaks to the essence of their humanity, you'll be contributing to an entirely new communications paradigm that has the potential to change the timeline of human endeavor. Oh yeah, and you'll end up making lots of money.

MOVING TARGET

Traditionally, films targeting the ever-changing trends of the 12-to-17 year old youth market have always needed the most expensive advertising campaigns and account for the vast majority of ticket sales. Now that this demographic also represent the fastest-growing segment of the Internet market, the motion picture industry is scurrying to adapt.

According to the latest MPAA estimates, Web marketing has doubled from last year and now accounts for 1% of the 30 million dollars spent marketing a contemporary theatrical release. Is this an example of how cost-effective Web marketing has become or of how obtuse Hollywood is?

THE STUDIO JUGGERNAUT

There seems to be a prevailing mindset in the independent film community that the studios are the enemy; they are not. It has been my experience that some of the sharpest minds and most genuinely warm people in the business work for them. It is only after you step outside their gates into the swampy marshlands that you must watch out for the snakes and vermin.

The studio system has given us some of the industry's greatest talents on both sides of the lens and created such a mythos out of our little manufacturing process that you'd be hard pressed to find anyone, anywhere in the world, who wouldn't love to be part of it. And yet even I can't help taking an occasional poke or two at such a plodding beast.

When I first started working in this industry, I shot on short ends that were left over from studio productions and donated to emerging filmmakers. When I first started experimenting with using personal computers in motion picture production, Universal Studios gave me an office on the lot at a <u>greatly</u> reduced rate.

More recently, Warner Brothers was gracious enough to let us shoot Faye Dunaway's Hi-Def movie on their back lot. For them it was a chance to see how the new technologies integrated into cinematic studio methodologies. For me it was a chance to work with friends on my favorite set.

<<<<< Warner Brothers, Mid-Western Town (*Gilmore Girls*) set was the location of the first concerted effort to use cinematic Hi-Definition within the conventional back-lot studio superstructure. It was a lot less painful than we all imagined.

There is a tendency to hold the studios accountable for every problem a filmmaker encounters. Lack of support, lack of funding, lack of resources, lack of distribution. This misperception stems from a basic misunderstanding of the way the current studio system works.

Studios do not make movies anymore. They make deals, and serve as a hub for numerous "mini-majors" who generally further subcontract to production companies (my own Electric SandBox Productions is one), who then hire freelancers to augment their own in-house staff. In the big five major studios, there are probably less than a few thousand actual employees, but they in turn support millions of people as their connections expand.

In a way, the movie studios are the ultimate metaphor for the Internet. A central hub connecting smaller, more mobile versions of itself, who in turn rely on numerous, smaller independent companies to actually create the content. Problem is, new distribution mechanisms start at the bottom and don't need the top. The feet simply disconnect from the rest of the body and walk away.

The new generation of studios will be online. More of a group of people who agree upon a common set of digital standards than a physical environment. The new studio is unencumbered by the need to maintain a physical property and the obligatory staff of lawyers and MBAs.

More than half of my most recent movie was shot on a chroma key sound stage, which meant that an enormous amount of environments and virtual set pieces needed to be made. All but two of the fifteen people who comprised my post-production crew live in either Spain, France, Italy, or the U.K., and none of us have ever met personally.

We used a private area of my PixelMonger website to exchange data sets and coordinate our designs. By standardizing our computer platform and applications we only needed to post a single, low-resolution reference frame and FTP the application's setup file. Since I did all of the rendering here in L.A., the actual data transfers were quite small.

As I write the second edition of this book, we are in production on a half dozen shows for Discovery Channel. They are all very ambitious and cinematically engaging projects that deal with the recreation of significant events in the timeline of human history. Our production crews are in Lithuania, Greece, and the U.K. When they wrap out of their present locations, they'll head to Hawaii, Argentina, and the Orient. We communicate daily via the

Internet, and coordinate the hundreds of plates and elements that will comprise this ambitious project.

Because of its global proximity, virtual studios are able to resource a high-density mix of production people and creatives. With increased efficiency comes increased economy.

The ability to collaborate globally has opened the very process of production up to the point where nearly every significant motion picture in the last several years has elements that were created outside the gates of Hollywood, a trend that will only escalate.

2 ⋮⋗ LIGHT BEAMS & PIXEL STREAMS

"Those who know will always have a job.
Those who know why, will always be in charge."
Pete Fasciano

Whether your movie is destined for celluloid projection or pixel streams from the latest digital projector, there are common sets of production methodologies that prevail. Once you've got a handle on the basics, all that is left is craft.

We've all been to a store where numerous video cameras are hooked up to video monitors. Many people make qualitative judgments based on this information and are disappointed when the final image quality falls well short. The images of a four-hundred dollar consumer video camera could well look comparable to a forty-thousand dollar DigiBeta under these consumer-orientated conditions. All that you're really seeing is the output from the CCD, pumped through a composite encoder, and projected on a poorly adjusted, low-end consumer monitor that is being bombarded with florescent lights.

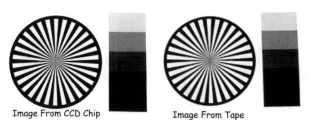

Image From CCD Chip   Image From Tape

<<<<< The higher the resolution of the recording format, the closer the taped image resembles the image off of the chip, but unless you're recording uncompressed 4:4:4 RGB, there will always be a noticeable difference.

The only way to truly evaluate the signals of different cameras and formats is off of the recording medium. If the system you're considering is a direct-to-disk system, then the signal off of the disk is all that matters. If the system uses video tape, then that image is all that matters.

Shoot a natural scene under natural light and then shoot a scene under artificial lights. Make sure to include a person, some plants, some brightly colored plastic items. Then shoot a chart.

CHART YOUR COURSE

If you've got a high-quality color printer you can download one of the charts from the camera section of *www.PixelMonger.com* and print them out, but remember that the color rendition will have jumped through a lot of hoops by the time it gets in front of your lens.

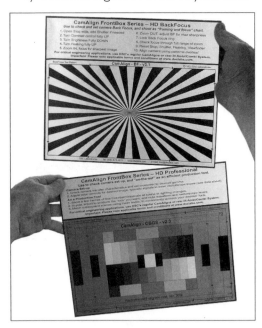

Better yet, shell out a few bucks and buy yourself a chart. It will serve you well for years to come and go further toward helping you develop and define a consistent "look" than any other single investment

My most hearty recommendation for emerging digital moviemakers is the CamAlign FrontBox Series - HD Professional chart which has a Back Focus chart on one side (checks focus and sharpness) and the industry standard CamAlign chart on the other (*www.dsclabs.com*).

>>>>> Calibration is the most noticeable difference between an image acquired by an amateur and one acquired by a professional. The key to professional quality calibration is not so much in *owning* a professional quality chart as it is in *using* one.

Buy yourself a blank videotape, or several if you're comparing formats, set up your chart and shoot it with everything you can get your hands on.

Immediately after shooting a few seconds of chart, get someone's face in the picture, even if it's just the pimply-faced stock boy. Regardless of how much I might blither on about the importance of comparative calibration, cinematography isn't about making charts look good.

Once you've got your tapes, run your images through the Waveform Monitor in Apple's Final Cut Pro, Avid's XpressDV, Adobe Premiere, or Synthetic Aperture's Color Finesse. If you don't have access to these programs, find someone with a Vectorscope and a Waveform Monitor and ask them to help you check out your tapes.

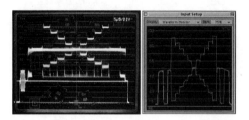

<<<<< **The truly revolutionary aspect of digital technology is that it gives us such easy access to high-quality diagnostic tools.**

Since the care and feeding of the Waveform Monitor/Vectorscope requires more pages than a meager tome such as this can do justice to, I'm going to defer you to (*www.adamwilt.com*). Adam Wilt is a highly respected Bay Area cinematographer and journalist with extensive credentials in both arenas. My favorite explanation of how to calibrate and standardize your video signal using the WFM & V-scope are from a two-article series that he wrote for *DV* Magazine, both of which are linkable from his site.

I have also included a separate chapter (in Reference Section) on alignment that was written specifically for the readers of this book by the founder of DSC.

I've heard a lot of excuses from new shooters for not aspiring to this level of signal analysis, but have never seen a shred of quality content from any of them. On a professional level there are a number of people who use a high-quality monitor to set their shots, but their system was almost certainly run through the WFM & V-scope prior to their shoot. Add to that their years of experience and the fact that their eye can actually see so much more than the eye of someone who doesn't understand calibration.

A professional-looking signal quite simply demands professional analysis. There are hundreds of people, wherever you live, that understand the true value of qualitative comparison and will be glad to assist you.

Even if you have to drive around with a camcorder in your car looking for the local news truck, production people all belong to the same family. They have a passion for this industry or they'd be doing something else more financially rewarding. Don't hesitate to head off to the nearest disaster waiting for an opportune moment to ask the location engineer to patch you into the WFM.

I've worked with, and known a lot of ENG (Electronic News Gathering) folks, and have always found them to be eager to help people trying to upgrade their capabilities. More often than not you'll walk away with a better knowledge of your chosen system's potential as well as a very practical update of the industry trends.

PRODUCTION TWEAKS

Walk on to just about any high-end digital production and you'll find a person who is responsible for the constant monitoring and calibration of the recorded signal. More often than not, the DIT (Digital Imaging Technician) is a professional cinematographer who on this particular job is responsible for the overseeing the technical aspects of using the digital camera.

The DIT position on the crew was created by the IATSE Local 600 digital contract (itself a new agreement) and is specific to a single-camera, film-style crew. The responsibilities include setting up and maintaining the digital settings that will create the look specified by the Director of Photography, as well as cable and monitor wrangling.

On larger or multi-camera shoots, the feeds from the various cameras are generally routed into the engineering station where the individual signals are fed into dedicated monitors and then into a switchable Waveform Monitor with a feed into the God monitor. With multiple cameras to balance, as well as the prime responsibility for squeezing every drop of imaging capability out of the format, the DIT is called the CCO (Camera Control Operator).

Having served as DIT, CCO, EIC (Engineer in Charge), and Director of Photography (not at the same time) for a wide assortment of HD productions, I can assure you that the ability to do them all simultaneously is impossible.

<<<<< Location
calibration can be
eloquent or simple.
It all depends on your
budget and your
comfort level with gear.
Sony's resident HD
guru Jeff Cree shows
Sean Fairburn how far
off my settings were.

For economical location calibration with higher resolution formats such as DigiBeta, MPEG IMX, DVCPRO-50, or any of the flavors of HD, I some-times use a little $99.00 adapter from Belkin that takes the composite feed out of the down converter and pumps it into my laptop via the USB port. You're not looking to record a sequence, and pixel count is not really important at this time. All you want is a general idea of how the various signals compare quantitatively.

>>>>> Today's laptops pack an
entire studio
full of portable
diagnostic capabilities.

It is probably safe to say that you should never take any advice regarding signal quality from anyone who doesn't own or use some form of WFM & V-Scope on a regular basis.

The decision of which format to shoot your movie on and what method-ology to use to produce it are far too important to leave to the vagaries of opinion. Learn to think for yourself. Gather your own data from reliable sources that aren't trying to sell you something or looking for company in their own misery.

One of the saddest aspects of this industry is that when someone makes a bad decision, or worse yet, a series of them, they'll tout their shortcomings as if they were state of the art. Misery loves company and there are an awful lot of miserable people out there who would absolutely love your company.

Once you have the field narrowed down, take the time to digitize a few frames from your final contenders and see how they handle as they pass through your edit environment. Some video compression schemes are more compatible with various edit environments than others.

THE DAYS BEFORE TAPE

Keep in mind that when video standards were first introduced, there wasn't any videotape yet. All the early television shows were shot live and broadcast directly to the home. If you wanted to record a show for posterity you simply filmed the television screen with a motion picture camera (kinescope). If you wanted to rebroadcast a kinescoped show, you simply projected it on a wall and aimed a video camera at it.

One of the reasons that there are so few old shows and movies around is because the motion picture film back then was still constructed from Thomas Edison's original cellulose nitrate formula (we now use cellulose estar). In addition to being fragile and sensitive to humidity, the stuff was combustible, explosive really, and many old shows and movies soon went the way of an errant match or cigarette butt.

THE TECHNOLOGY OF RUST

Years later (1955), after experimenting with all kinds of recording mediums, (metallic wire was one of my favorites) Ampex came up with the "rust scrapings on Scotch Tape" concept and the era of videotape had begun.

SCOTTY'S HOME SCIENCE PROJECT

Take a piece of rusty metal and sandpaper off the metal oxide (rust) until you've got yourself a nice little pile. Then take a roll of Scotch Tape and stretch out a good yard or so with the glue side facing up. Sprinkle your rust dust over the tape until the whole thing is covered up and work it in real good with a soupspoon.

Let the whole thing sit for a hour or two and then brush off the excess oxide with a paintbrush. Take a soft cloth (T-shirts work well), and buff up the side with the rust on it. If you run this tape across the heads of a tape recorder while in record mode and then run the same tape across the head at relatively the same speed in play mode you'll hear an amazingly good rendition of what you just recorded. (NOTE: It's a good idea to have a bottle of isopropyl alcohol and a cotton swab on hand to clean up the mess.)

SIZE DOES MATTER

All things being equal, tape real estate is one of the bigger factors in video image quality. The more area that a frame of information is spread out on, the more inherent resolution can be recorded. There are three ways to get a lot of real estate: size, speed, and compression; although real estate alone does not guarantee a good image.

All analog and most digital videotape formats record their data in a series of diagonal stripes. These helical scans are placed on the tape by one or more record heads mounted in the outer rim of a spinning drum. Both the drum and the tape are at opposing angles so that the path of the record head writes a track of information diagonally across the tape. The faster the drum moves, the tighter the tracks can be stacked. The faster the tape moves, the more real estate can be written to.

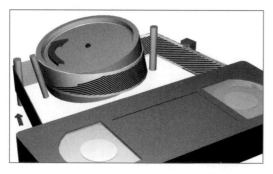

<<<<< After the tape passes by the rotating drumhead it generally passes a set of fixed heads that write the audio tracks as well as time code and control information.

Originating in the mid '60s, and using a terribly inefficient analog, color-under system, the 3/4-inch U-matic format is in wider daily operation around the world than any other format. Even now, as we stand firmly rooted in the 21st century, the 3/4-inch U-matic is so ubiquitous that you'd be hard pressed to find a post-production house, studio, or ad agency that didn't have one in daily use. In many countries of the world it is still the broadcast standard.

The 3/4-inch tape appears to have far more real estate, yet the image from the DVCPRO is far superior while taking up less room. Both formats use a helical scan drum to read and write the video signal to and from the video tape, but DV has greater resolution because of the speed of the tape through the system and the higher rpm of the drum, combined with a sophisticated compression scheme.

<<<<< Digital technology is the great equalizer. The tiny DVCPRO tape format drastically outperforms the much larger cassette's 3/4-inch U-Matic.

While the U-matic system moves the 3/4-inch tape through the system with a drum speed of 3,600 rpm, the DV moves its 6.3mm tape through at 33.813mm per second with an amazing drum speed of 9000 rpm.

The higher-output Metal Particle and Metal Evaporated DV tape supports narrower tracks without degrading the signal-to-noise ratio in analog formats (carrier-to-noise ratio in digital formats). High output tape also enables the capture of shorter recorded wavelengths for the higher recorded frequencies that are essential for digital video.

The biggest difference between these two formats, perhaps even more important than the resolution issue, is the fact that U-matic is analog composite and DV is component digital. Each successive copy of an analog format gains contrast and loses resolution while the DV can theoretically be cloned hundreds of times without degradation. Notice I said "*theoretically.*"

THE SOFT EXPLANATION OF DIGITAL

Perhaps the best way to explain digital is to first compare it to analog. Life itself is analog. Vision is based on infinitely smooth gradations of tone, from pitch black to blinding white, while color spans the spectrum from infrared to ultraviolet in billions of frequency values. The oscillations and amplitudes of air pressure that transmit sound are a smooth succession of accelerations and decelerations infinitely divisible into smaller and smaller units of mass/energy. Analog is analogous to infinite.

From the moment we're born to the day we die, every move we make, every sound we hear, every sight we see is processed in analog. From the ebb and flow of the relentless tides to the very cycle of life that frames our existence, we are analog creatures.

Digital on the other hand is quite finite.

Digital is the representation of analog in binary quanta. Any physical event that can be seen or heard can also be reduced to numbers. The more numbers you use to describe something, the closer to the analog form it comes, but it can never describe the analog event exactly. There is of course Blumenfeld's Theorem 86 which states, *"Given enough bits/resolution you could sample down to the molecular level and restate reality in the digital domain."*

I am particularly fond of the Dutch Masters and can easily stand for hours in front of a Pieter Claesz painting while the flow of humanity silently washes around me. Using a simple search engine you can pull up one of his surreal masterpieces. It will, of course, be a digital representation of the original and, as such, is limited to the color palette and tonal limitations of your particular computer system. Is it a good indicator of the original? Yes, but no matter how high the resolution of a digital recording gets, it will never be able to capture the true depth of color and texture that are present in the original analog painting.

All of digital recording technology comes down to creating a "good enough" approximation, and what is good enough for viewing on your home television is quite simply not good enough to print to film or project on a large screen.

THE HARD EXPLANATION OF DIGITAL

Digital is an electronic method of expressing an analog event in numeric equivalent. Visual elements within the digital domain are translated into a cluster of PIXELS or PIcture ELements. Contrary to popular belief, a pixel is not a resolute or finite amount of data, but rather a potential of resolution. It is not a 1:1 map out.

By using recording devices that can translate sound or light waves into voltage, and then sampling those voltages, we can arrive at numeric equivalents for the analog values. This is called Analog-to-Digital (A/D) conversion.

These values are then expressed in a binary code composed of ones and zeros (actually electrical impulses in a mostly-on state or a mostly-off state). Binary is the language of computers. It is a language of just two words, yes and no. It isn't so much that computers have found their way into the entertainment industry as film and video have found their way into the computer's realm. Anything that uses a two-word language is essentially a computer peripheral or a New York City cab driver.

Each digit in this binary code is a bit (Binary digIT). Each mathematical bit can define one of two states, on or off, black or white, yes/no, 0 or 1. Two bits can define four levels, three bits — eight, four bits — sixteen and so on using the simple formula 2^n (two to the nth, or two to the power of n), where n equals the number of bits. To imagine just how much information can be expressed in binary terms, consider human DNA, which is a four-bit code (A-C-G-T).

Eight bits together make a byte, which can describe 256 levels of brightness or color. A signal that is converted into a 10-bit number can describe over a thousand levels of brightness or color. Obviously, all things being equal, a 10-bit system will generate better-looking images.

Unlike the base 10 decimal system we all grew up with ("dec" meaning 10), the binary system of digital computing is base 2. Since it can only describe two states (on/off) it requires a far greater number of digits to express a value. The base 10 number 230 is expressed in binary form as 11100110. The result of a binary multiplication contains the sum of digits of the original numbers so: 1100100 × 11100110 = 101100111011000 (in 10 base, 175 × 212 = 37,100).

This preponderance of digits that the binary system generates is where the initial opportunity for compression becomes most evident. Given too low a bit depth, large areas with subtle variations in color have a tendency to create distinct bands.

<<<<<   Compression artifacts become more evident with greater compression. The image here was compressed at 50:1.

COMPRESSION SCHEMES

Compression is a very difficult topic because the results are so subjective. With television and desktop video it generally comes down to the eye of the beholder. Does it look good or not? Once we get into the realm of video-for-film or digital cinema however the subjective critique becomes far less relevant and we need to look at mathematical justification for platform and methodological decisions.

Talk to any relatively knowledgeable video engineer and you're going to spend a lot of time on the topic of compression schemes. They are, after all, what make nearly everything digital possible. We're still years away from being able to record, broadcast, or store the enormous amounts of data that we deal with every day without these sophisticated algorithms. The important word in "compression scheme" is scheme. The Dictionary defines a scheme as:

1.) NOUN: a method devised for making or doing something or attaining an end.
Synonyms: plan, blueprint, design, game plan, project, strategy.
Related: conception, idea, notion, ground plan, intention, platform, purpose, means, method, way.

2.) NOUN: a secret plan for accomplishing a usually evil or unlawful end.
Synonyms: plot, cabal, conspiracy, coven, intrigue, machination, practice.
Related: collusion, complicity, contraption, contrivance, artifice, maneuver, ruse, stratagem, trick.

Now it would be nice to think that the first definition is the one we're dealing with but I'm afraid not. Compression is a war fought by really big corporations and the winner makes all the bucks. Compression engineers spend nearly every waking hour trying to figure out how to get a video signal to look good without really being good. The first rule of compression is to remove everything from the signal that you possibly can.

From birth, the human eye is tuned to subtle shifts in the gray scale. It is these subtle shifts of light and shadow that transmit the play of emotion across the human face. We are so subliminally sensitive to these subtle shifts that our eyes can detect a mere .1% shift in luminosity. Fortunately for the compression mongers, we're simply not as sensitive to the color spectrum, so this is where they focus their efforts.

Since the human eye is most sensitive to green, the red and blue elements of the video signal are sampled at half the rate. The unfortunate result of this scheme is that it deeply affects the quality of skin tone. Even in the very best video environments, skin tones lack the depth and subtlety that we find in film images. This, perhaps more than any other factor, is why so many digital film projects end up in black and white.

If you understand the basics of compression and how it affects the color-space of your image, you will be able to create a production environment that not only meets your financial limitations, but also maintains what little color information is left in today's highly compressed digital video formats.

THE MANY FLAVORS OF COMPRESSION

There is absolutely no way to fully explain the convoluted world of compression without filling many pages with multi-syllabic words. Basically, higher compression factors allow data to flow faster while lower compression ratios give a better picture.

Anyone who's worked with Adobe Photoshop or one of the other personal computer graphics packages is already familiar with the basics of compression as it pertains to a single image. JPEG is quite rightly the most popular flavor of single image compression and stands for the Joint Photographic Experts Group, ISO/ITU-T, while MPEG stands for Moving Picture Experts Group, ISO/CCITT.

JPEG baseline compression essentially transforms images into 8x8 pixel blocks of frequency and amplitude data. Since digital data is essentially written in ones and zeros, this scheme looks more closely at the less visible high frequencies and compresses them by a higher factor than it does the more visible lower frequencies. Many normally dense data blocks can subsequently be reduced to a single one or zero.

Consumer implementations of MPEG add inter-frame compression to the basic JPEG scheme, essentially looking for similarities between frames and averaging common elements. There are several flavors of MPEG, the most common being MPEG-2, which is the backbone for HDTV, DVD and digital TV. MPEG-2, with data rates between 4 and 100 Mb/s, is essentially designed to be a transmission strategy utilizing decoders at the reception end of the data stream.

MPEG-2's method of using inter-frame compression to remove redundancy within sequential frames creates long groups of pictures (GOP). This method of producing strings of pictures containing I (header), P (predictive) and B (bi-directional) frames, makes it tricky to use as a digital film production tool.

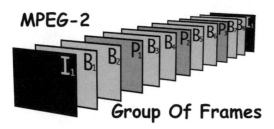

MPEG-2

Group Of Frames

<<<<< Although an efficient method of compression, the sequential GOPs cause difficulty when trying to create frame accurate edit points.

To get around the problem of trying to edit between the full frames of the conventional GOP structure, a number of MPEG based production systems are emerging that only record a series of header frames. The common name for this is Zero Inter-frame Compression, although you just know the marketing guys are going to have a blast coming up with some tragically hip variations.

The new (insert tragically hip name here) format records equally well onto tape and hard media such as hard drives and ram disks. Sony's new MPEG IMX system sits between Betacam SX and Digital Betacam and uses MPEG-2 with a 50Mbs intra frame system. The translation in common vernacular means that the image is crispy and every bit a contender for taking over the high-end of video production.

BINARY SHELL GAME

After years of marketing misdirection, there is an understandable and carefully orchestrated confusion between sampling rates and mathematical compression techniques.

Any "digital" image is, by definition, compressed in the sense that there is less information contained in it than there was in the analog original. From this point on, every time you read or hear the word "uncompressed" used in respect to motion imaging, a little echo in the back of your head should whisper *"bull shit."*

The degree of compression or data rate reduction is primarily determined by the sampling rate and the bit depth of the original image as compared to the data rate, capacity, and system resolution of the storage medium and working environment. The only way it could be truly uncompressed would be to sample it with a theoretical infinite sampling rate at an infinite bit depth (*Blumenfeld's Theorem 86*). Since neither of these are currently possible, compromises are made.

Compression is hard to get away from because software companies have established a precedent for using words like "transposed" and "calibrated" instead of "compressed." What this means in the real world is that basically everything gets compressed and recompressed all the time, so even "uncompressed" video streams (as in FCP "uncompressed mode") are stomped on.

But compression isn't really the biggest problem. As you now already know, compression is merely the application of algorithms that detect redundancies in the image's code and restructure it with less bits. The big damage is done in colorspace transpositions.

The thing you really need to keep an eye on is the lowest common denominator. The lowest bandpass you put your signal through is the finite quanta of your signal from then on.

THE BASICS INGREDIENTS

There are many ways to describe a video signal. Resolution is an obscure term that is wielded more often by ad agencies than production professionals. There are four main quantifiable aspects to a video signal and they must all be taken into consideration simultaneously to be relevant. (We'll get deeper into each of them later.)

1.) The number of pixels or picture elements which are generally described in a horizontal to vertical ratio such as DVCAM 720 x 480 or HDCAM 1920 x 1080.

2.) The amount of luminance and color information which is almost always described by three sets of numbers separated by colons such as DVCAM @ 4:1:1 and Sony's HDCAM @ 3:1:1.

3.) The amount of data that it creates each second. Panasonic's DVCPRO-50 records data at fifty Megabits per second.

4.) The compression ratio is basically the degree to which the data set has been reduced numerically.

You could hear someone say that miniDV with its 4:1:1 colorspace has more resolution than HDCAM at 3:1:1. But this is totally wrong — a comparison of Standard Def apples to Hi-Def oranges. In fact, the HDCAM has lots more information for both luminance and chrominance.

So if the data rate of D5 HD is 235 Mbps with a 4:2:2 colorspace and a 996:235 compression ratio you might see it represented as: D5-HD, 235 Mbps, 4:2:2 @ 4:1.

If you take a nice fat 4:2:2 DVCPRO-50 signal and you squirt it through a conventional 4:1:1 FireWire based capture application into a 4:2:2 edit environment, you only have a 4:1:1 end product.

It will be swimming around in a 4:2:2 colorspace, but the data you lost can never be recovered. This is especially true of plugins and graphics filters which are generally written in 2:1:2 or 3:2:1 three-space color. Once you apply them to your video, that's your colorspace from then on.

In the case of 4:1:1-ish, FireWire'd miniDV — that's what you've got. You can't increase the resolution by squirting it into a 4:2:2 colorspace, but it does help protect what you've got if it isn't "recontextualized" yet again to fit into another "native" compression scheme.

Resolution is finite and unrecoverable under the Newtonian Laws of Physics. Once you've transposed it away, it's gone. You're going to get beat up any way you move, so look for the guy with the smallest club.

THE I.T.U. AND YOU

With all the myriad formats and compression schemes out there, someone had to step in and start dealing with standardization issues. The CCIR (Comite Consultatif International des Radiocommunications) was widely considered the last word in transmission standards but the unmistakable French twist that was put on everything became tiring and broadcasters and manufacturers the world over looked to the United Nations for some relief.

The UN came through and formed the International Telecommunications Union (ITU) as a regulatory body covering all forms of broadcast communication. The CCIR was absorbed into the ITU after a judicious amount of whining from ze French, and the rest as they say, is history. We now have an internationally recognized body of egghead engineers that sets standards that everyone adheres to.

The reason that I bring up the ITU at all is because without a point of reference, there is really no place to start.

601 VIDEO, NOT 601 JEANS

The granddaddy of all video standards is unquestionably ITU-R 601, formerly known as CCIR-601. This international standard for digitizing component video in both 525 and 625 line systems is the basis for numerous video formats including D1 (uncompressed) and Digital BetaCam (compressed). It deals with both the RGB video signal that comes directly off of the imaging chips in cameras and image generators like computers, as well as color difference systems like (Y, R-Y, B-Y). If you've got access to a personal computer with a high-quality video digitizer board you'll most likely find connectors for one or both formats on the system's breakout box.

<<<<< The business end of the highly popular Targa3000.

Every relevant form of digital recording has its own compression schemes. ITU-R-601 accommodates the highest practical compression standard for modestly budgeted video-to-film purposes. Essentially the 601 standard breaks the visual spectrum down into three units using either an 8-bit or 10-bit system. As the electronic signal comes off of the three CCDs of a professional-quality video camera, it is described in ITU-R-601 lingo as a RGB 4:4:4. The first "4" describes the luminance value of the picture and second two describe the color differences between red and blue.

If you were to up-convert that image and print it directly to film you would be amazed at the quality of the projected image. It would possess tonal gradation and color saturation that would rival the projected image of a fast 35mm stock.

On the flip side, if you take the same image, sample it at a high compression ratio, record it to a low bandwidth recording medium, decompress it, and re-compress it thorough several different schemes, and then print it to the same film stock, you will understand why the vast majority of video-to-film projects end up looking the way they do.

I've been up-converting and printing the 601 signal to film for more than a decade now, and every year better and better algorithms show up to further facilitate the process. The first 601 up-conversion algorithm I used was written by Price Pethal, a true luminary in the digital film industry and cofounder of Jim Cameron's highly successful Digital Domain.

Pethal's code allowed me to create more than sixty-five visual effects for Roger Corman's *Fantastic Four* in ITU-R-601 and then up-convert and print to film. Unfortunately for our micro-budgeted movie, Twentieth Century

Fox bought out the rights after just one screening. They figured that if we could do that much with no budget then they could do something really great with the budget of a small country. And there it sits.

>>>>> Ben Grimm turns into *The Thing* in the first "Big Screen" morph sequence.

I've used 601 up-conversion more than a hundred times since that 1990 project, in movies with both large and small budgets. The substantial number of up-conversion algorithms and printer drivers that now deal with the ITU-R 601 protocol and have made it the most widely used video-to-film format in the industry.

Hi-Def is coming on strong, and by the time this book goes into its third edition, it will no doubt have become the standard but for now ITU-R 601 is the irrefutable, qualitative, and quantitative standard. Once you understand the technical aspects of 601 you'll be able to make solid judgments regarding your own production platform choices. Without a qualitative reference to base your decisions on, you're only guessing, or worse yet, following someone else's advice.

While RGB theoretically creates the most robust ITU-R 601 signal, the most common reference to 601 is as color difference, component digital video, sampled at 4:2:2 at 13.5 MHz with 720 luminance samples per active line, digitized at either 8- or 10-bit.

Whew, it hurt to write it, too.

We're going to spend the remainder of this chapter deciphering that last sentence because once you understand 601 you'll have enough information to begin making educated decisions... and hopefully you'll never have to turn your work of art into a retro-artsy-fartsy, black and white motion picture... unless you really want to.

The ITU-R 601 signal can have either an RGB or color difference format.

As light enters the camera's lens it is focused on to a light sensitive computer chip called a Charge Coupled Device (CCD). The surface of the CCD is composed of thousands, if not millions, of microscopic cells that act as tiny light meters, each generating an electrical charge proportional to the light striking it. The relative current from each element is then sent to an encoder where it is converted from the analog RGB video to digital component and streamed down a wire where it is inserted as binary information into the steady flow of ones and zeros that represent the data structure of the recording environment.

The vast majority of the video acquisition formats that digital filmmakers use convert the RGB signal into a (Y, B-Y, R-Y) component video signal. Although not 100% accurate, without going into several pages of really boring technical palaver, think of (Y) as representing the analog luminance or inherent light range of the image while (R-Y) and (B-Y) represent the two color difference signals. (R-Y) is RED MINUS LUMINANCE and (B-Y) is BLUE MINUS LUMINANCE. Since Y encompasses R, G, and B, a simple math equation (R-Y + B-Y = G) will yield G (green).

ITU-R 601 signal is component digital video.

There are several methods of maintaining the initial integrity of the video signal by keeping various elements of the signal (components) separate. The most common way of doing this is by simply using individual wires for each signal component.

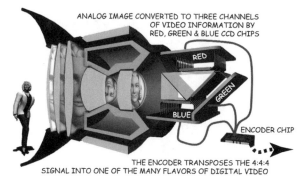

ANALOG IMAGE CONVERTED TO THREE CHANNELS
OF VIDEO INFORMATION BY
RED, GREEN & BLUE CCD CHIPS

RED

GREEN

BLUE

ENCODER CHIP

THE ENCODER TRANSPOSES THE 4:4:4
SIGNAL INTO ONE OF THE MANY FLAVORS OF DIGITAL VIDEO

RGB is the most robust signal type due to the purity and wider palette of its colors. The Red, Green, Blue, and Sync (timing) signals are generally carried on separate wires. The major drawback with RGB is that it is a very fat signal and there really isn't any video tape based mechanisms that are capable of recording it.

Most component video formats separate each of the three colors and luminance by one of several methods. These are used in BetaCam SP, Digital Betacam, D1, DVCPRO, and other high-quality formats. A component signal is generally expressed as YUV, but you'll also see it written as (Y, R-Y, B-Y) or (YCrCb).

Component video signals, such as ITU-R601, retain maximum luminance and chrominance bandwidth for a much longer time. They are far more robust within editing and graphic environments, and if you ever need to pull a chroma key or do any sort of luminance mapping, you're definitely going to want to the extra colorspace that component signals provide.

S-Video is often considered a component signal. Technically it does keep the color and luminance routed through two separate wires but the inherent quality of the signal is so low that it is unfit for consideration as a digital production format. Unfortunately S-Video systems like Hi8 are quite popular due to their low cost, and while they are generally far better than using a standard composite video format, they fall far short of a true component systems signal.

<<<<< BNC, S-video and RCA (bottom) are all various types of video connectors while FireWire and USB (top) are data connectors. Generally, if you see BNC connectors, you're dealing with a professional system.

Composite Video merges the R, G, B, luminance and sync information into a single wire. The lower quality image is intended for "end-use" and does not make a viable production environment. The television broadcast standard for the United States, in fact anywhere in the world that runs on 60Hz electrical power, is NTSC (National Television Systems Committee also known as Never The Same Color). NTSC specifies a composite signal with a total of 525 vertical scan lines, 40 of which are used for vertical blanking. This leaves a visible image area 480 lines high.

ITU-R 601 signal is sampled at 4:2:2 at 13.5 MHz.

4:4:4 is the highest practical ratio of sampling frequencies used to digitize the luminance and color difference components of a video signal at this time. All arguments and discussions about which video format prints to film best end here, because uncompressed, 10-bit, 4:4:4 is essentially the Holy Grail of digital filmmakers. In the 4:4:4 signal, there are equal numbers of samples of all components. (Y) gets four samples, (R-Y) gets four samples, and (B-Y) gets four samples = 4:4:4 .

There is of course 4:4:4:4, which includes an alpha channel, as well as various über-resolutions such as 8:4:4 and 27Mhz:13.5:13.5, but for the foreseeable future, 4:4:4 is going to do just fine.

Since most television and video systems operate on lower-quality ratios like 4:1:1 or 4:2:0, we rarely get to see 4:4:4 resolution video in our daily life. Most quality personal computers use a native 8-bit, RGB 4:4:4 system, but the signal is generally down-sampled by video I/O boards to a far less robust resolution. When 4:4:4 images are generated within a computer and then taken directly from the computer's hard drive as data files, up-converted and printed to film, the resultant images compare well to images originating on film.

It would be really great if ITU-R 601 maintained the color information that came off of the chips and sampled at full 4:4:4, but it doesn't. ITU-R 601 is generally considered a 4:2:2 system where the color is sampled at half the rate as the luminance information. The 4 represents a sampling frequency of 13.5MHz while each of the 2s represent a sample frequency of 6.75 MHz. 4:2:2 has half the color information of the more robust 4:4:4.

Most consumer and prosumer DV cameras transpose their signal into a 4:1:1 configuration, which essentially has 256 levels of sampling, compared with the 1024 levels of 4:2:2. So a 4:1:1 number may be a representation of luminance sampled at 13.5MHz and the color differences sampled at 3.375 MHz. So for every four samples of the luminance channel, there is one reference sample of the blue and red.

ITU-R 601 generates 720 luminance samples per active line.

In analog monitors, a scan line is called a raster (to be technically accurate a raster is actually the entire screen) and a frame is made up of two sets of them. The cathode ray sweeps across the screen and after completing one horizontal scan line the beam shuts off (horizontal blanking) and returns to start the line after next.

In an interlaced system (like television) every odd-numbered raster (line) is written as a field and then the beam goes back to the top and writes the even numbered rasters. These two fields create an interlaced frame. In NTSC there are thirty of them (really 29.97) per second offset by color burst.

ODD + EVEN = INTERLACED FRAME

<<<<< It takes two sets
of interlace rasters to
build a solid frame of video.

In a progressive scan environ-ment (similar to a computer monitor) each line is written in succession until the beam hits the bottom and snaps back up to the top.

<<<<< Progressive scan
builds the image using a
continuous succession of rasters.

In LCD and Plasma monitors the fields are always on rather than being traced on one at a time. This is why you don't need any special accommodations to film or videotape them. In standard NTSC digital systems the visible image area is 480 pixels high and 720 pixels wide.

The ITU-R 601 digital signal generates a separate and distinct luminance sample for 345,600 pixels, thirty times a second.

ITU-R 601 signal is digitized at either 8- or 10-bit.

ITU-R 601 allows for both the luminance and chrominance information to be sampled at either 8-bits or 10-bits. The vast majority of televisions as well as PC computers, Macintosh included, are 8-bit. This means that each com-ponent in the (Y, B-Y, R-Y) signal is represented by 256 levels of information.

A 10-bit system creates a palette that has more than a thousand levels of information. Since you stand a good chance of losing information every time you move or manipulate your information, it is in your best interest to give serious consideration to using a format with the greatest bit depth you can afford.

Many times, motion picture effects work is digitized in 10-bit log and generally needs to be done on a 10-bit system like Silicon Graphics. Recently, software applications such as Puffin Design's Commotion, Adobe After Effects, and Discreet Logic's Combustion have appeared on the PC and Mac platforms allowing 10-bit work to be done in an 8-bit world.

The single most important thing to keep in mind when working on the desktop is that using a poorly written plugin or filter can cut your resolution or colorspace in half. Just because you're working in After Effects at 10-bit doesn't mean a thing if you use Joe Blow's 8-bit filter. Your shot is now reduced to 8-bit resolution and once it's gone, it's gone.

For David Lynch's motion picture *Mulholland Drive*, I scanned the film-based elements for the 34 visual effects shots into data files using 10-bit, SGI/RGB file format at full sample (4:4:4). Since the RGB image format was compatible with the software systems we used, there was no further degradation of the image. Having been degrained during the visual effects process, the images were printed back to the same camera stock as the original acquisitions. The resulting frames cut in seamlessly.

In the motion picture *Barb Wire*, we had far more shots to do than our meager budget would allow. Rather than scan each frame individually, we took the numerous shots that originated on 35mm film stock and telecined them to 4:2:2 RGB image files. Unlike scanning, where an electron beam painstakingly records each individual frame three times (R+G+B), telecine runs the film through in real time, turning each frame of film into a ITU-R 601 image file. The resultant data file is much smaller than a scanned file and far less expensive. (NOTE: For what it's worth, the first day of shooting on the movie was done with my miniDV camcorder.)

Since the majority of effects were layered elements to which matching grain had been added, we printed to a good intermediate stock using a laser recorder. Two different methodologies, two different file sizes.

If you figure around a megabyte per frame, with an average effects sequence running five or six seconds, plus head and tails, chimes in at several hundred megabytes a shot. Ten years ago that was a lot of storage, but nowadays you can slip it into a shirt pocket and have room left over for a phone and a palmtop computer.

After we added effects in various software applications, the images were up-converted, sent to the printer as 4:2:2 RGB data files, printed to film, and edited into the motion picture. Many of the effects shots were cut in amongst the non-effects shots without any noticeable resolution difference.

Point being... even with serious limiting factors, a well-maintained digital signal is capable of being matched back to film. What this means to the digital moviemaker is that resolution is only one factor in the visual integrity of your picture. You must fight to keep every bit of information that composes your signal. Colorspace must become as important to you as sharpness.

EVEN BLACK AND WHITE ISSUES AREN'T

The color system defined by the ITU-R 601 video specification is based on an 8-bit-per-channel luminance range of 16 to 235. Most digital video systems, from DV to D5, generally rate black at just under 7% brightness with an RGB color value of 16/16/16, and white at just over 92% brightness with an RGB color value of 235/235/235.

The vast majority of 8-bit-per-channel, RGB-based computer graphic programs use a luminance range of 0 to 255 which rates Black as 0% brightness or 0/0/0, and white as 100% brightness, or 255/255/255. With these desktop systems, you can't get darker than black or brighter than white.

Since the 601 system allows for colors that are darker than black and brighter than white, you have the opportunity to pull detail out of hot spots and shadows before hitting the video legal wall.

One of the major contributors to the "DV Look" is caused when DV footage is transposed incorrectly or effects are added that use the extended luminance range of the computer environment. The resulting image generally has crushed blacks and blown-out whites, and any extra effort you undertook in production is negated.

WHERE DID ALL MY COLOR GO?

MiniDV is the format of choice for a vast majority of digital filmmakers. It uses a native compression scheme of 5:1 from a 4:1:1 bit sampled source. The luminance channel receives four samples at 13.5MHz while the two color channels only receive single samples of 3.75MHz each. The relatively high compression scheme (5:1) of DVCAM strips much of the color information from the otherwise robust signal. When combined with the low sample rate (4:1:1) you end up with a signal that looks great when played back on your monitor but performs quite poorly in chrominance values when up-converted and projected or printed to film.

PAL consumer DV and DVCAM have 4:2:0 color, which has some additional advantages for cinema over the 4:1:1 color of NTSC consumer DV and DVCAM. The 4:1:1 system samples color on every scanning line, but only for every fourth luminance pixel. You get 180 H x 480 V samples for R-Y and B-Y in NTSC.

The 4:2:0 system samples color on every second scanning line, for every second luminance pixel. You get 360 H x 288 V samples for R-Y and B-Y in PAL. This means you have more color samples on the horizontal axis, which is better for wide screen cinema production.

In a 4:4:4 sampled signal, 66% of the information deals with color. In a 4:1:1 sampled signal with 5:1 compression, only 33% of the signal deals with color. After just a few seemingly harmless conversions and transpositions, the delicate signal often ends up with only a fraction of its original color.

By shooting your movie digitally, you stand to save considerably on processing when compared to the inherent costs of film-based production. What you lose are the wide-ranging advantages inherent in film itself, the look, the texture, the resolution, and the subtlety. While this book will endeavor to get you as close as possible to the classic cinematic look, it should be obvious that it entails a significant amount of craft to emulate the richness of film. We are locked in a battle of perception, and every wrong step will take you further away from a cinematic image.

3 ▸ FORMAT WARS

"The truth is more important than the facts."
Frank Lloyd Wright

There has been a fierce, global battle raging for the latter half of this century. The battlefield is littered with dead or dying formats and you have just parachuted into hostile territory. Your survival depends on developing a set of strategic objectives and avoiding the land mines of propaganda.

Technology before the chip didn't move all that fast. Yeah, there were innovations, but real breakthroughs were few and far between. Back when countries were trying to figure out what television standard they were going to use, there was a lot of confusion, competing formats, some good, some not so good, all backed by companies touting the benefits of their particular electromechanical hodgepodge.

NTSC vs. PAL

Bottom line was that everyone was basically selling the same thing with a regional twist. In the end, countries that had an electrical infrastructure based on 60Hz, like the U.S., Japan, Canada, and Central America, went with the 30 frames per second (60 fields) of NTSC. Countries with a 50Hz infrastructure, like most of Europe, Great Britain, Australia, and China, went with the 25-frames-per-second (50 fields) format of PAL. Then, of course, there was France, who as a point of national pride had to do something totally contrary, so they came up with SECAM.

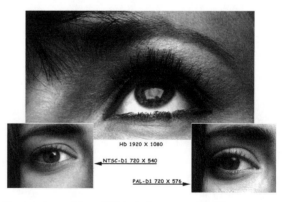

Iraq and Iran didn't want France to feel alone, so they adapted SECAM as well. Except for the holy trinity of retro-tech, what we essentially ended up with was a world split by two formats, NTSC (National Television Standards Committee), and PAL (Phase Alternating Line).

Mid-century analog technology wasn't based on exotic materials or micro-miniature componentry. You took a little of this, and hooked it to a little one of these, put on a couple'a lights and a nice set of dials and *Voila!* A new, improved thing. Still firmly rooted in the last fading vestiges of the mechanical age, engineers all used the same raw materials to create the various video production environments.

Back in those technologically slower days, signal flowed pretty much the same speed for everyone. Well, except the French. Processors, whether NTSC or PAL, still pushed their analog signals through copper wires at relatively the same speed. Since NTSC was pushing more frames per second through the same copper wire, (30 as opposed to 25) it reduced the signal bandpass (the amount of information each frame carried) accordingly.

There are really so many valid arguments for using PAL over NTSC that I could fill an entire book with them. Instead, I have assembled my favorite arguments and offer them here, greatly abbreviated, for your consideration.

DROP-FRAME

NTSC generates 525 visible lines of image at 60 fields a second or 525/60. Remember that two fields make a frame. When color was introduced to the NTSC system the frame rate was changed from an even 30 frames per second to the current 29.97 fps (Drop-Frame). Two frames were dropped every minute to compensate for a timing metaphor used in commercial programming. Nothing so technically involved that your basic chimpanzee couldn't figure it out and accommodate, but back then they figured that reducing time by .1% would make things easier for people even dumber than simians, network schedulers.

Drop-Frame is only one of the many reasons that I'm not a big fan of using NTSC for film applications. Many cameras can operate in DF (Drop Frame) or ND (Non-Drop), and while it has no effect on the actual frame rate, it does cause problems everywhere along the production process. Not only does this complicate everything from synchronizing peripheral production equipment to computing edit points, but it also brings a nice hairy fly into the ointment of video-to-film transposition as well.

FRAME RATE

While NTSC uses a wonky frame rate of 29.97, or 525/60, PAL generates a very solid 625 lines of visible lines of image at 50 fields a second or 625/50.

When you process your NTSC video for up-conversion to film's 24 frames per second, you first need to drop six frames out of the thirty (a whopping 20% reduction) in total information right off the start.

The frame rate of PAL is 20% more efficient than NTSC.

Since film generates 24 frames per second, anyone with an above room temperature IQ will see the obvious benefits in establishing a video production environment based on 25fps as opposed to 30fps, when producing for a 24fps end product. I've been using PAL for motion picture applications for many years and in all that time I've never had anyone mention or notice the extra frame.

I'm often asked about synchronizing sound between the 24 and 25 fps frame rates. To start with, there is no such thing as perfect sync. Not in film, not in video, not in life. The further away you are physically from another person, the further out of sync they are. Any form of locking the audio to a picture entails a bit of work and artistry. I prefer to do that work on a signal that is significantly superior.

VANILLA VIDEO

There are so many flavors of resolution, and so many ways it can be stated that you can almost feel your leg being tugged every time someone mentions the word. Since resolution is affected initially by the camera's lens (a topic I'm quite fond of ranting on about), as well numerous other factors in the image stream, let's first talk about the theoretical, all-things-being-equal type of resolution that the system is supposed to have.

LINES OF IMAGE

Essentially, resolution is a measure of the detail that can be resolved, or reproduced in the image. The ITU-R 601 digital video standard defines the NTSC 525/60 signal as having 486 active vertical lines, each with 720 horizontal samples. ITU-R 601 defines the PAL 625/50 signal as having 576 active vertical lines, each having 720 horizontal samples. There are 51 more vertical lines of image in the PAL system than in NTSC.

PAL has 20% more spatial resolution than NTSC.

SAMPLE RATE

The transposition of the analog image voltage off of the camera's CCD chips into a series of digital values is called sampling. The more samples there are per second, the higher the number of bits the image data can be resolved into.

ITU 601 calls for a 13.5 MHz Y sampling rate in both PAL and NTSC. PAL has 20% higher spatial resolution 576/480 = 1.200. NTSC has (approximately) 20% higher temporal resolution 60/50 = 1.200. This is how PAL and NTSC flavors of the same videocassette can have the same recording time. But NTSCs 20% superiority in temporal resolution gets thrown away when you convert to 24 fps for projection or printing to film.

PAL has a higher sampled resolution than NTSC.

Both NTSC-D1 and PAL-D1 use non-square pixels. While this generally doesn't cause any problem as long as you maintain a native format data path, the moment you divert the signal into a non-native environment, like, say, a computer program, you're going to need to deal with the variations in pixel aspect ratio.

NTSC-D1 uses a 0.9 pixel aspect ratio that is 0.9 wide and 1.0 high, orientated in the vertical direction. PAL-D1 on the other hand, uses a pixel aspect ratio of 1.0666 that is orientated horizontally.

Aspect ratio issues aside, PAL is by far the simplest format to work with, even in the United States of NTSC. Computers just don't care and easily adapt to various pixel aspect ratios. Nonlinear edit systems don't care and the vast majority of professional monitors have a simple switch on the faceplate to switch from NTSC to PAL.

So am I advocating the use of PAL over NTSC? Depends. For me it is as simple to work in as NTSC with big payoffs in resolution. But then I've been working in this environment for quite a while. I've also got a rather firm grasp of the technologies involved and my own rather odious production system that has evolved over the years.

For someone who has a good practical understanding of the technologies involved, PAL is a no-brainer, but for someone starting out, the best NTSC system you can get your hands on is probably going to serve you well. The important thing to keep in mind is that with NTSC you're starting out with a significant handicap.

ASPECT WARS

The aspect ratio is the frame's width divided by its height. When movies started out they were almost square. Gradually they became wider, until they were roughly the same shape as a contemporary NTSC television signal, which is four to three, or 1.33:1. European and American cinema have been dueling back and forth about standards for quite some time, Europe adopting the 1.66:1 aspect ratio and America the slightly narrower 1.85:1.

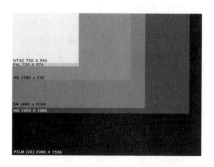

<<<<< There are of course many other aspect ratios that I have intentionally omitted. It's confusing enough.

NTSC television uses an aspect ratio of 4:3, an image four units wide and three units tall. Then along comes HDTV. Numerous size and resolution options flew around since its initial introduction in the late '60s, and now, after more than thirty years of bickering, they've decided on a 16x9 aspect ratio.

The Internet provides us with even more choices. Since the majority of compressors don't really care what the aspect ratio is, it's open season on format. While most sites prefer the conventional 4x3 of analog television, the new "virtual" formats like i-View, QuickTimeVR, and iPIX offer a viewer definable aspect ratio and framing environment.

The only thing I can offer is that it's going to get even more confusing from here on out. Personally, I'm a 16x9 kinda guy.

Since the final image that we are aiming for is film or digital projection, it will theoretically be projected in the widescreen aspect ratio of 1.85:1. The future of home television and video formats like HD, DVD, and broadband lie in the realm of the 1.78:1 aspect ratio usually referred to as 16×9.

The majority of contemporary digital cameras now come with 16×9 aspect-ratio capabilities. The better quality systems generally use a wider chip with more horizontal pixels, while the majority of DV camcorders merely stretch or crop the image without really increasing the inherent resolution.

FUTURE PROOFING

This may sound obvious, but the number of people who are taken by surprise when they finally see their image cropped to the wider aspect of cinema is astounding. If you've shot in standard NTSC 4:3, then you've got to throw away upwards of 20% of your hard-earned image. Talk to any company that prints DV to film and they'll have a wealth of stories about digital filmmakers who lost important information in their scenic composition.

Take your pick of 1.85 or 16×9 and stick to it. If your viewfinder doesn't have a cinematic reticule (framing template or outline) then make one. I'm predisposed to the 16×9 format because it makes your movie inherently more marketable to cable and network.

Whatever it is that you intend on making probably has a far better chance of being distributed on cable than it does theatrically. With an eye to the future, forward-thinking distribution mechanisms such as HBO, Showtime, Discovery Channel, Bravo, Sundance, SciFi, IFC, TLC, and Lifetime are looking to HD distribution as their primary delivery format. Shows shot in 16×9, even if they are originated in DV, have a much better chance of integrating with the new standards than something shot with even a higher resolution but presented in 4×3.

Keep in mind that even though networks and channels are starting to ask for shows to be shot in HD, what they really want is 16×9. It will be several years before the HD format actually becomes a transmission standard that is used for its pixel count. Since you'll now match the standard Hi-Def broadcast aspect ratio very little side information is lost in projecting to the more cinematic 1.85 if you do go theatrical.

Keep in mind that most prosumer cameras don't really generate a true 16×9 image but rather crop upwards of 25% of the signal off of the CCDs to get the "wide look." Some other camcorders stretch the conventional 4×3 image to the wider aspect ratio. Be sure you're dealing with a true 16×9 image system and not throwing away precious resolution before committing to a wide aspect format. D-Beta and most high-end DVCPRO camcorders use a true 16×9 CCD to record the image.

If you are using a camera that records to the conventional 4×3 aspect chip consider using a good anamorphic adapter that optically squeezes your image horizontally. A typical 4×3 image that uses an anamorphic squeeze in production and is then fit into a 16×9 aspect in post will have 33% more vertical resolution than a 4×3 image that is cropped to 16×9.

4x3 Native

4x3 cropped to 16x9

16x9 Anamorphic

<<<<< Anamorphic adapters can effectively double your available resolution, when used correctly.

Arguments can be made with regards to the commercial broadcast of a movie shot in 4×3, but when you look at all the options, weigh all the pluses and minuses back and forth, you'll generally come to the same conclusion. It is far better to maintain all the inherent vertical resolution that you can for as long as you can. The new world order of 16×9 will be around for a long, long time. Anything shot or released in 4×3 is, quite simply, ancient history.

BOTTOM LINE

Don't get obsessed with numbers because it makes you an easy target. We are living in a world where large corporations find it much cheaper to hire a marketing firm to rearrange and redefine specifications than to actually improve their product.

Electrons essentially flow at the same speed for everyone. Math is the shell game used by companies to confuse the issue. The only way to tell what is right for you is to shoot the same exact thing with numerous cameras and formats. Digitize them all with the same card or system and then do whatever it is you want to do with the images and judge for yourself. Everything else is BS.

THE FLAVORS

Most NTSC miniDV, whether single or three-chip, and all single-chip PAL miniDV, represent CONSUMER GRADE video. An exception to this is well-shot, three-chip, NTSC miniDV that is processed with Magic Bullet, which then becomes PROSUMER GRADE.

8mm film and top-of-the-line miniDV cameras fall into the ever-trendy PROSUMER category.

Super 8mm film starts the PROFESSIONAL category along with DigiBeta, DVCPRO-50, and the new MPEG IMX as the mainstay digital resolutions. A CanonXL series camera that has been outfitted with a P+S Technik Mini 35 adapter and is using cine style lenses is the only miniDV camera that makes it to this category. Conventional 16 mm film closes out the high-end of the PROFESSIONAL category.

CINEMA QUALITY starts with super16mm film, and DVCPRO-HD and continues up through all of the flavors of Hi-Definition and then continues on up in film resolutions to VistaVision and IMax.

4 ∴ TOOLS

"We shape our tools and they in turn shape us"
Marshall McLuhan (1911-1980)

Choosing the right tool with which to tell your tale is perhaps the most confusing aspect of digital production. With film, it's a relatively easy decision. Budget, format, crew, and location all combine to give you two or three basic choices which are then narrowed down by personal preference.

In the film world there exists a methodology that has changed little in the past century. An enhanced level of professionalism has taken advertising hype out of the decision-making process because manufacturers assume that the vast majority of cinematographers have already been shaped by their tools.

The industry's slow growth allowed parallel systems to evolve. The same piece of 35mm film fits into a 1949 Mitchell BNC or a 2003 Panavision Millennium. There are many different camera manufacturers, all catering to different preferences based on what you shot and where you lived. Panavision, Arriflex, Aaton, and Cinema Products took the high ground with other smaller manufacturers picking up the niche markets of high-speed, ultra-light weight, underwater, stunt, and so on. All in all, a rather mellow, high-quality field of competition.

THE THEOLOGY OF TECHNOLOGY

"Just as the wheel is an extension of the leg, and radio is an extension of the voice, so too, is the camera an extension of the eye, the computer an extension of the brain, and wiring, circuits, and the Internet an extension of the nervous system." As Steve Mann suggests in his Keynote Address at the *McLuhan Symposium on Culture and Technology*, your tools are an extension of your body and mind. The only way to evaluate what tools are right for you is to poke around and try them yourself.

Which tools do you feel are destined to become an extension of your body?

Marshall McLuhan was often referred to as the "Oracle of the Electronic Age." His fundamental belief in technological determinism is one of the central themes of his best-selling book *The Medium is the Massage* (no, that's not a misspelling, he just had a whack sense of humor). In it he proposed the notion that the message is greatly impacted by the delivery system. In his view, "how" we say something is more important that "what" we say.

He divided content into two distinct categories, "hot" and "cold." Hot media represented higher resolutions which lowered audience participation. Cold media (with much lower resolution), causes the audience to fill in missing information and thereby become more participatory. To me, the cinematic dividing line between hot and cold media is miniDV/DigiBeta.

FORMAT CHOICE

I'm assuming that you've plowed through the Tech section and now have a profound understanding of what constitutes a robust signal and how important it is to nurture and maintain it. If, like so many creative, right-brained people you've skipped that section entirely, there is a bit of review in this chapter as we consider the benefits of the various production environments.

For me, the actual decision of which format and computer platform to go with comes down to a subtle mélange of McLuhan-esque influences and the Price/Performance ratio. What is the most affordable system and methodology that has a chance of becoming a natural extension of your being?

Technically you need to consider signal quality, resolution, colorspace, and data rates. Humanistically you need to consider controls, features, form factor, weight, design, and ergonomics. Computer platform decisions should concern ease of use, selection of software applications, data rates, and cost factors.

Every aspect of design can be used to trigger emotional connections. Every aspect of signal quality can be used like a game of Three-Card Monty. What might sound like the best quality based on compression might actually not be the best based on data rates.

While I obviously can't crawl inside your head and help you with emotional and psychological decisions, I can help you with the technical ones.

Obviously, you want to use the highest resolution that you can afford, but there's a whole lot more to resolution than just the number of pixels on your CCD chip. Digital acquisition is a process, and the images must pass through a number of hurdles.

If you hook the video out from a number of different cameras to identical video monitors, they'll all give you a relatively nice image. What you don't see is what that image looks like once it is recorded. Different formats may suffer due to inferior electronics or poor lenses. The actual speed of the tape has a major effect upon the signal's integrity, as does the methodology employed to record color and luminance information.

Taking this all into consideration, why would you want to go through all the trouble of making a movie (which, by the way, stands a thousand-to-one chance of being the only movie you'll ever make) on an obviously inferior format?

As long as you have freedom of choice, exercise it. And most importantly don't believe any salesmen, advertisements, articles, or books (even mine) that offer a quick and painless solution.

EVERY BUCK YOU WASTE ON EQUIPMENT IS A BUCK THAT DOESN'T GO UP ON THE SCREEN, SO...

1.) GET YOUR HANDS DIRTY: You can delegate the process of gathering information and trying out various systems, but you can't delegate the final decisions. Before you open the checkbook, or decide on a format, at least one person whose ass is on the line needs to actually learn and understand the technologies and the basic operation of the systems that you're going to use. If you rely on a salesperson or someone who isn't invested in the production, then you're too far removed and a world of pain and disappointment are waiting just around the corner. There is far too much snake oil in this industry to rely on anything but hands-on, trial and error.

2.) ONLY BUY WHAT YOU NEED: The actual production process of a movie easily runs a year while the time that you spend shooting generally lasts several weeks. The predisposition to purchase your camera is an affectation of advertising and that strange, predominantly male gene that loves to tinker. Get over it! You can rent a good DigiBeta or DVCPRO-50 for less than a hot miniDV setup would cost and then put the extra money you save up on the screen.

3.) BUY IN THE "SWEET SPOT:" If you absolutely feel the need to own your camera, then please have the common sense to buy in the negotiable area between too expensive and too old. Don't necessarily go for the most expensive or newest gear you can find because you're going to end up paying through the nose. Who wants to be in the middle of production when their spiffy new camcorder is recalled?

4.) BUY OR RENT GOOD EQUIPMENT FROM A QUALITY VENDOR: Those deals in the back of magazines might look tempting, but where are they when your nifty new camcorder starts eating tapes for breakfast? The vast majority of individuals who rent out production packages are generally former victims of the urge to buy. They simply can't compete with the maintenance and instant replace-ability of a quality vendor. Service, even for battle-weary old curmudgeons like me, is as important as the technology.

5.) BEWARE OF BUZZWORDS: Don't allow buzzwords to serve as verbal shortcuts until you've clearly communicated that you understand exactly what they're supposed to mean. Phrases like "enhanced resolution" or "widescreen emulation" may sound great, but generally mean that the manufacturer is just trying to keep up with the market without actually improving the merchandise.

6.) STICK WITH SIMPLEST TECHNOLOGY THAT WORKS FOR YOU: The whole thing about computers and digital technology is that it's supposed to make things easier, yet nearly every industry magazine spends page after page comparing tweaky little features between competing products. 90% of the people use 10% of the features of any given digital product, whether hardware or software. Let's say you have a choice between two cameras, and they both create identical images; the one with fewer features is probably not only going to save you money but will probably be far more dependable and much easier to use. You don't want to be on a hot set reading the instruction manual.

7.) FAVOR "PROVEN" OVER "BREAKTHROUGH:" After "doing time" out on the bleeding edge of digital production, you'll start to recognize a certain type of person who is always extolling the virtues of the "newest hardware" that's "supposed to be" better than everything else on the market. Don't risk system downtime on something that isn't proven. Time after time, a battle-proven system will get you to the premiere more dependably, and that is what it's all about.

8.) IF IT AIN'T BROKE, DON'T FIX IT: Avoid all upgrades once you're in production! The real cost of a major hardware or software upgrade is lost time and productivity. Even though the manufacturer, sales people, and every magazine in the industry tells you that the new, improved upgrade is ten times better, stick to the flavor that works. There is also the chance that one small, seemingly insignificant change in the linking together of disparate systems (concatenation) can have a compounding effect on the final image quality.

From miniDV to HD, the choices are endless. Like any determination regarding major investments, you want to make your decision based on qualified and quantifiably sound information.

PROSUMER VS. PROFESSIONAL

There is a billion-dollar industry invested in having you believe that miniDV is a professional format. It isn't. Yes, Steven Soderbergh shot some elements of *Full Frontal* with miniDV, but he was going for a specific look. The motion picture was shot in 35mm film, and the DV was used to give a sense of separation. Yes, I shot David Lynch's PlayStation2 Commercial with a PD150 DVCAM, but he's David Lynch and you and I are not. He liked the look and the way the tiny camera moved in tight spaces.

Without a long and successful career to back up your format decisions, everything you do is going to be judged on its professionalism. The format that you choose to work with will speak volumes.

PIXEL JUICE

The real power of desktop production lies in the broad pallet of tools, which can contribute elements to the final production. The ease of use of this environment must include connect-ability, system administration, and management of peripheral devices such as scanners, hard disks, FireWire drives, CD-ROMs, cameras, and any other gizmo that tickles your fancy.

I don't particularly like computers. They're great as far as tools go, but a tool is just a tool. I can't ever remember a time when I went out to the garage and "played" with my Makita 110mm circular saw. With a top end of 11,000 rpm at 7.5 amps, it's every bit as cool, in its own electromechanical kinda way, as any of my computers.

Tinkering and tweaking your computer system takes time and energy away from other, far more important endeavors. If a system takes you more than a couple hours to set up and get running, then you have just gotten the wrong system. Some people are naive enough to think that it will get easier but it never does, and the few dollars that you saved by going against conventional wisdom will haunt you for a long, long time.

Once you embark on the binary path of digital production, you automatically become a computer dweeb. Even if you're a card-carrying Luddite and don't intend on using a computer for titles, graphics, effects, or even editing, the camera is a computer peripheral. It records binary data. The friendlier your computer system is, the better your life will seem.

I use my own IBM Intellistation NT quite often for software applications that don't run on the Mac like Maya (Yes, Maya now runs on the Mac, but it needs a render-farm to kick out big projects and all the good render farms are PC based), SoftImage, and the Realviz SFX Studio (which is abso-freekn-lootly awesome). My beloved palmtop is a Windows-based David of Goliath proportions. For high bit-depth and ultrahigh resolution film projects, I fire up the Silicon Graphics workstation. The bottom line is that when it comes down to moving digital video around, nothing even comes close to a Macintosh.

Price point is the king here. The cost effectiveness of modern production tools is quite literally reinventing communications on a global scale. One of the main characteristics of digital technology is how it blurs the lines of previously disparate endeavors. One box can make commercials, motion picture effects, music videos, CD-ROMs, DVDs, Web design, corporate videos… it's endless.

PUTTING THE PEDAL TO THE METAL

'Nuff theory, let's start designing your production environment. From DV to HD the choices and costs are endless. Like any determination regarding major investments, you want to make your decision based on which price performance ratio is best for you. The following chart is intended as an aid to help you determine your platform preferences.

	RESOLOUTION	SAMPLING	COLOR	DATA RATE	COMPRESSION	CAMERA PRICE
HUMAN BRAIN	3,000+ LINES	4:2:2	16+BIT	1GBS	DEPENDS	-----------
FILM	4,000+ LINES	4:4:4	20+BIT	1GBS	NONE	@$10,000
VIPER	1080 LINES	4:4:4	10BIT	2.9GBS	NONE	@$110,000
D-5	1080 LINES	4:2:2	10BIT	235MBS	4:1	-----------
HD-CAM/24P	1080 LINES	3:1:1	10BIT	140MBS	5:1	@$90,000
DVCPRO-HD-P	720 LINES	4:2:0	10BIT	100MBS	6.7:1	@$60,000
D-1	525 LINES	4:2:2	10BIT	166MBS	5:1	-----------
DIGITALBETA	525 LINES	4:2:2	10BIT	90MBS	2:1	@$45,000
DVCPRO-50	525 LINES	4:2:2	8BIT	50MBS	3.3:1	@$40,000
DVCPRO	525 LINES	4:1:1	8BIT	25MBS	4.1:1	@$12,000
MINI-DV	525 LINES	4:1:1	8BIT	25MBS	5:1	@$3,000

>>>>> This chart is only an approximation as prices and specifications change constantly.

WHEN IS THE RIGHT TIME TO BUY?

We've all done it, wanted something but felt we should wait until the newest version came out. The huge advances in technology are behind us. This is the post-digital age, a time when technology starts getting simpler to use and harder to see. This could be called the age of technological ubiquity, but then that's an awfully pretentious title for a simplified paradigm. We need to start taking this technology for granted and focusing on what it can do for us. We need to start focusing on the methodology and less on the technology.

So when is the right time to buy? Answer: When you need it.

While we're on the topic of price performance… Gordon Moore, co-founder of Intel, hypothesized back in 1972 that the speed and performance of computer technology would double every two years while the size and price would halve. This formula has proved extremely accurate and is used almost unanimously in the computer industry as a basic rule of thumb.

For illustration, if the automobile industry performed at the same level, today's Mercedes sedan, which in 1972 cost around $10K, would cost $.12, get 10,000 MPG, and travel near the speed of light. With the industry-wide acceptance of digital, the motion picture industry has just plugged into that formula. Hang on!

INTERLACED VS. PROGRESSIVE

As you should remember from Chapter Two, the difference between progressive and interlace is that progressive is generally defined as a single frame of solid image which is displayed in successive lines of image. CRT computer monitors operate this way, and it's one of the reasons why type is much easier to read on a computer than on a television. Film is analogous to progressive.

With interlace, the frame is built out of two separate fields of even and odd numbered lines of image that are separated in time by 1/60th of a second. This time difference can cause a serrated edge to appear on objects that are moving along at a good clip. Not bloody-well cinematic.

There are several cameras that are capable of shooting both interlace and pseudo-progressive video. While a very few of the newest cameras such as the Panasonic DVX-100 actually give you a true progressive frame, the majority of miniDV cameras that claim to give you a progressive frame are merely doing some rather toxic math. While the essence of the manufacturer's claims are correct, without the carefully worded disclaimers, you're looking at a convoluted image that is difficult to project or print to film.

A far better choice is to simply declare yourself a moviemaker and go with one of the new 24P cameras. With the exception of some mathematical manipulation, the bandpass is spreading the same information over 24 frames that it would normally be spreading over 25 or 30 in PAL and NTSC. The enhanced resolution as well as the native progressive component to the signal projects and prints far better than any interlaced signal of equivalent colorspace, bit-depth, and pixel count ever could.

Let's say that you've got an interlaced camera, and that's all there is to it. There are a number of excellent methods for transposing (there's that word again) interlaced frames into progressive frames without reducing the vertical resolution. They all require post processing the image, which can quite often get quite expensive.

For the adventurous do-it-yourselfers, there are a few really cool sub-apps (plugins) that work in conjunction with applications such as Adobe AfterEffects and give amazing results. One of my favorite post process filters is the MagicBullet from the San Francisco-based Orphanage (*www.toolfarm.com*).

What started out as a rather pricey post process for up-converting inter-lace 601 has hit the wonderful world of desktop plugins. The Bullet uses fuzzy logic (intelligent algorithms) to align luminance groupings which turns your NTSC or PAL interlace footage into progressive frames. Very cool little hack because now you could get a killer deal on some used "i" system and turn your footage into "P" in post.

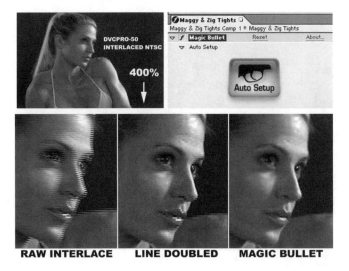

RAW INTERLACE   LINE DOUBLED   MAGIC BULLET

<<<<< The Bullet makes a great-looking face (actress Maggie Myatt) even better, by removing interlace and reducing artifact.

(PAL or NTSC instantly become 24P using the Bullet's spooky code.)

In addition to possessing the ability to turn 60-field-per-second NTSC or 50-field-per-second PAL into 24-frames-per-second progressive, the Magic Bullet has a very powerful artifact-reduction process that comes in handy when it's time to project or print your project to film.

Once processed, a solid frame of digital information equals a solid frame of film. If, however, you're using an NTSC system, remember that 1/5 of your frames must be thrown away for every second that you transpose to film. That's six out of every thirty frames, totally discarded.

FLAVORS OF DIGITAL VIDEO

At the high-end of the video spectrum is Hi-Definition. As far as I'm concerned it is the ultimate video format and a darn good cinema format as well. My good friend Sean Fairburn has one of the more homespun points of view with regard to this new standard and I get a chuckle every time I hear him describe it.

"I come from southern Louisiana where fresh water and salt water meet in the bayous... it's neither fresh nor salt, but rather a combination of both that's called brackish water," he says with his southern drawl. *"In my opinion, 24p HD is similar to brackish water in that it's neither film nor video. It exists in both worlds simultaneously. In interlace mode, it's really, really good video... better than anything out there. In progressive mode, it's darn near indistinguishable from film, but it's also a heck of a lot cheaper and a heck of a lot faster with the added advantage of being able to see exactly what you're getting."*

<<<<< Sean on set.
Homespun meets Hi-tech.

CAMERA SELECTION

Let's say you've got a relatively unlimited budget for your project and you want to get the best possible video image so you've decided to shoot in Hi-Definition. The nasty little secret in the high-end of digital imaging is that the cameras themselves are capable of generating a much higher quality image than the onboard cassette recording mechanism is capable of recording.

There are a number of ways around this data bottleneck, but the most popular method to date is to run the signal from the imaging block out through the HD Serial Digital Interface (HD-SDI) connector to a D5 machine. In most cases, the resulting image has nearly twice the colorspace of the same image recorded to the onboard cassette.

<<<<< The contemporary HD camcorder is a soda fountain of data streams, so belly up to the bar and tap into the flavor that works best for you.

The highest resolution camera in general use is the Thomson Viper Filmstream camera, which generates an uncompressed, 4:4:4 RGB signal that is so dense that there currently is no tape-based system capable of recording it. The current method of recording with the Viper's datastream uses a hard disk system called the Director's Friend.

>>>>> Without the encumbrance of an onboard cassette recorder, the Viper becomes a more cinematic tool.

This is the end of the video-for-film discussion because by the time your image is printed or projected, it will almost assuredly compare well the vast bulk of conventional theatrical projections.

Now let's say that your budget is not necessarily less limited, but rather, you need the added convenience of a camcorder. The Sony-HDW-F900 is a multi-Format, HDCAM Camcorder featuring 24/25/30 frames per second progressive and 50/60 interlace recording modes. Panavision has created their own version of this camera complete with Panaflex lenses and a Panavision viewfinder.

Photo: Minky

<<<<< The author fires a fully loaded HDCAM under the command of David Lynch.

Next step down the budgetary pathway leads to the Panasonic DVCPRO-HD with a data rate of 100 Mbps. After this comes the world of 4:2:2 Standard Definition. While there are many flavors, two outstanding performers are DVCPRO50 and MPEG IMX, both of which operate at 50 Mbps.

>>>>> Joe lines Maggie Myatt up for a chroma key shot with the DVCPRO-HD while 1st AD, Art Cohan, readies the slate... or... Joe and Maggie luxuriate on an exotic tropical beach as a lowly beach boy crawls up to take their drink order.

As I've mentioned before, the current litter of HD camcorders are capable of recording much higher quality signals than the on-board cassettes are capable of recording. For this reason, many people are choosing to record their signal to a D5 machine through the camera's SDI port and then use the onboard cassette for back up.

The D5 machine of choice is the AJ-HD3700 which records in 16:9 aspect ratio at full bandwidth, 10-bit component with a 180MHz sampling rate and 960 lines of resolution switchable to 1,920 at 24 fps at 2:1 on-the-fly compression. It has eight-channel PCM audio at 20 bits and does all flavors of HD at 10-bit quality with 4:2:2 color and mild Bit Rate Reduction.

A D-5 tape, storing full-aspect 16x9 at 10-bit and 1,900 lines of resolution will give you around 40 minutes for slightly under $300.

>>>>> Ralph Fairweather records the SDI feed from the 27V, into the onset, D5 Recorder while pulling a down sampled tap into Apple's FinalCutPro for onset edits.

If the world of 4:2:2 is out of your reach and the esoteric realm of progressive scan is too spooky for you, then consider the high-end of the 4:1:1 category, the Sony DSR570WSL. With almost 800 lines of 4:1:1 resolution sampled at 10-bit and an impressive 62db signal-to-noise ratio, this system creates the best signal in the entire 4:1:1 line. The increased bit depth translates to a significantly better retention of color information. In many instances (up-conversion, chroma key, and visual effects) the 4:1:1, 10-bit signal outperforms many 4:2:2, 8-bit signals.

Sometimes you've got to take a look at the big picture to figure out what is really going to work best for your specific application. The best bang for the buck in video-for-film production today is BetaCam SP. Yes, I know that it's an analog acquisition system, but keep in mind that analog is analogous to infinite, while digital is fixed. Colorspace digitizing schemes don't transpose well from one format to another.

In many instances, shooting in analog and then digitizing at your highest data rate will give you much better results in colorspace. Since everyone in production is so biased toward everything digital, there are many golden opportunities awaiting the savvy moviemaker in the analog world. An aggressive and innovative person could conceivably put together a good used BetaCamSP system that would drastically out-perform many, if not all, of the prosumer quality DV systems for a similar budget.

Keep in mind that one of the major factors in the inherent quality of the image comes from the quality of the lens. An industrial-quality BetaCamSP lens is many times superior to consumer lenses while a broadcast-quality BetaCamSP lens is almost immeasurably better.

My undisputed pick of the litter is the Sony-BVW-D600 BetaCamSP. Sony ImageWorks did a test where they up-converted the BVW-D600 image and printed it to film. The projected test was far more film-like and had a more pleasing image than a comparable test done with DigiBeta.

So, you don't really have a budget after all? But hey, you did just get approved for a new credit card and you see in the paper where Costco is running a special on miniDV camcorders. All right, you're going to make a movie, dude!

Doesn't really matter which of the 4:1:1 systems you use, they're all going to give you basically the same thing. If you want to spend energy stressing over advertising hype, well then be my guest. The reality is that a chip's a chip at that resolution. The true limiting factor is the lens. Don't be fooled by the ability to change lenses. They're all still just prosumer-quality inter-changeable lenses. At least get a camcorder that allows you to override the auto functions.

<<<<< One of the smallest 24P camcorders in general use, easily overrides the auto functions for more professional acquisition.

Panasonic AG DVX100 was the first 24P palmcorder to hit the store shelves. It boasts outstanding sensitivity: F11 @2000 lux, min illumination: 3 lux (at +18dB) and supports 480i/60 (NTSC), Cinema-style 480p/24fps, and 480p/30fps image capture. Although I prefer the look of the camera's 30P mode with cine gamma, the 24p does deliver as promised. It comes with a very crisp wide-angle lens with Servo/Manual Zoom that has stops and easy-to-read barrel markings.

With so much juice packed into such a tiny form-factor, they had to keep it from disemboweling their healthy ENG market so they saddled it with the horrendous *focus ring from hell*. It is impossible to get professional results with a lens that has a focus ring that just keeps on turning. Since there is no quantifiable or repeatable point at which you can actually generate a true follow focus, any camera with a focus ring that doesn't stop turning is not suitable for professional production. PERIOD!!!

Even though the DVX100 boasts a 16:9 aspect, it shoots a conventional 4:3 and merely cuts off the top and bottom of image. Echoing the trend in higher resolution, cine-style cameras, the DVX 100 has both conventional video gamma and cine-like gamma operational modes. The audio accommodations include two-channel XLR audio inputs with phantom power supply (48V) and manual audio levels. On of my favorite additions is that it holds six scene files and two User Sets that can accommodate a wide range of shooting situations. The cameras IEEE-1394 FireWire™ interface accommodates both in and out transfer of digital video/audio to and from NLE platforms.

In the world of interlaced miniDV, the PAL version of the Canon XL series is one of the better choices. It costs a little more than its NTSC cousin but is designed around the same professional modular approach that allows the user to change lenses. One of the hip things about this camera is that it lets you shoot in 25-fps, quasi-progressive mode and has an anamorphic setting that actually compresses the image horizontally. While the XL progressive mode projects well, everyone I know who's tried to print it to film has had problems. Proceed with caution!

>>>>> A Canon XLI dressed up with a manual lens just like the big boys. Body Brace, Follow Focus and Matt Box by Karl Horn at (*www.cinetechonline.com*).

Even though the XL chipset is much older technology than any other camera in the high-end of DV, it has become the de facto stan-dard because of its rugged construction and the option of using a mechanical lens. No auto-focus, no image stabilization, no power zoom, in fact nothing to degrade the video image outside of the limited bandpass of the miniDV format itself. The XLs mechanical lens is composed of fully coated glass elements that offer an unusually crisp image through its entire 14x focal range. (See actual comparisons in the TEST section of the PixelMonger website.)

With the advent of the XL2 and its 16×9 native chip set, the playing field of miniDV production will truly infringe on professional standards once and for all.

My biggest concern with the XL series is that since the last edition of this book was published, only six people I know of, out of several thousand who have used the XL, have used the mechanical lens. I'm sorry but I just don't get it.

YET ANOTHER LIST

Here are my several technical particulars that could help you maximize your cost/resolution factor.

1.) If you're serious about shooting in digital video and then digitally projecting or up converting and printing to film, give serious consideration to building a PAL system. Computers and software don't care. Basically any format in PAL will outperform the same format in NTSC in both resolution and colorspace. There is simply 20% more data in each frame of PAL.

2.) If you're hell-bent on owning your camera, you can quite often buy a used ENG system like BetaCam SP for the same price as a spiffy new DV system. What you'll get is a robust system that was built for professional use. It will most likely come with a really good lens. The component signal will look much better when digitized through a high-quality video card into your desktop edit environment than the FireWire DV signal. Just about any of the BetaCam SP family of cameras have really nice CCDs that give a better tonality and a more filmic look than the tiny miniDV chip sets ever could.

3.) Learn the difference between 4:1:1 and 4:2:2 and then apply that knowledge to all future decisions.

4.) If you can't afford an Inferno on an SGI then get a Macintosh. I have, and use, top of the line UNIX, Windows, and MacOS systems. Nothing moves video as well as a Mac, especially since it's morphed into a killer little UNIX system.

5.) Shoot everything in 16×9.

6.) Only digitize once! Don't import something with FireWire or a component-capable video digitizer and then re-compress it so you can use it on your Avid. Look out a window. Look out a window with a screen on it (digitized). Now, go get another screen and hold it in front of the window with the screen already in it (re-digitized). If you actually did this, the pattern that you would see is called a *moiré*. Get it?

7.) The best inexpensive video-to-film methodology is to shoot on a rented DigiBeta or DVCPRO-50 (16×9) and digitize (Serial Digital) into your nonlinear system. Keep everything on the same system and don't recompile your data files. When you're done take your files on a hard drive over to a lab that has a Panasonic D5 and dub in SD to the D5. And use a company that has a lot of experience with pixel jockeys.

8.) The price/performance leaders in each resolution category, in my order of preference are:
(A) Thomson Viper HD recorded direct to disk via Director's Friend at 4:4:4.
(B) Sony - HDWF900PAC multi-Format, HD Camcorder at 143 Mbps. Recorded via HD-SDI to a D5 Deck.
(C) Panasonic DVCPRO-HD 27V, 4:2:2 color sampling at 100 Mbps. Recorded via HD-SDI to a D5 Deck.
(D) Panasonic AJ-SDX900 DVCPRO50-24P/30P/60i, 12-bit 4:2:2.
(E) Sony MSW-900P MPEX IMX, 25P, 12bit 4:2:2.
(F) Sony DSR-570WSL 800lines of 4:1:1, DVCAM.
(G) JVC MPEG2 Hi-Def Palmcorder w/native 16:9 (or which ever system shows up first).
(H) Panasonic AG DVX100 24P miniDV camcorder.

Acquisition is only half the battle. While the bulk of the higher resolution platforms are still better served using their dedicated conventional post-production environments for the online, there is a notable emergence of high-resolution desktop solutions. One of the more popular of these tools is the CineWaveHD Macintosh/Pinnacle system. Based around the 64-bit TargaCine card and utilizing Apple's own Final Cut Pro non-linear editing application, the system offers a true 16×9 environment with YUV processing, which eliminates the luma and chroma clamping issues that plagued earlier users.

>>>>> The business end
of the high-end
CineWaveHD desktop.

Combined with a Terabyte of
massively fast storage provides
ample resource for the bulk of
production scenarios. Weighing
in at under $20,000 for the
entire HD system, we are truly
witnessing the emergence of a
new era in moviemaking as these tools continue to get cheaper and more
powerful with every week that passes.

CAMERA SELECTION

I've answered well over a thousand e-mails from readers of the first edition
of this book and one of the most often asked questions was, *"I'm making a
movie and I've got (insert dollar amount here). Which camera should I buy?"*
While first-time moviemakers generally stipulated dollar amounts in the
three- or four-thousand dollar range, there were a significant number of
readers who had managed to secure substantial financing and were
embarking on serious projects. More often than not, their camera budgets
were in the ten- to twenty-thousand dollar range, some as high as forty
thousand dollars.

If we're talking about a miniDV camera that only costs two or three thousand
dollars, that's one thing. Long after your movie is in the can, you can still use
it to document your kids, shoot a friend's wedding, do some freelance
porno work... However, when you start getting into camera packages over
ten thousand dollars, you're in an entirely different league.

I know that the prevailing mindset is that you're making an investment and
that you can rent it out later or that you'll use it to make your next movie
with. Believe me, I've heard them all. If your goal is to become a professional
moviemaker, then focus on making your damn movie.

In the three years since the first edition of this book came out, I've counseled
readers through almost a hundred projects. Slightly more than half of them

were shot on miniDV and about a dozen were shot on HD. Everything else was done on DigiBeta, DVCPR-50, or some ENG or broadcast format. Problem is, by the time the vast majority of those projects were finished, the budgets were up in the range where they could have been done very efficiently in HD. Six of the projects specifically would have enjoyed a very respectable commercial success had they been shot in HD.

The most rudimentary problem with moviemakers emerging from the world of miniDV is this uniquely American predisposition to own everything you use. Perhaps it's a result of living in the most media-saturated country in the world, but the urge to own is an entirely inappropriate concept for motion picture production.

I know quite literally hundreds of cinematographers, but few have put back into the industry like the noted British cinematographer, Geoff Boyle. If you want a crisp vision of the level of quality and integrity that you should be aspiring to, check out his site (*www.cinematography.net/geoff*). If you have questions with regard to cinematic technique, methodology, or technology, check out the adjacent CML resource which he founded and is internationally regarded as the definitive last word.

Being a no-nonsense Brit, a truly great cinematographer, and a person who has been through the equipment-owning aspects of production for many years, I asked him to contribute a summary of his experience with respect to ownership.

>>>>> Geoff Boyle, FBKS

"I've owned or part-owned kit for the last 25 years. This has included the original Sony tube cameras, 1" portable recorders, the first Betacams, the first CCD Betacams, the first of the one-piece Betacams, and the last Betacam that Thomson made, in all around 10 top-of-the-range broadcast cameras. There have also been Aaton LTRs and XTRs, as well as an Arri 435 along the way.

The video cameras never made much money. They basically just paid for the next generation in an area where a two-year-old camera is obsolete.

The film cameras made money because they have a much longer write-off period, but not the kind of money you'd like to make.

The problem is that most people don't cost camera ownership accurately, because once you've got the camera you need all the other bits that people expect you to have and not charge extra for — and don't forget insurance! My current insurance bill is $8,000 per annum.

Let the rental companies take the risk on the major items.

If you have money to invest in kit, then spend it on the specialist bits that rental houses don't carry and that you can charge an outrageous amount of money for. In terms of return on investment, my 15-way VGA splitter is the most profitable piece of kit I've ever owned, it's returned its cost 20 times.) Specialist lenses are good as well. One of my ACs bought his own wireless focus and now has three, as they were so popular.

It's easy to do the math; cost of kit and upkeep and insurance and transport and storage of kit, expected life of kit, return on sale of kit when obsolete, daily hire rate you can expect for kit, hassle of collecting that rate, bad debts.

Buy equipment that you can rent/use long term, lenses are particularly good in this respect."

So, unless you are a well-respected cinematographer, who shoots as your primary occupation, and knows damn near everyone in the business, and are known and respected for the excellence of your craft... well then maybe you should just rent.

TOP TEN REASONS TO RENT
1.) It's the professional thing to do.
2.) You'll get a whole lot more resolution for your buck with renting than you ever will with purchasing.
3.) You won't be constantly worried about damaging your "baby" so you'll go for more interesting shots.

4.) You can upgrade your grip, gaff, and lens packages with all the money you save.

5.) If there's a problem, you can swap out the camera and keep shooting.

6.) You've got a built-in technical support staff.

7.) You'll be free to utilize the most contemporary methodology on your next movie.

8.) You are assured of proper alignment and functionality.

9.) Your purchase won't devaluate upwards of 70% by the time you finish your project.

10.) You can continue to work toward your goal of becoming a moviemaker without the distraction of becoming a rental house.

TOP TEN REASONS TO BUY

1.) You love acquiring possessions.

2.) You love to tinker with stuff.

3.) You think that you're being clever by getting your financial backers to buy you a camera.

4.) You already know that your movie is going to suck so you're hedging your bet.

5.) You secretly want to be in the equipment rental business.

6.) You love having your friends constantly asking you to borrow your equipment.

7.) The hours you spend maintaining your gear gives your pathetic life meaning.

8.) You're a multimillionaire and you need the write-off.

9.) Your rapidly antiquated format fulfills your need to defend lost causes.

10.) It's a good conversation starter at parties.

There is a very basic assortment of tools that you should consider owning, in my opinion. They are: a video graphics-capable computer, a light meter, a small lighting kit, a chart (preferably a DSC CamAlign FrontBox), a roll of chroma key fabric, and a miniDV camcorder to experiment with. Everything else should be rented.

In the end, many of your choices will be dictated by your budget. Or, in the immortal words of Randolph Bourne, "*He who mounts a wild elephant goes where the wild elephant goes.*"

5 ⋮ THE HI-DEFINITION TRANSITION

"Digital Cinematography must abandon all links to Television.

Overwhelmingly, the majority of the constraints and compromises we are faced with have their roots in trying to fit a square peg (film) into a round hole (tv). The needs of Digital Cinematography have a very small area of intersection with the needs of the broadcast television world. One of them has its basis in art. The other, from inception, has been about using the cheapest and lowest-bandwidth methodology to deliver an acceptable image to the masses. The first asks 'How can we create stunning imagery to convey this story?' The other is content with using MPEG-1 delivery with lots of compression artifacts."

Martin Euradjian

There is just so much hype and misinformation flying around about Hi-Definition that I'm going to start off this chapter quite remedially so that there aren't any gray areas. I use nearly every flavor of HD on a daily basis, from high-end network commercials and Acadamy Award nominated motion pictures, to my own ultra-low budget movie. HD is a powerful tool but there is a lot of opportunity for confusion.

David & Goliath

<<<<< From the tiny JVC HD palmcorder to the Thomson Viper über-camera, Hi-Definition is a yin/yang mélange of binary decisions.

Hi Def is the bastard child of film and the epitome of video. It is digital acquisition with organic texture. It is fun to shoot and the biggest pain-in-the-ass that you could imagine. It is the future of cinema.

A story told with HD will look bigger, feel more present, and stimulate the senses far more than any lesser format choices ever could. The content and emotion of your story will play across the actor's faces with far more empathy than lesser colorspaces could ever muster.

So, for the record, let us consider Hi-Definition as a global HDTV standard for both production and programming. In its most formal description it is known as ITU-R BT 709-3. In the streets and on the sets it's generally called 1080 or 720 and then "i" for interlace or "P" for progressive. The "i" is generally kept small so that it doesn't get confused as another number, while the "P" usually seems to end up in caps.

HD "i" seems to be the flavor of choice for sports, action, and television fare while HD "P" has taken the dramatic high ground... and then there's the numbers. 1080 actually refers to an image that is 1920×1080 pixels in size, which if you divide by 120 will equal the future of all aspect ratios, 16×9. 720 is actually 1280×720, again, 16×9. One generally giving you more pixels, one giving you more color. HD pictures actually come in a variety of sizes while standard television pictures tip the scales at 525 lines in NTSC and 625 in PAL.

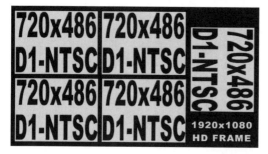

<<<<< Obviously there are many more considerations than just image size, but this graphic representation sets a good mental image.

Compared to the standard NTSC signal, the HDTV image is 250% wider and has twice the luminance definition both vertically and horizontally due to its more cinematic aspect ratio of 16×9 as opposed 4×3.

One of the greatest appeals of HD is the clarity of its image. When you get up close to a standard television screen, you can see the individual rasters that compose the image, while the HD image looks like a photograph from the same distance. The densely packed HD image not only contains much more picture information than a standard television picture, but has CD quality, multi-channel sound as well.

Perhaps sensing inevitable onslaught of digital movies, Kodak took out a series of ads in technical industry magazines stating that in the official

'Kodak' view, film has 4,096 pixels × 3,112 lines of resolution per 35mm frame. That totals up to a whopping 12.75 Megapixels and, when compared to the seemingly impotent 2.073 Megapixels of the standard 1920×1080 HD frame, it looks like an easy victory for film. But hey, do I smell smoke?

A full frame of film is just about the same aspect ratio of a standard 4×3 television. The cinematic framing of 1.85:1 crops heavily into the top and bottom of the "full" frame of film bringing the pixel count down to around 4,096 by 2,214, or just at the 9 Megapixel mark. Is that a mirror in your pocket?

In the past fifteen years, my wife and I have done almost a thousand visual effects for motion pictures ranging the full budgetary spectrum. Out of the 142 motion pictures that we worked on to date, only three requested that the effects be done at 4k (4,000 line) resolution. The rest were all done at the far more common 2K resolution. In real world terms, that's either 1828×1332 for a total of 2.4 Megapixels, or 2048×1556 for a total of 3.18 Megapixels. So, that's 2.073 Megapixels for HD and 3.2-ish Megapixels for your average run of the mill studio fare. See what I mean?

It gets even more confusing when you try to compare the more subjective aspects of film and HD. Of course film looks more film-like, no contest, but perhaps the real question is, "Will the audiences care?" The subliminal nuance of grain does seem to enhance the perceived quality of a motion picture, but then, I was raised with film as being the qualitative standard. Today's market spends a majority of their free time in front of computer screens. They have other priorities and simply don't see grain as a qualitative Holy Grail.

Of course there are a number of postproduction filters that can emulate every film emulsion ever made. The Panasonic D5 machine has a little switch that processes in a number of the most popular flavors of film on the fly. So the way is seems to me is that you can get HD to look like film, but you can't get film to look like HD. Hmmmmmmm...

With a theoretical 4:4:4 sample rate, film has far more color information than say, Sony HDs 3:1:1 color sample or Panasonic's 4:2:2. But now, with the introduction of disk-based 4:4:4 HD acquisition systems, the gap is closing dramatically. As we already know, color degrades with every analogue transposition and there are few things more analog than film.

In the conventional motion picture methodology, the original camera negative must be copied and reversed five times before it gets in front of an audience's eyeballs. With digital you're essentially looking at the camera master, and being digital, it is going to hold its color and resolution. Film, on the other hand, starts to degrade immediately upon the first screening.

DIGITAL PUBERTY

I have been fortunate enough to work with a number of consummate filmmakers and the single unifying factor in their methodology is that they are driven by a need to engage the audience. The more resolution you throw up on the screen, the easier it is for your audience to become involved in your vision.

Higher resolution is the hallmark of professionalism. Projecting miniDV to an audience that is expecting cinematic quality is a potentially career-ending faux pas for anyone who doesn't have the resumé to back it up.

At some point in your career, you will cease to be a digital moviemaker and just become a moviemaker. The change is something that will sneak up on you and change your view of the industry and your place in it. For many, it comes the first time they stand at the back of a theater full of people who paid money to watch their movie. For others, it happens the first time they walk into a Blockbuster and see their movie up on the shelves.

Whenever it hits you, it will feel as though you've just gone through puberty once again. Old habits won't fit the way they did before, as you reevaluate your motivations. Hopefully you'll become a defender of the experience where every project you get involved in, every shot you take, is driven by a desire to give the audience an enjoyable and worthwhile two hours.

Let's say that you've already managed to make a couple of shorts, maybe even a passable long-form feature. The fact that you've actually gotten the train to leave the station and brought it back with cast and crew intact qualifies you as a professional.

Maybe you had a little success at a festival, maybe you didn't — it doesn't really matter. The fact that you actually took a project from concept-to-can is really the only relevant qualifier. Whether or not your movie was any good, that's not for me to judge.

Since you're now a professional moviemaker, you need to make professional choices. The problem comes when the information you make your decisions on comes from ads and articles rather than experience. People like myself who write articles for magazines can only get those articles published if they sell something or support the publication's mythos. This isn't a bad thing, it's just commerce.

Now obviously there are a lot of magazines that require a lot of articles. The reality is that production people are generally too busy making a living to write articles every month. We end up with far too many articles written by people who have little-to-no real world experience and who are simply reformatting a manufacturer's articulate press release.

Please don't misunderstand, there is a lot of misinformation in books as well, but since they aren't driven by advertising, the info is generally a bit less commercially motivated. This is one of the main reasons that I value books so much. So after shooting many projects on every flavor of Hi-Def, from every manufacturer, here is my very best attempt at the bottom line of HD.

HD FAIRY TALES

MYTH: You need less crew to shoot HD.
FACT: Since cinematic methodology remains the same, the number of crew in every department required to create a comparable level of quality also remains the same. The essential difference is in the camera department where the Film Loader is replaced with an HD Engineer at a pay rate between a Camera Operator and the DP.

MYTH: You need fewer lights to shoot HD.
FACT: If you rate the HD Camera at 320 ASA for best performance, you will need the same number and type of lights as if you were shooting 320 ASA Film.

MYTH: HD is cheaper to shoot than film.
FACT: With shorts, the savings in film and development is generally offset by the added amount of footage that you shoot. Takes tend to go much longer with HD because they can. The benefits in not cutting are generally mirrored in more consistent performances. With features, there is a slight savings, but nothing that should amount to more than 2% of your budget.

MYTH: HD saves an enormous amount of money in post-production.
FACT: This is true. Upwards of 70% in effects-heavy projects. (However, don't forget that these savings can disappear when it comes to on-line and other post-processes, where HD equipment may be relatively scarce and definitely expensive.)

MYTH: HD Camera Packages will be less expensive to rent than film packages.
FACT: Industry writer Glenn Estersohn did research on camera rental prices in New York, Chicago, and Los Angeles. In August 2001, he contacted Abel Cine Tech and LVR (New York), Fletcher Chicago and Clairmont Cameras (Chicago), Panavision, and Plus 8 Video in L.A. He compared undiscounted published "rate card" prices and found that the average Sony HDW-F900 rental was 9% more expensive than the average rental for an Aaton 35-3, Arriflex 535B, or Golden Panaflex GII, all with color video assist. His findings seem to be holding steady.

MYTH: HD looks better than film when projected.
FACT: Good HD looks much better than old film. Head-to-head it is a personal choice.

ART AND COMMERCE

Factory presets represent the "safe zone." Art isn't safe.

What we've got here is a new art form, not just a new brush. The thing to keep in mind is that the people who made the brush whether Sony, Panasonic, Philips, Ikegami, Thomson, or JVC made a very good, middle of the road brush, with the finest components available.

As of the publishing of this book, Sony HDCAM has more pixels but less colorspace than Panasonics DVCPRO-HD, while Thomson's Viper beats them both because it isn't hindered by reliance on an onboard tape recorder.

So... for the sake of argument, and despite enormous marketing efforts to contrary, here is the way it breaks down for me, with a bit of review from Chapter Three.

A video signal with a representation of 4:1:1 has its luminance sampled at 13Mhz and the color differences sampled at 3.375 MHz. For every four samples of the reference channel, there is one reference sample of the blue and red. So...

BetaSP is the rough analog equivalent of 3:1:1. DVCAM is 4:1:1 in NTSC and 4:2:0 in PAL. Digital Betacam, DVCPRO-50 and MPEG IMX are all 4:2:2. Moving over to the world of Hi-Definition, you'll also see ratios like "4:2:2." But be aware that the HD data rates up to 5.5 times higher. So 4:2:2 in HD has tons more picture information than 4:2:2 in SD. 'Nuff said. With that in mind, HDCAM is 3:1:1. DVCPRO-HD is 4:2:2, and the Viper is 4:4:4.

>>>>> The author shooting some footage with the Viper that is to be printed to 70mm IMAX film format.

The Viper builds a frame with a full sample of 1920 x 1080 in RGB, gen-erating a full 4:4:4 signal. Since there isn't any tape format that will record this much information, the signal is recorded to hard disk.

D5-HD, having 1920 x 1080 in luma, and 960 x 1080 in each chroma com-ponent, generates a 4:2:2 signal and is currently the highest resolution of any tape format in general use. (I don't consider D6 and D11 to be "general" at this time.)

Both HDCAM and DVCPRO-HD camcorders are capable of generating much higher quality images than the onboard tape cassettes are capable of recording. If you route the signal from either of the cameras to a D5 machine via their (SD) Serial Digital taps, you will get full pixel count sampling at 4:2:2.

Sony's F-950 is so close to the mechanical threshold of recording tech-nology that D5 needs to split the signal and record each frame as two sep-arate elements. This system of recording is called Segmented Frame (HD/SF) and the two separate pieces are glued together on-the-fly to be viewed as a single frame.

Since the DVCPRO-HD frame is physically smaller than the HDCAM frame (720 × 1280 vs. 1080 × 1920) the D5 is capable of recording it whole, even though it does contain almost 20% more color information.

>>>>>   In this case HD stands for High altituDe as Minky shoots the Panasonic AJ-HDC20A 1080i DVCPRO-HD camcorder. The durability, light weight, extended battery life, and small form-factor of the new generation of HD camcorders make them ideal for *remote* location work.

When using the onboard HDCAM recording medium, the video signal is sampled with 1440 × 1080 in luma and 480 × 1080 in chroma, which becomes 3:1:1.

When using the onboard DVCPRO-HD recording medium of the 27V Varicam, the video signal is sampled with 960 × 720 in luma, and 480 × 720 in chroma, which becomes 2:1:1.

There are always new formats springing up and before this book goes into its third edition, we'll have 4:2:2 HD palmcorders for under $3,000. The only rule of thumb that I can offer that will stand the test of time is to follow the bandpass.

The Sony F950 imaging unit pumps out a video stream at 1.2 Gb/sec., but you need to use a D5 machine or disk recorder to record that signal. The on-board HDCAM recorder captures a data rate of 140 Mb/sec. DVCPRO-HD is a close second at 100 Mb/sec. DigiBeta is next at 90 Mb/sec, while DVCPRO-50 and MPEG IMX both create and record data at 50 Mb/sec. I hope you're starting to see how confusing this all can get if you get wrapped up in letting numbers make decisions for you instead of your eyes.

THE ZERO BS TEST

A quick, although not altogether scientific test, to quickly see which system will work best for your needs is to get a piece of navy blue foam core at your nearest art store or Office Depot. Even though they will also have a really nice green foam core, you should use the blue because it is the nosiest channel.

With foam core in hand, head over to your rental house. Borrow a small light and bring it in at a 45 degree angle from about seven feet off of the floor so that you've got a full slash on the foam core and a hard, hot, angular hit on your subject, who should be about three feet in front of the foam core. If you're feeling artistic you can bounce a little card fill from the opposite underside of your subject's face, but this isn't about art.

Have your subject hold up the case for the video tape that you're shooting on. Trust me on this... without this step you're screwed. Get some big Post-It Notes, stick'em on the case, and write any unique info on it so that it is recorded along with the clip.

Pop off a few seconds of your subject with everything that they'll let you get your hands on. The cost for this little test is one cassette of every format that you're considering. If you've got a little extra cash, shoot stuff you're not even considering just so that you'll have the knowledge. Try some different lenses if they have them. Maybe a few primes, maybe a different frame rate. Make sure you write it all down on the Post-It.

As one of my favorite directors is fond of saying, "It's all just money in the bank."

If you're lucky, the rental house will also rent desktop systems, in which case just have them transfer a second or two from each format to a CD-ROM. If not, find someone who will do it for you. The important thing is to use the same system to digitize all of the footage. Something like the Pinnacle CineWaveHD system can digitize a number of component signals as well as all of the popular Serial Digital flavors from DigiBeta to HD 24P. There will obviously be signal truncation, some re-compression, maybe even bit-depth reduction, but since everything jumps through the same hoops, it's apples-to-apples.

If you can't find someone to capture a few frames for you then you are not only in the wrong end of this business, but you really need to work on your people skills. Consider this not only a test of your formats, but a test of your ability to be resourceful and creative.

Your success or failure as a digital moviemaker will in no small part be dependent on your resources. So start hanging out with the nerds, baby.

So let's say that you've got your little CD-ROM full of clips. Pop it into your desktop computer and pull a chroma key. That's it. Forget the numbers, forget the ads, forget the hype... I've used this little test for many years and have yet to have it lead me in the wrong direction.

"But wait," you say. *"My movie doesn't have any visual effects or chroma key shots in it."* Doesn't matter. What you've just done by this little process is find a colorspace, format, system, and lens that gives the best image you can afford. By lighting your shot poorly, you can see how the system handles falloff across the face, how it handles the blacks and whites, the sharpness of the lens, and the quality of the colorspace. You've also played with a number of systems and now hopefully have a better idea which camera best suits your needs and is *destined to become an extension of your body.*

A significant advantage with this little test is that you've now established yourself with the rental house as someone who is serious about the quality of their signal. They will most likely treat you more seriously, and since they have a better idea of your grasp of the technologies involved, they know where to offer help.

For moviemakers moving up from the user-friendly world of miniDV, the professional workplace is a daunting venture. The most important resource you'll have is the quality of service and the added security of support that a good rental facility offers. There are a lot of deals on "packages" that an individual might be renting. While some of those systems are well maintained and constantly upgraded, the unfortunate reality is that many of them are not.

Don't trust your future to the lowest bidder.

GUN FOR HIRE

Quite often a DP will have their own system. If you've checked this person's work, talked personally to people who have used them, and feel comfortable that they can give you the look you want, then this is quite often a great solution. By using a DP who owns their camera, you'll generally get a good break on the system and they'll most likely have a good relationship with local rental facilities. This is all good.

The most important thing is to hang out with this person socially first. Have a few beers, or just sit around and chat about things other than the project. The lines of communication need to be crisp and clear, and all the resolution in the world can't make up for "misunderstandings" once you're in production.

At the risk of stepping over the lines of political correctness, I'd like to add that if you're a Guy, (capital G is intended) and you're embarking on a project that actually has some social dynamics to it, may I suggest hiring a female Director of Photography (DP). I am fortunate to know a number of them and can tell you for a fact that they bring a sense of texture and subtlety to a story that your basic capital G guy would be hard pressed to capture. Just a thought, and something that I feel really needs to be said.

The rapport between the DP and the Director is the most important collaboration that there is in the entire motion picture manufacturing process. There are too many stories about projects that went adrift because of cultural, generational, or emotional differences that only became apparent after production started.

Out here in California, if you marry the wrong person, you can get a divorce. Unless there's some extenuating circumstances you'll generally lose half of what you own... no harm, no foul. But if you hire the wrong DP you're generally stuck with them, in many cases longer than a California marriage. With a hostile production you stand a good chance of losing everything, which will affect your career for the rest of your life. Now it isn't that I'm necessarily cavalier about marriage (my own is going on a very happy 15 years), it's just that I'm obsessed with the initial structure of the production.

Without a happy little production family you are screwed from inception. The added limitations of resolution, budget, and the added vocabulary of technology, quite often bring an element of dissension into even the happiest of endeavors.

Having shot HD in every conceivable way, from studio back lot with an old-school crew, to one-man, run-and-gun, my most sincere advice is to evaluate every option carefully before making your decision.

I consult to all of the studios as well as many production companies, and in nearly half of the projects that I am asked to evaluate, I recommend that they shoot in film. Nearly every production that has taken my advice has met with success while nearly every production that hasn't has run into major problems.

This may sound like heresy coming from some guy who is arrogant enough to write a book called DIGITAL MOVIEMAKING, but my recommendations are not only based on the technologies involved but rather on the circumstances of KEY CREW and ENVIRONMENT.

Everyone in Hollywood is anxious to go "DIGITAL" although few if any have a firm grasp of the realities involved. If you've got the money to shoot film, in most cases, you're far better off shooting film. Digital production, especially HD, has a wide spectrum of advantages, but if you don't understand those advantages they all become disadvantages. Without the extreme latitude of film to cover your mistakes, you're screwed.

DIGITAL OFF-ROADING

Native HD is a rather bland affair. The factory presets are designed so that the camera performs well in a wide number of lighting and production environments. Manufacturers must also take into account that since this is a cinematic production tool, the signal must be configurable to a wide range of distribution modalities (broadcast, digital projection, tape-to-film, DVD, and so on). Each of these distribution modalities has different signal profile requirement, and this is where it gets even more confusing.

If you were to take a Hi-Def camera and either DigiBeta or DVCPRO-50 camera with equivalent lenses, and then shoot the same exact scene, the signals would look almost identical when displayed on an NTSC monitor.

HD-for-broadcast works well straight out of the box.

The latitude, colorspace, and gamma curve all transpose well to the 601 standard while HD destined for digital projection needs to have special attention paid to resolving the denser areas as well as a few contrast management issues. HD that is destined to be printed to film depends on just how you're printing, and what kind of hoops you intend on making your signal jump through.

Let's face it, you use a Sony DigiBeta or a Panasonic DVCPRO, you can rest assured that basically anything you shoot is going to look really good when broadcast. The cameras were made for broadcast, the factory presets are all dedicated to jumping through SMPTE hoops and I've yet to hear a dissenting voice with regard to the signal integrity of any of them in conventional video production.

HD, on the other hand, especially 24P, is an image spec that is by its very nature destined for a myriad of distribution modalities. Are you shooting your HD for network broadcast, or satellite distribution in MPEG, or DVD-ROM, or perhaps a theatrical release is in your plans? If so, are you planning on printing your HD to film using an intermediate stock on a laser recorder or camera stock using a Celco? Maybe you're planning on a digital projection. Will that be using a DLP, LCD, or light valve technology? So many choices, and every single one of them requires a different kind of signal. A different palette, if you will.

The HD equipment manufacturers are all faced with the same problem; with HD being distributed in more than a dozen different ways, what constitutes an appropriate factory preset?

The image that comes directly out of a professional HD camera via the HD-SDI (Serial Digital Interface) connector will look crisp and full on both the Waveform Monitor and Vectorscope, as well as NTSC monitors. Keep in mind that this image essentially represents only the factory preset.

<<<<< The author prepares to shoot the opening sequence of director Irving Schwartz's latest motion picture *LArceny*, with the Panavised CineAlta HDCAM. *"Nothing I likes more than shoot'n dancers, 'cept meybe fer shoot'n mimes."*

While the WFM and V-scope are fine tools, they both have their roots firmly entrenched in the analog world. Since digital cameras are essentially computer peripherals, doesn't it make sense to analyze the signal with the addition of computer graphic tools?

At the very top of the list is the histogram. If you're familiar with Adobe Photoshop, or nearly any professional image-processing software, you're probably already familiar with this powerful image-analysis tool, which is sometimes called Levels. It essentially gives you a visual representation of the luminance values of the image.

Think of the histogram's box as representing the potential bandpass of your signal, with the far right representing white, the far left representing black, and the vertical dimension representing the number of pixels of that voltage or density.

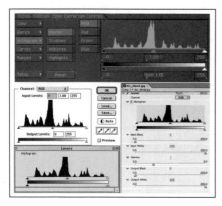

<<<<< Histograms from four different software applications all displaying same DSC chart. At the top is the histogram from Discreet's Combustion and then immediately below on the right is Adobe After Effects. The chart on the far left center is Adobe Photoshop and then below that the Pinnacle Commotion chart.

I'll use Adobe PhotoShop's Histogram to illustrate my point, but all professional graphics applications that I am aware of use this metaphor.

If you download the actual frame from (*www.pixelmonger.ref_frame_1*), import it into any professional graphics program on any computer platform, the histogram will be identical. Keep in mind that there will be the tiniest variation due to JPEG compression.

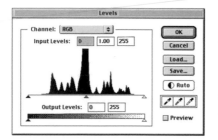

<<<<< Factory Presets.

This is the histogram of a chart that was shot using the Sony F900's factory presets. Notice how nice and "middle-of-the-road" the image is, not just in the visual spectrum, but all the way down to the binary essence of the signal. The space to the left and right of the data group represents wasted bandpass, in this case more than 20%.

With an HD signal that is destined for NTSC, this is not such a big deal because parameters for broadcast greatly truncate the edges of the voltage potential.

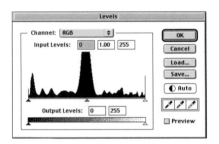

<<<<< Timed on set.

This histogram is from a chart that was timed or "painted" using the F900s Matrix adjustments and a WFM. Notice how much wider the signal is. It has significantly more usable dynamic information in it than the factory preset signal.

While you might not see the difference if you were to broadcast this signal on NTSC, when projected or printed to film there is a notable variation. In postproduction your keys will be nearly 20% cleaner when using a signal that was expanded or "painted" in the acquisition stage.

Since the knee was brought up near 90 and ped down to 1, the resultant histogram could be considered an optimum production setting for a wide variety of uses. Maybe a little punchy for NTSC, but definitely a better signal for printing to film or projecting using a DLP type system.

>>>>> Timed in post.

This is the histogram of the factory preset signal after it was "timed" in post. Notice that the envelope is almost exactly the same as the painted histogram but the white vertical bands represent missing data. The histogram is

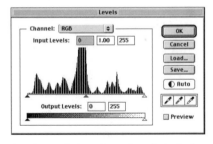

not an approximation, it is an exact reproduction of the data that it is fed. By timing in post you get a signal that looks better to the eye but is technically inferior.

I urge you to try this for yourself. Simply download the raw HD frame, (I've reduced the size to 50%) and import it into Photoshop. In the menu go to "Image" and then scroll down to "Adjust." Select "Levels" from the pop-up menu and then slide the black and white triangles in to the foot of the image data. Save the image as another name and then open up the histogram again. What you'll see is a signal that encompasses a wider swath of the histogramic range, but is noticeably missing entire frequencies of spatial data.

Keep in mind that this comparison is solely designed to show the potential resolution differences between timing in post vs. timing in the field and there are numerous considerations that must be taken into account before embarking on any radically new approach.

Charles (CR) Caillouet is an instructor at the highly-regarded Santa Fe Workshops where many cinematographers go to digitally upgrade their toolsets. In a conversation with CR about my histogram timing concept, he was quick to point out:

"There are pads at the top and the bottom of the HD dynamic range, one put there originally in the CCIR 601 spec in the '80s to allow for proper filter oper-ation. There is also some pad in the camera design at nominal settings. You can safely recover some of this range in the field by careful setup. In post, you can regain the rest BUT you may introduce edge artifacts down the line if you don't leave the room at the top and bottom of the range for proper filter operation."

<<<<< A tiny AJA or Miranda converter can quite easily get a down converted signal into most laptops where you can run it through a variety of image analysis tools.

"Digital filters, like analog ones, need a little space for overshoot to retain enough information to make the signal fully recoverable. Otherwise, if you just clip the signal and throw away the overshoot, you may generate a nasty 'video-looking' edge down the line when a reconstruction filter tries to use the data that you have now synthesized.

One of our nasty video artifact problems is caused by saturated colors hitting the limits in red or blue channels and not being very obvious in the luma display. A gamut limit warning would clue us into that condition."

While there are a number of indispensable color management tools on the desktop, Astro Systems makes a great little monitor that fits on your camera and provides a WFM and V-Scope overlay of your image in the field.

<<<<< From the smallest shoot to full blown productions, signal analysis is a serious element of your personal commitment to excellence. Shown here is the ASTRO WM-3001 HD WFM with graphic overlay capabilities mounted on a Sony F-900 HDCAM.

It seems as though a simple addition to the camera's user presets that allows us to switch the camera's response profile in the field to more closely match the distribution mechanism for the project would give us 20% or more usable resolution. Until this simple addition begins to arrive, we must choose between Vanilla Video and field timing methodologies.

THE ANATOMY OF A CINEMATIC HD PRODUCTION

There are two schools of thought (warring factions, really), with regard to the integration of Hi-Def into the motion-picture manufacturing process.

"Run-and-Gun" is very popular with single-camera productions. It involves working with the chief engineer of your camera rental facility to create a number of preset looks that can be recalled for various situations. The basic looks involve both interior and exterior settings, as well as accommodations for various lighting instruments, visual effects work, and any special atmospheric effects or filtration that the Director of Photography or Director may wish to utilize.

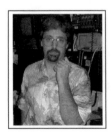

<<<<< Steve Lucas threatens to "*Pop me one, real good*" if I don't stop bringing back his cameras with super glue on the gain switch... or... Steve Lucas tries in vain to get my friends away from his calibration system while we check out some of the gear that's laying around.

One of my favorite Run-and-Gun settings is from Steve Lucas at Wexler here in L.A. He has developed a very popular variation of the IT-709 setting which many people, including myself, take credit for on a regular basis. The Wexler setting extends the blue range ever so slightly into purple, which expands the range of your red and flesh tones as well as giving you a little more wiggle room and texture in shadow detail.

Once you've rated your HD camera and loaded it with your looks, you shoot much the way you would any film camera. By creating a suite of timings for your HD production, you will end up with at least 10% to 15% more resolution and colorspace up on the screen than by using the factory preset... Maybe more.

While a library of presets works well for single camera shoots, it is a blatant waste of resolution on multi-camera shoots.

Color matching is a subtractive process and since nearly all lenses have a color cast to them, there is always a considerable amount of correction to be done in post on projects that don't use on-set engineering. If one lens is greenish and another has a reddish cast, you must subtract green from the green image and red from the red image until they match. You can't just add some color. It doesn't work that way.

Timing in post can often cost you upwards of 10% of your colorspace, while match timing your cameras in the field can *increase* your colorspace as much as 20% over factory presets. That's 30% more colorspace up on the screen!!!!

Hi-Definition engineering is a new department on the conventional motion picture set, and while it doesn't require as drastic a restructuring as many people envision, there are a few accommodations to be made.

Much like any department, there are keys or supervisors, and there is a hierarchy associated with each. Whether there are two or twenty-two in the department, a clear breakdown of job description and responsibilities is helpful to everyone to get the work done efficiently and to understand who is responsible for what.

The HD Engineer needs to consult with the DP early in pre-production to design the look of the project with regard to the director's goals, VFX, production design, and the style of shooting and lighting. Engineering must also work closely with the First AC in coordinating and acquiring all of the necessary gear from the rental house.

HD Engineering is a subdivision of the camera department and should not be confused with the video department, which is an entirely separate sub-division. Video is responsible for video playback and 24-frame video that needs to appear in a scene if needed. Video will receive a down-converted

HD-to-NTSC signal from engineering for normal distribution to the producer's area and to the director's monitors.

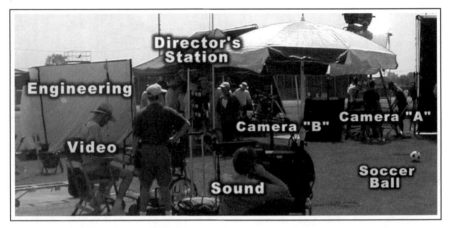

>>>>> A well laid out production environment is a pleasure to work in.

The base of operations for hi-definition is generally referred to as the engineering station (please don't call it video village), and since it is where the look is generated and maintained, it is ideally manned by someone who has a background in both cinematography and engineering.

The terms Digital Image Tech (DIT), Video Controller, HD Supervisor, and Vision Engineer are often used to describe this position, but regardless of the title, this person is the engineer and is responsible for the proper set-up, performance, consistency, and modification of the digital cameras and the look of the image that they record.

<<<<< The Camera Control Unit (CCU) can affect every aspect of the camera's performance and look. It is a loaded weapon with a hair trigger, handle with caution!

Quality control on a Hi-Def shoot isn't automatic. Something as simple as a white balance can radically change the matrix of a camera and its ability to render consistent color values. For this reason, you'll generally find Engineering hunkered down in some dark corner, or cloistered away in a light-tight tent. Needless to say, fourteen-hour days in 100 degree heat can really turn your little hideaway into a portable sauna.

The idea is to keep the engineering station dark so that you can best judge the quality of the signal. Biggest problem of course is that you've now got this really great, ultra-high quality image, that is several orders of magnitude better than anyone has ever seen, so traffic management becomes a real problem.

In addition to the chores of air traffic controller, the Engineer performs changes related to the camera and its performance and keeps the DP aware of how those changes will affect the image.

The master time code generally comes in from the sound department and is then distributed to all other devices that must receive sync. The engineering station is responsible for insuring that multiple cameras all have proper time code during both free run and record run operations as well as setting order of action with the AD to insure that post has enough pre roll. Engineering is also responsible for making sure that all cameras are color matched and phased.

Upon arriving at a location, the HD Engineer coordinates with the Director of Photography to determine where the cameras will be set and to establish the looks necessary to achieve his vision. The Engineer then works with the AD to determine the most advantageous position for the engineering station. Since both cameras are physically connected to, and controlled from it, positioning becomes a critical element.

The rest of the camera crew follows the basic film methodology with a few very specific amendments. So here is the basic methodology that seems to be evolving in conventional HD motion picture production.

Camera Section:
Camera Operator — Insures proper composition and movement of the camera and that all frame line generators are set. Also responsible for making sure that the back focus is properly set and that tape is properly cued up in the camera, so as not to roll over any previously shot footage. At the end of each shot, the Operator hits the RET button, playing back the last five seconds to ensure the camera recorded the scene.

First AC — The First is responsible for the gear related to the camera, as well as its configuration, much like a First AC in film. Also rigs the cameras, loads the HD tape into the camera, and sets time code for new tapes, making sure the feed gets tone from sound and bars from engineering. The First then records 30 seconds of bars and tone on the head of each tape, aids the Engineer in shooting necessary test charts per scene and assists the camera operator in setting back focus. Following a shot, the First insures proper labeling of all filtration, ND, and color correction in front and in back of the lens, along with shutter angle and frame rate.

Second AC — The Second slates the takes, keeps the camera report, and assists the First AC and Engineer. Also runs any necessary cables to the camera and ensures an efficient signal on both ends of the cables.

Cable Puller — Assists the Second by running cables, plugging monitors, and retrieving batteries, cables, and tapes. As the job title would indicate, they are responsible for insuring that cables are not caught in wheels of big dolly moves. The Cable Puller also works like a Digital Grip by loading in and wrapping out on moves to new setups. Since there is usually quite a bit of gear involved, everyone on the HD crew generally helps with moves.

>>>>>   Engineer Sean Fairburn leads off the HD train while Tony Salgado wrangles the "snake." Notice the two fully loaded Sony F-900 cameras that are pulling up the rear.

ENGINEERING:

Engineer — Is responsible for the effective operation of all hardware related to recording as well as distribution, monitoring, down converting, upconverting, analog-to-digital, and digital-to-analog transposition. This gear must not go down! *EVER!* The Engineer is also the supervisor overseeing all other aspects of the department including First AC and Second AC, and proper implementation of signals and recordings.

HD Shader — Physically manipulates the master control units (Paint Box) for the cameras to maintain a particular look prescribed by the Director of Photography. The Shader must insure proper and consistent performance of the look within each scene prescribed. The Shader tweaks and sets up the camera's color, black, white balance, scene files, and menu adjustments each day after the First AC gets the camera powered up. The Shader rides the look during the shots to ensure no shift or glitches occur and insures proper recording of picture and sound with proper time code and labeling of all tapes.

PIXEL PUMPING

I have found that it is harder to shoot excellent HD than it is to shoot excellent film. On the other hand, it is easier to shoot mediocre HD than mediocre film.

Technically, HD is little more than glorified DigiBeta, but the transition to HD is cinematographically biased by more than just frame rate and the fact that you're paying $80 for a cassette that looks damn near exactly like your $24 BetaCam cassette.

At one time the thought of HD on the desktop was daunting. Now it's generally little more than an upgrade away. In my opinion, the leading contenders in the dedicated desktop category are the BOXX system on the PC platform and the AJA-Kona on the Mac, while the best multi-format system is the ever-present Pinnacle CineWave system.

BOXX TECHNOLOGIES

The *HDBOXX* is a turn-key, PC based system that offers uncompressed HD editing, compositing, and playback and is equally at home in film, digital cinema, and HDTV production.

The *HDBOXX* interface is built on a full suite of powerful 10-bit editing and compositing tools, which get it around many of the colorspace bottlenecks that must be addressed on other systems. It is unusually fast, robust, and in my experience, bug-free. The *HDBOXX* works equally well with conventional software applications such as Adobe AfterEffects, DigitalFusion, and Discreet Combustion.

Some of the more notable features include real-time 3:2 pulldown, real-time colorspace conversion, and support for both the Panasonic variable frame rate and Sony 23.98 at 10-bit uncompressed recording.

AJA

Kona-HD card mounts inside a Macintosh computer and supports native 10-bit resolution using the QuickTime V210 10-bit YUV format. Since the Kona captures directly to 10-bit YUV files the sequences that have not been processed with colorspace reducing effects are output as exact clones of the original digital input.

Even when working with graphics/effects programs like Adobe AfterEffects in 8-bit RGB, Kona's 10-bit video/8-bit RGB codecs provide significantly higher quality as compared to 8-bit video. Kona also supports 10-bit video/16-bit RGB codecs and is widely considered the best quality image on a dedicated desktop system.

PINNACLE SYSTEMS

CineWave was the first usable software and hardware system to offer quality Hi-Definition on the desktop. It is based on the time proven TARGA Cine Engine and uses both 8- and 16-bit YUV and 8-bit RGBA codecs.

CineWave is QuickTime native and designed to work with a wide range of formats including: DV, DigiBeta, uncompressed 601, PAL, NTSC, 1080i, 1080p, 720i, 720P, 4:3, 16:9, DVD, and Web compressions. Being fully QuickTime compliant, CineWave allows you to view your uncompressed SD or HD footage on an external NTSC/PAL or even HD monitor from QuickTime compatible applications such as Commotion Pro, After Effects, Combustion, and Pro Tools.

MOTIVATION

There is the reason you're shooting HD in the first place. Are you shooting it because it's cool and the very hippest thing to do? Are you shooting it because you're a videographer who's migrating to the movie business? Are you shooting it to try to gain creative independence or just give your project longer shelf life?

As many people as there are choosing to shoot HD, there are an almost equal number of reasons for doing so.

On a recent HD-for-film project, we were shooting on the Warner Brothers back lot using the "Panavised" Sony F900 HDCAM at 24P. We had a full film crew and shot everything very conventionally. Basically the only difference was that the conventional film loader had now been replaced with a far more expensive HD Engineer.

The look of the final project when projected was almost indistinguishable from that of film. Was it cheaper? Not really. Was it faster? Nope. Why then, you may ask, did we shoot on HD? *"Because it is what's happening,"* replies Faye Dunaway, the film's director. *"There are, of course, the practical givens; you can go out and shoot a lot more because tape doesn't cost as much money... but that's not why I did it. We did a very sophisticated budget and HD was only about a thousand dollars less. We shot in HD because, quite simply, it is what's happening. This is a transitional time in motion picture production, it's exciting and fresh."*

<<<<< Director Faye Dunaway in her character as Aurora Beavis.

"We're out there on the leading edge of technology and art. I've been watching the stuff that people like Mike Figgis and Lars von Trier and Dogma have been doing, it's a new revolution. I guess it's the variety of expression that appeals to me. I like the challenge of it and the clarity and newness of the medium. I love the magic of film, and there's nothing like it. Perhaps I'll work with it again, but for this project I wanted to explore this new world of hi-definition. I'm glad I did."

The obvious advantage of recording on to an inexpensive medium (videotape) did not escape Dunaway as more than once the actors heard her calling out, *"Just keep on going and then roll right into it again. Tape is cheap."*

Perhaps no other incident so keenly drove home the inherent cost-effectiveness of the actual recording medium as when James Coburn, in his role as an evangelical preacher, got hung up on the word "Gethsemane." Time after time he'd work his character into a hollowed frenzy only to be stopped dead when he came to that word. In a traditional film production, the director would generally make accommodations after a failed take or two. Maybe even utter the popular *"We'll fix it in post,"* but not here.

Without the budgetary pressure of burning film, the urgency was gone, as the extras who populated the congregation chuckled politely with each botched try. When he finally did get it out, it was in a one of those "hell-fire'n brimstone" deliveries that you felt down in your shoes.

<<<<< James Coburn drives home some digital dynamite.

Cast and crew alike, all looked up at the tow-ering Coburn, who was on a roll and driving home a performance that was pure gold. After a moment of stunned silence, Faye Dunaway the actress, who was sitting in the congregation as her character, Aurora Beavis, remembered that she was also Faye Dunaway the director and called out (in character) "*Cut!*"

Once out of character, Faye was quick to point out the advantages of shooting in a relatively low-cost acquisition medium. "*It's an idea that I first got when I worked with Luc Besson. He would operate the camera and he would talk to the actors during and between takes. There's a great advantage to letting the film run and maintaining the connection with the actors. As an actor, the abili-ty to stay in character without breaking the energy lets you build on your per-formance. You get up for the scene but maybe you missed a little something or you want to come at it from another direction. Because tape is cheap, you're not as predisposed to cut, and so you keep rolling and refining the performance until you get everything just right.*"

"*With film there's always that pressure to cut, but when you do, everything deflates. Hair and make-up come in and start fussing with the actor, people start drifting off to craft services, and you end up losing everything that you worked so hard to build. If you can keep on going from one take to another, you start building on all the tension and energy that's in the air, and start generat-ing a higher caliber of performance. That was obviously the case with James, and just look at what we got.*"

The cinematic look that we got in the end was entirely due to the way we shot and the way we lit. When asked what he thought of shooting HD, the show's key gaffer, Ken Wheeland, shook his head with a smirk while pulling off his leather gloves, "*When they told me I'd be setting for HD, I figured this'd be a cake walk, but look at this! I've done film shoots that were easier to light than this; lots of 'em.*"

Those who look at HD as a way to replace the gaffer and grip and all of the associated equipment that their work entails should save their money, because HD isn't for you.

<<<<< Turn about is fair play as Faye returns the favor.

Six months later I was shooting my own highly experimental HD production. Being not only a consummate professional, but also a genuinely good person, Faye had consented to be in my humble production. As I'll cover in greater detail in Chapter Seven, due to schedule conflicts it was necessary to shoot Faye's scene against Bluescreen without the aid of her scene partner.

Several takes into a particularly involved monologue, Faye turned to me and said, "*Scott honey, why do you keep cutting? Tape is cheap, let's just keep it rolling till I get this right.*"

Touché!

6 SPIELS AND DEALS

"When you pitch a story, you are being judged
in two areas. One, how good is the story, and two, is this
somebody that I want to work with?"

Ken Rotcop

Do your dreams of moviemaking include endless pandering to minimum wage employees in the hopes of getting a face-to-face rejection from their boss? Do your dreams include the demoralizing quest for money that always seems to have been doled out the week before to someone not nearly as qualified as you?

Didn't think so, but without pitching and dealmaking your career is just that. A dream.

It isn't about "making" any more. Heck, anyone can make content. It's not even about equipment... that's what we have Good Guys and credit cards for. It's only about the deal, putting it together, writing or finding a good script, finding good people, getting distribution, tapping into emerging markets and, of course, schmoozing. Polish those skills and you'll be in good shape, without them you're just another log on the fire.

I've seen some really spooky stuff happen in this industry. Film school kids fresh off the bus, getting a movie deal on their first pitch... or some well-connected kid getting a multimillion dollar deal on their first script.

It is a rare occasion to go to a party in this town where there isn't some wide-eyed flavor-of-the-month holding court, spewing about how they're on the inside track, or how they're going to show us all how to make movies their way. Then there's all those red-hot, up-and-comers from the festival circuit.

Look around the industry a year or two later and they're gone. All of 'em.

The few smart ones use their festival success as a backstage pass into the clockworks of Hollywood. They jump in and jostle around until they find the niche where they belong, establish themselves and start swimming up stream with the rest of us salmon.

There is no secret to success in this industry and the ones that make it look easy are very often the ones who work the hardest. There are, however, some fundamentals of pitching and dealmaking that will assure you a better than average chance at survival.

PITCHING

It always seems to start with a pitch. You pitch the script to raise the money to make your movie. Unless you're making an experimental short or a project to use as an example of your abilities, it's safe to say that you should never use your own money unless you've got piles of it laying around.

The underlying, fundamental cornerstone of the motion picture industry always has been and always will be OPM (Other People's Money).

Making a movie is a difficult job; you'll have more than enough concerns vying for your attention. Balancing your checkbook and the fear of losing your kids' college fund should not be among them. Your only thoughts at this point should be the excellence of your script. Whether you wrote it, bought it, stole it, or paid to have it written, the script should be your singular obsession. Well, OK, you can skip the bit about stealing.

Your friends will tell you the script is great because... well, because they're your friends. Get any two of 'em together and one will lie straight-faced and then the other one will swear to it. That's what friends do. Investing, however, is an entirely different matter, which in the real world of business is rarely predicated on friendship. If you can't get even one investor or producer to see the intrinsic value in your script... well then, maybe it needs a little more work.

Let's face it, the only valid reason for making a motion picture is to make money. Even the project or two that you shoot to demonstrate your abilities are done to get you into the money-making world of professional moviemaking. As crude as it may sound, that is the bottom line.

If you want to make art, there are a lot of far less expensive mediums out there. If you want to send a message, or make some grand sociopolitical statement, may I suggest the plethora of opportunities the Internet has to offer.

If you approach the movie-making process as anything other than a money-making venture, you are a failure just waiting to happen and anyone daft enough to sign onto your little venture will get some of it on them as well.

While we're on the topic of pitching, perhaps I'm just being naive, but I've never understood why anyone would ever pitch a miniDV project when, for the same expenditure of time and energy, you could be pitching to make your movie in DigiBeta or even HD.

Apprehensive about shooting HD? Get over it. In the Sony world, HDCAM is just glorified DigiBeta and in the Panasonic world, DVCPRO/HD is the same size tape that's in your miniDV... it just runs a little faster.

If you've already demonstrated your craft and abilities and are in possession of a script that you feel like spending the next year of your life on... pitch the damn thing as an HD feature. Don't let the little weevils of doubt eat away your self-confidence. You're on a destiny vector that will irrevocably change the entire outcome of your life. Don't piss it away!

HOME COURT ADVANTAGE

In addition to my home court of Los Angeles, I've hung out in the filmmaking communities of New York, Canada, Australia, France, Germany, U.K., and Italy, and the one thing that they all have in common is that everyone is pitching everything all the time. So here is what I've come to know with regard to the fine art of pitching.

A well-pitched mediocre script will get made before a poorly pitched great script. Sad but true.

Nothing of any lasting value gets made without some serious pitching, and the fundamentals that sell a pitch in Germany are the same ones that work in Hollywood. They are: enthusiasm, structure, delivery, and of course, it always helps to have a good script.

You must believe in your story, you must care for your characters, and you must make your potential financiers feel as though you are someone who they trust with their money and reputation.

The key to trust, as any good car salesman will tell you, is the ability to mirror the sensibilities of the person you're trying to sell. If you find yourself pitching to a guy that works out of his beachfront home, your attire and style should be a lot more casual than a formal studio pitch.

Keep it short. Two minutes tops. If they want to sit around and talk about the characters or the story, fine, but the bottom line is that you want them to read the script, fall in love with it, and then finance your movie. The more you blither on, the more chance you're giving them to examine the chinks in your armor.

There are a number of formulas for a good pitch but the best game plan that I've found is to stick to the basics. Not only does it make you look like a pro, but the person you're pitching to is already familiar with conventional structure and will be far more receptive to what you're saying.

Start with a question that is related to the topic of your script and then follow that up with a brief story of how you came to write or acquire this particular screenplay. Once you have their attention, the two-minute clock starts ticking.

Any experienced person that you're likely to be pitching to is going to be looking for a number of specific things about your script. They'll want to know who the protagonist is, why we should care about them, and how they evolve over the course of the movie. Structurally they'll want to know what the central theme of your movie is and what unique variation makes your story marketable.

Open with your log line i.e. "This is a homespun murder mystery about an ambitious car salesman who gets involved with some unlikely crooks." If you can't get a solid description of your movie out in one breath, then either your script needs work or you need to cut down on the cigarettes. Wait a beat or two for any questions and then dive head first into your synopsis.

I guess it goes without saying that your log line and synopsis should be constructed in standard industry parlance. Regardless of how original you may think your project is, I can pretty much guarantee you that something like it has been done before. Go to *www.IMDb.com* and and look up some movies that are similar to yours. Use their log lines and synopses as a template for your own project.

The object is not to boggle them with your oratorical brilliance but rather to give them an honest glance into the world of your movie. By using standard parlance, they don't need to sit there and translate everything you're saying.

Be conscious of your body posture. A slight forward lean, lots of eye contact, an occasional hand gesture and a good volume delivered with a rhythmic pace will maintain a level of interest even if they're really just trying to figure out where to have lunch.

In most cases you'll be pitching a business venture to a successful businessman. Dress as though you're applying for a home loan and you should be all right.

In much the same way a salesman closes with a "call to action" so should you. Close the pitch by asking if they'd like to read your script. This way they not only know that you've finished the pitch, but it gives them a chance to ask you a few questions.

Generally, if you've done your homework and have managed not to soil yourself, the first question that you'll be asked is, "Who do you see in the lead role?" I really hated this question when I started pitching, partly because I didn't have a very good grasp of the commodity actors, and partly because I didn't want to see my project become another vehicle for some over-exposed flavor of the month.

Hundreds of pitches later, I've come to realize that writing a character for a commodity actor gives everyone a point of reference. It also helps give your character a unique voice that separates it from the other characters. Hey, Mike Myers isn't available, you can always pitch cast Adam Sandler. Adam's not available, well then how about David Arquette or one of the Baldwins. There's always a Baldwin available. I've been in pitch sessions that have basically rewritten the entire project through hypothetical casting.

For me, science fiction and action genre scripts are the easiest to pitch. When I started in this business my odds were less than 1%, now I'm averaging a little over 10%. I have a good friend of dubious sexual identity who can pitch the crap out of a romantic comedy, but couldn't pitch an action-adventure if his life depended on it. Pitch what you know.

Chances are that whomever you're pitching to has heard hundreds, if not thousands of pitches, and the odds are so terribly stacked against you that you'd better be working from your strongest position. Don't do or say anything that isn't brutally honest. You're the rookie and it's more important for them to trust you than it is for them to love your project. In some ways, a good pitch is more important than the project.

In 1995, I was pitching my heart out to a couple executives at Rysher Entertainment. I had this script that I'd written called *Rat Race*, and I knew that it was a perfect fit for their upcoming schedule. I finished my highly rehearsed and energetic pitch and then asked if they'd like to read it. They politely declined saying that it was very similar to something that they already had in the pipeline and asked if I minded if they pitched something to me. Personally I love curve balls, so I sat back while they pitched making a series out of the movie *F/X*.

The original movie was about a special effects guy who helps police solve crimes, but for the series they wanted to use more contemporary methodology like computers and visual effects. In addition to designing all of the technology for the series, I wrote all of the technical dialogue for all of the characters for the three years that the show ran.

From those connections I've written technical dialogue for more than a dozen major motion pictures and countless quickies for an almost endless number of network shows. Not bad for getting turned down on a pitch.

The secret to giving a good pitch is practice. No matter how much you cerebralize, and visualize the process, there's nothing like actually practicing your pitch over and over to get you in the groove. Pitch to your friends, your family, your dog... and when they won't have anything more to do with you, head out onto the street and pitch strangers.

Keep a close watch on their eyes and make a mental note of when they start to look off to the side. You've now identified a flat spot in your pitch that needs a little work. By the time you've ironed out all the flat spots you should be able to keep the attention of a teenager, and that my friend, is an indication that it's time to put on the tap shoes.

The object is to get your pitch perfect, get your delivery perfect, and to get accustomed to pitching in situations that aren't comfortable or familiar. Kinda like the office of a famous producer.

PITCHIN' FROM THE BOONIES

Keep in mind that I live in L.A., where there are literally hundreds of production companies of all sizes, just looking for their next project. You, however, live in Kenton, Ohio, where the only producers are standing out in a field on four legs. OK, so this is where your game plan comes in.

Start by joining IFP (Independent Feature Project - *http://www.ifp.org/*). As far as I'm concerned, there is quite simply no better resource available for the up-and-coming moviemaker. Try to take a seminar or two, or one of their intensive workshops. They have very active offices in L.A., New York, Miami, Seattle, Chicago, and Minneapolis, and maintain a presence at nearly all of the major film festivals. Once you start taking advantage of the opportunities that arise, you'll start becoming aware of the industry in a far more realistic light.

At an IFP/West sponsored Hollywood Networking Breakfast (held at the trendy Bel Age Hotel), I met a young moviemaker who had driven in from Arizona just to "stay in the loop," as she put it. While the monthly event is not intended as a "pitchfest," many people, including myself, consider this opportunity to pitch to your peers as perhaps one of the more enjoyable resources for honest feedback.

Although Ms. Arizona's networking skills were far above average, her actual pitching method seemed to be leveraging the fact that she was a very nice-looking young woman, rather than the content of her script. When nearly everyone at our table busted her on that fact, she understood it on a peer-to-peer, non-confrontational level.

A month later, there she was again; less provocatively dressed and she had her pitch down cold. We convinced her to pitch the guest speaker who was a well-known executive producer of a top-rated, network television series.

As this book goes to press, Ms. Arizona is a staff writer with a multiple-Emmy-winning writing team. Was it what she was expecting? I doubt it. Has she given up on her objective of making her movie? I doubt that, too. The point is that she is now a quantifiable part of the industry. Not only is she most likely pulling down some serious coin, but with her natural ability to network, I wouldn't be at all surprised to see her exceeding any of her goals.

My point is that you shouldn't be so focused on realizing the narrow definition of a moviemaker that you pass up golden opportunities that will actually help you achieve your goals in the real world of the greater motion picture industry.

YOUR ARSENAL

Let's assume that you've already made a miniDV movie or short or have some sort of reel that you can use to show your style and capabilities. Let's also assume that you're in possession of a red-hot script that is fresh, innovative, and full of well-sculpted characters that take us on a non-stop roller-coaster ride.

Hopefully you've got some coverage (industry critique) from a qualified source that attests to your script's commercial potential. Maybe you've entered it in a few screenwriting competitions, where it managed to pull in an award or two.

It is now time to start working double shifts at the local Burger King because you're probably going to need to do a little traveling. Not a lot, but some.

Keep in mind that what I'm suggesting is in a book that thousands of other filmmakers are also reading. Any tips I give instantly become general knowledge and therefore less effective as more books are sold. The real trick is to get the snapshot of the industry that we're working on here and then take the bits that you feel most comfortable with and improvise.

The basic tools you'll need are access to a listing of film festivals (use your IFP connections and their website), a subscription to the *Hollywood Creative Directory* (*Producers & Distributors*) and a subscription to either *Daily Variety* or the *Hollywood Reporter*. You'll need to put together your own game plan, but the essential methodology could be something like this.

Find a dozen or so medium-sized production companies who are making deals on films like yours. Find out who the festival acquisitions people are at those companies and then see if they're sending anyone out to any of the film festivals in your neck of the woods.

The upside of the burgeoning avalanche of DV production is it has spawned so many film festivals that every state in the U.S. now has at least a couple of them.

So hopefully you've got yourself a nice little list of contacts. The next step is to write them a letter. No e-mail, no phone calls... just a well constructed letter. If you aren't literate enough to cobble together a crisp single-pager, how do you expect them to believe that any script that you're in possession of will be much better?

You'll want to introduce yourself, mention that you've done some production work, and that you've got a project that you feel is appropriate for their catalogue. Mention that you'll be at such-and-such film festival, and ask if you could pitch your project to their representative. If you haven't heard from them in ten days, then try an e-mail or give them a call. Don't be too pushy, but then don't be a push-over, either. If only one out of ten says yes, it is well worth the trip.

Here's why. The people who cover the festivals for the various studios and production companies all travel together. They all go to the same festivals year after year and the same parties year after year. They're really very nice folks and you can usually find them standing together chatting at any number of festival get-togethers.

I wouldn't presume to speak for them, but I do know a few of these folks and I can basically tell you that if you pitch one of them well, it'll get around. Hopefully they'll see something in your pitch and invite you to pitch the head of acquisitions. On a rare occasion, with proper disclosure, they'll take your script to read on the plane, although this isn't something you should count on.

Even if you're turned down, you're now out there pitching and a bona fide part of the system. Put another pitch together, you're a moviemaker, this is what moviemakers do. No one takes offense, and believe it or not, a vast majority of people out there are rooting for you to succeed.

Another more direct approach is to participate in one of the numerous cluster pitches that take place nearly everywhere in the world. Sure, there's a lot of them out here in L.A., like Let's Do Lunch and Ken Rotcop's famous Pitchmart, but a few minutes with your favorite search engine is bound to turn up something in your neck of the woods. If *www.nebraskacoast.com* can sponsor the Hollywood Salon (Schmoozing Nebraska style) then no place in the world is sacred.

I've been both the pitch-ee and the pitch-er and can tell you that a good presentation of good material very often gets serious results. Your ultimate goal is to get the most accomplished producer that you can find to buy into you and your project, and then get out of the way.

There have only been a very few emerging moviemakers who have self-produced their own project and then realized any true measure of success. As I've said before and will say again, this is a very complicated industry. The number of people who possess the capacity to do both the creative and the business side of moviemaking well can be counted on one hand... with fingers left over.

The most valuable contribution to the success of your movie is the brutal dose of reality and proven methodology that a good producer brings.

THE DEAL

The basic purpose of the deal is to secure the best set of circumstances that will allow you to make your movie with the least outside interference and the best chance for distribution. A nice secondary goal is to emerge from the process with all of your body parts intact, but don't count on it.

Before you go looking for a deal you've got to have a game plan. Your basic choices are to form a corporation and do all the business yourself, or find a production company to help you make your little epic.

Having done both, I am totally in favor of finding a production company that already has staff, insurance, existing industry connections, and maybe even a nice line of credit with vendors.

A small company may only have one producer who is overseeing several projects in various stages of completion. Larger companies generally have a number of producers who specialize in various genres. Either way, it is at this point that it not only stops becoming _your_ movie but you start to be less of a moviemaker in the holistic context of the word.

Since you are now transitioning from the world of do-it-all-yourself, moviemaking-as-a-hobby to the world of part-of-the-industry, moviemaking-as-a-career, you'll need to start packing away some of the many hats in your wardrobe. The larger the production company you associate yourself with, the simpler you will find your job description becoming.

Financially, you stand to make less of a percentage but the total that the percentage is from will most likely be a whole lot bigger. With a professional producer covering your back you're also not going to come out of the process nearly as beat up. Since you're not going to need to spread your attention over such a wide area of interest you can now focus more on working with the numerous other professionals that are involved with the project.

I am always impressed by the occasional moviemaker who has done the whole process in-house. If you have the energy and inclination to be your own boss, then by all means consider forming your own production company and giving the route of self production, and maybe even self-distribution a try.

The vast array of considerations involved with forming your own production entity could easily fill an entire book. The good news is that it has. The single best resource I've ever come across for creating your own production company is a book called PERSISTENCE OF VISION: An Impractical Guide to

Producing a Feature Film for Under $30,000 (now updated and called *Digital Filmmaking 101*) by Dale Newton and John Gaspard. It should come as no surprise that they perform their ultra-low budget wizardry in the frozen reaches of Minneapolis, Minnesota.

Whichever way you go, you are going to need to get as much bang for the buck as you can manage.

FINANCING

Keep in mind that I'm not a lawyer (although I play one on TV), and that my advice is entirely predicated on personal experience and not cross-correlated research and study.

If you don't already have a lawyer, you can generally find one through your closest IFP chapter.

Whether you've now got a producer behind you or not, you're going to be looking at financing coming from one or more of the four basic food-groups of production: investor, lender, industry, or the truly wonderful world of foreign financing. All have their advantages and drawbacks.

INVESTOR FINANCING

This is quite often the first method of funding for the vast majority of moviemakers. It can be as simple as opening up your checkbook or as complex as forming a corporation and offering stock.

With any sort of investor financing, other than self-funding, you'll need a very good business plan as well as an investor-financing agreement. You can do all of this by yourself, but I find that it truly drains your energy away from the important task of making a movie.

A rich uncle or friend looking for the thrill and glamour of moviemaking might be all right for a small miniDV production, but when you get into serious production, you're far better off with a funding source with deep pockets.

If you don't have an experienced producer behind you, then you'd better have a good lawyer and an industry-savvy accountant, because the IRS is looking over your shoulder. I once had a "friend" working the books on an early project. The "misplaced funds" that didn't make it into the quarterly, and the hundreds of little shortcuts that my "friend" got creative with, ended up costing me almost as much in fines as the original production did.

Basically you've got two ways to approach investor financing: active and inactive.

Active participation deals are much easier to put together because the investor is part of the production process. In many cases, a joint partnership will cover the inherent legalities (again, check with a lawyer) and get you up and running with the minimum of delays. The downside is that you've now got someone who quite possibly doesn't have a background in moviemaking, but who is in a position to make creative and budgetary decisions.

When you embark on the road to sell stock, you not only need good legal and financial advice, but you'll now have the SEC (Securities Exchange Commission) in addition to the IRS looking over your shoulder. There are a number of different types of corporations that you can form, from an LLC (Limited Liability Corporation) to an S-1, NASDAQ-traded pachyderm and they all have advantages and drawbacks.

Since you generally can't accept any funds or even start production until the SEC has given its approval, production schedules are not something that you can nail down. The inevitable delays have caused more than a few productions to lose locations and talent due to schedule conflicts. Again, sage legal advice is imperative.

The advantages are that you have passive investors who don't have a say in how you spend their money. Another important advantage is that you've now set up a business that is well suited for long-term success. The fact that you've created an entity that can shelter you from much of the liability that is associated with unincorporated ventures is worth the effort in many instances.

LENDER FINANCING is basically the same as going to the bank and borrowing against your mortgage. A lot of really great homes show up on the L.A. market from this kind of financing, and while I've never been inclined to pursue it for my own projects, I did buy a house that was on the market because of it.

Consider this as a last resort because even if it isn't your house on the block, someone has something hanging out there and they want to get it pulled back in as soon as possible. Those creative additions or that last sweetening session are going to fall by the wayside in an attempt to stay ahead of the bank.

The two main advantages to this type of financing are that the lender doesn't participate in the profits and they don't have any creative control. They get their interest on the loan and that is generally that. Of course the downside is that if you screw up, someone is likely to be living in a hotel.

One of the most popular methods of securing lender financing is with a negative pickup. The basic concept is to get your production package as tight as a drum and then go to a distributor and get a nice distribution deal. Your producer and the distributor will then lock themselves in a padded room and proceed to beat the crap out of each other. The distributor will want the exclusive rights to as many markets as possible, your producer will try to get as much money as possible.

In the end they'll generally agree to whatever the distributor first offered in return for a promise to pay the full amount upon pickup of the finished negative from the lab. Hence, negative pickup... get it?

With production package and distribution deal in hand, your producer then heads off to a private lending institution and pitches your project to a glorified bank teller. As soon as he signs on the dotted line a huge theoretical alarm clock starts ticking and doesn't stop because of holidays, marriage problems, or your kid's music recital. You need to get your movie made before the alarm goes off. Or else!

INDUSTRY FINANCING is generally available in no short supply to production companies that are consistent sources of marketable material. At the high-end of the market you could find yourself on the lot where your producer can network your distribution while you're busy manufacturing the movie.

If you ever find yourself in this position, enjoy it and work your ass off. Shooting on one of the studio back lots is an entirely different world than any other form of production. Every time you set the camera, chances are that Hitchcock, Ford, Huston, or some other historic director placed their camera in that same spot. You are truly standing on hallowed ground.

Far more likely is the possibility that your producer or production company has a relationship with one of the independent mini-major distribution companies like New Line, Phoenix, Spyglass, or Artisan.

Now without getting myself into hot water, there is an ever-widening definition of independent distributor that should not be confused with the old definition. Very often a project is developed by a studio and then handed off to an "Indie" to produce. In addition to maintaining a significantly lower liability, the Indie is free to pursue avenues of production that a studio simply couldn't get away with.

If you have hitched your honey wagon to one of the mini-majors, you've got to keep up with a production schedule that is built on time savings, not financial economy. These guys don't care about saving bucks, so don't even bother pitching your cost-effective, leading-edge methodology. All they want to know is if you can deliver on time. If you say yes, you'd better mean it.

The upside is that you'll get some good distribution that generally has a lot more creativity to it than the conventional studio blockbuster. Since they don't have as many projects on their plate, you'll get a lot more personal attention. This can be good or bad, depending on the way you look at it.

The downside is that these guys generally don't get that big a piece of the domestic pie, so the foreign sales are really important to them.

Be prepared to water down any dominant female leads and keep in mind that Europe isn't an equal opportunity employer. If this offends your delicate principles then you are in the wrong industry, baby.

FOREIGN FINANCING is by far my favorite form of capitalization for a number of reasons. With many countries willing to subsidize upwards of 80% of your actual manufacturing costs, the potential to dramatically increase your movie's production value is very real.

Since the American dollar is generally quite strong in foreign markets, the money you do end up spending will have a far greater return, quite often upwards of 50% or more. A shot that could easily cost $50,000 to shoot on the streets of L.A. might cost only two or three thousand in a beautiful city like Prague. So you do a little rewrite. No big whoop.

On a recent shoot in Budapest, the government supplied all of the crew, the studio, and all of the equipment in return for Eastern European distribution rights and a small stipend. A month of shooting there cost less than a day of shooting in Hollywood. Since the movie was a gothic horror genre piece, the added savings in set construction were an added bonus.

When you're looking for a producer, keep an eye out for someone who does a lot of foreign production. They'll generally have a number of "balances due" from former production subsidies, which can be applied to your movie. This "hip pocket" financial boost has come in quite handy on a number of productions that I've been connected with.

A rarely discussed avenue in independent films is utilizing Restricted Funds. In an attempt to improve local economies, there are quite a few countries that impose limits on the export of money that was accrued within their borders. Since product that was created there is free to leave, but the money that was generated by sales and investments is not, there are a number of banks and corporations that have large Restricted Funds accounts just sitting there.

More than a few smart filmmakers have tracked down these companies and purchased a block of those funds (at a considerable discount) to use for below-the-line production within that country's borders. Since the restrictions only apply to money and not product, the film that you shoot is not restricted.

Since the list of countries that engage in blocking funds changes daily, you could start your investigation by contacting film commissions and trade councils. Keep in mind that corporations with substantial cash tied up in blocked funds are not going to be taking out ads advertising the fact. A little creativity here could have enormous payoffs in the production value of your picture.

Perhaps my favorite part of foreign financing is that it generally gets you out of Southern California. Did you ever notice how 80% of TV and most of the big movies all look like they were shot within fifty miles of downtown L.A.?

There is a wonderful difference between going to a foreign country as a tourist and going as part of a film crew. By shooting in a foreign location you not only add tremendously to your foreign sales potential, but you get a chance to travel the world on someone else's dime. Is this a great business or what?

There are, of course, a large number of you who live in foreign countries where there is actually a culture and an environment that supports the arts. Consider a teenager living in New Zealand who got his friends together and started making cheap, gory effects movies. Then one day the Kiwi film commission gets hold of one of his quirky little movies and gets it shown at the Cannes Film Festival. Next thing you know, little Peter Jackson is writing, producing, and directing *Lord of the Rings*.

7 ∴ DIGITAL CRAFTSMANSHIP

*"Filmmaking is like lovemaking, you can't forget
your audience and you can't be in it for yourself."*
Elyse Couvillion

Digital moviemaking parallels traditional filmmaking with the addition of understanding where and when accommodations for resolution, crew, and production inertia must be taken into consideration. You've also got to have a firm grasp of both video and computer technology.

Combine this with a drastic reduction in the number of people whom this expertise must be spread out among and you'll realize that good digital film is potentially far more difficult to create. Not only do you have fewer people as a resource, but they each need to have a working knowledge of several aspects of conventional production methodology, and then be able to incorporate the vague nuance of technology and budgetary limitations into the process.

Each aspect of the production process involves many years of evolution and refinement. It would be foolish to embark on a film project without having just a smattering of understanding with regard to the established methodology of conventional cinematic production. You won't just be wasting your own time but the time and resources of all those around you.

Low-budget film production generates a lot of stress and frustration. Never enough money, never enough time, never enough of anything but problems. It's all too easy to let it get to you and start becoming a tyrant. As soon as this happens, you'll start losing momentum and all your mealy-mouthed apologies the next day won't get you back on track.

Always treat your cast and crew with respect. Take time to acknowledge their contributions and include them in decisions. Even if you know in your heart that you are the rightful heir to the Speilberg throne, be humble.

LINGO

Like all professions, filmmaking has its own languages. These languages, or lingoes, are essential building blocks that are all too often overlooked or misused. The contemporary film production unit is a complex organization of numerous specialized groups interacting with a common goal.

The director needs not only to understand what each group is capable of doing but also how to communicate with that group so that his requests are understood. Of the many subset lingoes involved in contemporary production, the four languages that the director must be fluent in are the Literary Language, the Actor's Language, the Production Language, and the Visual Language. There are others, but these are the ones that I feel are most relevant.

LITERARY LANGUAGE

The Literary Language deals with character development, structure, and timing. It is the vernacular of the screenplay. The essential foundation of any motion picture is described in this language in terms of empathy and structure.

Empathy is the essence of a good screenplay. Will the audience bond with, and care about, this character? All too often, the inexperienced writer reverts to a series of hysterics or gratuitous confrontations to get the audience worked up, but this is just a cheap imitation of the true craft of evoking the most powerful of audience connections.

A truly empathetic character portrayal will cause the viewer to project their own personality into the character's situation and live the story vicariously through them.

Structure is the style of architecture by which your script is constructed. There are formulas and rules of thumb, but the essence of any script's structure comes down to the central theme. In the simplest of terms, it is what the movie is about. Every element and character that you can attach to it moves your story along. The plot is the sequence of events that move the characters along and create the ups and downs that identify a good story.

The way you put it all together and the voice you use to tell your tale are the style. Great writers, great directors, great actors all have a style that sets them apart from the others in their field.

Audiences go to movies to experience situations and sensations that will generate strong emotional reactions and insights. The structure, the characters, and the conflict of the script must engage the audience and give them a revealing insight into the human spirit.

A great script moves the audience along with a series of compelling visual elements (a picture is worth a thousand words) and uses the dialogue to glue the pictures together. This is true even if your movie never makes it any further than the Net. <u>You must engage the audience</u>!

All the technology in the world won't make up for a lack in the basics of cinematic storytelling. As filmmakers we've really only got two tools at our disposal. Sight and sound. Since digital moviemaking involves substantial sacrifices, particularly in the visual dynamics of the finished product, we must seize every opportunity in the production process to enhance the perceived value of our final product.

The essential unit of measure is the "shot," where an action or performance is recorded until the director calls "cut." A group of related shots create a scene, and a group of scenes form an act, of which there are generally three in a conventional motion picture. The shot is visually described by the angle from which it is recorded, such as subjective, objective, or point-of-view.

Continuity is the flow of elements that carry the audience along. Good continuity never lets up or offers the viewer a chance to disconnect with the story. Each new scene or location is established with a master shot that tells the audience where they are and hopefully how they feel about it. After the situation is established, the camera moves in for a series of closer observations of the action or situations involved.

If the scene involves dialogue between two people, you might go in for a two-shot, which is a medium framing that shows the proximity of the two characters. You might then move in for a "close-up" of one of the characters faces or an "over-the-shoulder" shot to further explain context and proximity.

Continuity also deals with the essential time base of the film, the color palettes, physical direction, lighting, and tempo of the action and eventually editing.

The lingo of editing is evolving daily as new production metaphors become accessible. Many of the terms from the mechanical age of film editing have made the transition into the digital age. Once a linen bag hung from a metal frame, the nonlinear environment still uses the term "bin" as a holding place for shots and sequences.

The selection, arrangement, and timing of the various shots into a continuous story is the essential goal of editing, and the lingo that is involved spans the spectrum of narrative influence, timing, and aesthetics.

ACTING LINGO

The Actor's Language is as varied as the methods by which they've learned their craft and many times you'll have actors from different schools on the same project. Developing a rapport and artistic bond with the individual actor is dependent on understanding what motivates them.

To even brush lightly upon this topic is to incur the wrath of acolytes of the various schools of acting, and the industry in general, but here goes.

In 1898, Constantin Stanislavsky founded the Moscow Art Theater, which was Russia's first ensemble theater.

"The program protests against the old manner of acting and against theatricality, against artificial pathos and declamation, and against affectation on the stage, and inferior conventional productions and decoration, against the star system which had been a bad affect on the cast, against the whole arrangement of plays and against the poor repertoire of the theaters."

Constantin Stanislavsky

Greatly inspired and influenced by Stanislavsky, Lee Strasberg recruited 30 actors, in the summer of 1931, to form a permanent ensemble dedicated to creating social change through acting. The newly formed Group Theater combined Gestalt psychology with the ensemble approach which developed into a series of physical and psychological exercises called "The Method."

The purpose of these exercises was to break down the actor's barrier between life on and off the stage. If a part called for a specific emotion, the actor needed to recall the feelings and circumstance of a similar event in their life and then bring this honest emotion to the stage.

Despite its relatively short life span, The Group Theater is perhaps the single most significant experiment in the history of American theater. Along with Lee Strasberg, the group's founding members included Stella Adler and Sanford Meisner who went on to found their own schools of acting.

The essence of these teachings is to give the actors tools by which they can access their own emotions in the unconscious mind. Since the unconscious mind can't be controlled directly, students are involved in various exercises that are designed to evoke specific emotional correlates.

Even though the schools are all in some way based on interpretations of the teachings of Stanislavsky, their ideas are often considered to be in conflict with each other. Stella Adler's interpretation is considered closest to the original Stanislavsky, then Sanford Meisner, and then Lee Strasberg.

If I, a non-actor, were to attempt to describe the basic theme of the various contemporary schools it would be this:

Adler is built upon Imagination.
Meisner is built upon Immediate Experience.
Strasberg is built upon Sense Memory.
British is built upon Observation.

The Meisner system seems to produce actors who pay attention to their partner better. Some of the basic Meisner exercises include the Yes/No, and various repetition and back-and-forth exercises that tend to "bond" the actors together. *"Acting is living life truthfully under imaginary circumstances."* *"The emotional life of a scene is a river and the words are the boats."*

The Strasberg system or Method system tends to produce actors that are a bit more tightly wound. The system is based on Sense Memory, which is the process of recalling all of the attributes of an object, and Emotional Memory, which is the process of recalling significant events and situations from the actor's own past.

This produces the best actors for bluescreen and effects performances, but often at the expense of the actor's mental health. Stella Adler once said about Lee that "*He would push people into spaces that they should not go without a licensed therapist present.*" Strasberg would often tell actors that they should get some therapy. Personally I feel the best improv exercises use sense memory. It catapults you into a sense of belief. Privacy In Public. "*Visualize a real situation in your own life and do your lines within that frame of mind.*"

Stella Adler gives us the process of action verbs and is based on imagination as being the best motivation for a good performance. The imagination is very powerful in the presence of a director who loves to tell stories. "*Get the verb of it, don't worry about the emotional thread.*"

The British approach to acting is an odd one. Not that it doesn't generate spectacular performances or consummate actors, but rather is based on the actual achievement of acting. Rather than becoming the character emotionally or mentally, the British system actually emulates a character by adopting all of the physical traits and characteristics.

ACTORS AND THEIR NEEDS

Music videos, although not necessarily an appropriate metaphor for cinematic construction, deal with limited bandpass constantly. Many people whose videos play regularly on MTV and VH-1 also have robust cinematic careers. Madonna, Will Smith, Sting, and others are constantly dealing with the duality between film and video.

The almost unlimited latitude of film can generate thousands of gradations that constitute the range of expression while most video only has several hundred shades of gray to work with. It is these subtle gestures and expressions that convey the hidden agendas and emotions that are so important to creating empathy and emotional connections.

Do your actors have more film or video experience?

One of the easiest and most effective ways to allow an actor to adapt his style to your environment is to tape improvisations. The important point to remember is to professionally light the set or area where the improv is to take place. The simplest method would be to stretch a large diffusion panel above the area with a few crossed key lights.

<<<<< Lighting and recording your improvisations gives everyone a test run.

You're killing several birds with one stone here. You're getting the actors comfortable with each other and you're allowing them to metamorphose within the context of the production environment. Generally in very low-budget movies, someone's girlfriend or wife is the designated make-up person. This generally entails little more than a smack with the powder puff and some light colored lipstick for the guys while the gals always seem to want to do their own.

By videotaping the improvs and rehearsals, you not only give the actors a chance to make modifications and adjustments but you also get an excellent opportunity to actually print a test if you intend to finish on film. Take your best shot directly to your film printer of choice and have them make a minute or two projection test.

Don't worry about sound and 3:2 pull downs, just have them print a frame of video to a frame of film. Not only will you see just how much potential resolution and colorspace your chosen video format has to offer but you'll also be able to let your actors know how their make-up choices are transposing.

Imagine if you got all the way through production and postproduction and finally up-converted and printed to film only to find that all of your actors looked garish. Oh, they looked great on the video monitor but up there on the screen... Don't be foolish. The two golden rules of digital video.

Don't stop shooting. Don't stop testing.

There is a big difference between improvisation and rehearsal. Improv is an exercise in developing rapport between the actors and most importantly it creates a shorthand between the actor and the director. Once you start shooting you'll have so many things to keep track of that communicating with the actor will become a whole lot easier if you both have some previous common reference.

The goal of improv is to connect the subconscious of the character to the subconscious of the actor. A good improv should stress that there is no right or wrong approach. You simply can't do an improv incorrectly. Some may be better than others, but if you send your actors into an improv without obligations or judgments you'll end up with a much happier kennel of puppies.

Rehearsal on the other hand deals with the actor's attempts to identify the emotional truth and core of the character. This process is best not practiced too much because it can have the unfortunate effect of flattening out the performance. Your actor may feel that they've got the character nailed and merely regurgitate it back for you rather than struggle with it and letting it evolve before the lens.

In the end, you're going to want to look for performances that are truly different and compelling.

PRODUCTION LANGUAGE

The Production Language essentially deals with the real-time business of making the connections, telling the story, and getting the bills paid. This language starts with the budget and includes all the vagaries of finance and deal making on an extremely sophisticated level.

When you're dealing with studio or distribution company executives, they most likely will be throwing around business school lingo. Don't fake it! What might sound like a really good deal in Harvard-ese might actually be the worst deal of your life. While there's no way to cram a six-year education into the development cycle of your movie, a great shortcut is to read the Friday copies of the *Wall Street Journal* and the *Hollywood Reporter*, front-to-back every week for a month.

The ability to make movies based on an innovative script is one of the primary motivations to the digital moviemaker, but if you're submitting your script to a studio, it often causes problems. As I've already mentioned, the studios don't actually make movies anymore, they make deals.

As a result, the executives that your script must pass through are all lawyers or MBAs. A deeply revealing or emotionally insightful script is frightening to them. They're just not mentally equipped to deal with the subjective realities of deeply revealing interpersonal revelations.

Many of them try to adapt by finding ways to express subjective concepts quantifiably. There's always some new and tragically hip formula floating around Hollywood. It's like they all go to the same parties and hear the same neo-theological postulate and next thing you know you're sitting in a pitch meeting listening to the Harvard Business School interpretation of the mise-en-scène.

Instead of actually going out and developing promising actors, they merely recycle the "safe bets" to the point where you'll see the same faces in four or five movies a year. Is it any wonder that the growing trend is to write bigger and bigger effects into the script or more spectacular obstacles to the character's goals? This formulaic, knee-jerk manner of writing is merely an accommodation to the horrible lack of industry acumen.

An independent script has far more latitude and should be wholly different than a studio script. There is no excuse for not developing the strong combination of revelation and sensation that creates the dramatic center of your script. The problem comes with the lack of subtlety that is available with digital productions because video simply doesn't have the dynamic range of film.

While motion picture film can capture the hundreds of thousands of subtle shifts in expression that echo pages of dialogue, the script destined to be shot in video must convey these thoughts more through speech and gesture. The greatest challenge for the digital scriptwriter is to create a boldness of action that treads the delicate balance between too much and not enough.

Unfortunately, the dramatic center is based on subtle revelations and digital video is far from being a subtle medium. Instead of focusing on making the script or scene "commercial," concentrate on evoking a series of emotional responses from the viewer. Creating an atmosphere in which the viewer can emotionally bond with the character is perhaps the hardest and most important objective in a video-for-film or video-for-net script.

Don't keep the audience guessing about the character's persona. The more time it takes you to bond your audience to your main character's life and predicament, the more time they'll have to find fault with your film's technical shortcomings.

A 35mm feature can afford to spend time showing the audience around, getting them used to the environment, and basically feeding them eye candy. You can't. Get down to business, get them involved and do it quickly. If you haven't sucked the audience into your world in the first few minutes, chances are very good, unless you've got a real barn-burner of a script, that you won't be able to reel 'em in at all.

It's not a bad idea to hold off on the title sequence until after they've had a chance to become vested in your principal characters. An even better solution is to suck in the ego a bit and put them all at the end. Titles are generally slow and plodding, a perfect time to analyze the quality of your image.

And once you're moving, don't let up, momentum is critical to the digital script. A 35mm film project can afford to back off of the action here and there and allow the characters to breathe and have those small moments that offer up deeper insight into their hidden motivations. Not you. Stay on 'em and don't let up. If you keep the audience involved in the emotional roller coaster of the story they won't have time for anything else.

And when you're writing that witty repartee, don't forget to maintain a uniqueness in the character's voice. By keeping the lead's voice separate, you can keep it tied into the movie's dramatic center with less reliance on the audience picking up on the more subtle indicators that would generally be used in a film script.

Where a film script would normally rely on dialogue primarily to express thoughts and the actor's craft to express feeling, the digital script needs to incorporate subtle emotional indicators into the dialogue. Don't tell them what the character's feeling but perhaps elaborate on the peripheral motivations involved.

Too often scripts become expositional in the third act, trying to tie up loose ends. This is the failure of establishing a solid base. Any basket weaver will tell you that a small mistake in the base will only get more notable as the basket progresses. With digital moviemaking this is particularly dangerous because it lets your audience off of the bus before the movie is over. Any glitches or shortcomings that they missed earlier will leave with them.

SHOW ME THE MONEY!

A lot of people might disagree with my putting the budget under the CRAFTSMANSHIP chapter heading, but anyone who's been through the process will be glad to tell you that a good budget is a thing of beauty. It's not just numbers on paper, but rather the numerical expression of your vision.

A decent script with a funky budget has less chance of getting made than a mediocre script with an outstanding budget. Put a good script together with a great budget and you've got a true formula for success. Good budgets instill a sense of reliability and confidence in those silly enough to invest in your little venture.

With a red hot script and a realistic budget in hand you'll have the essential tools you need to go out and start raising money. Unfortunately, a good script is, in many ways, easier to generate than a good budget.

At the point at which you start to solicit money for your movie, you become a business and as such, should start acting accordingly. Get your-self some legal representation. I know it sounds dreary and expensive, but there are numerous alternatives such as Volunteer Lawyers for the Arts and the many guild and professional organizations that have legal counselors who sometimes help the occasional loose cannon. IFP maintains a current list of legal resources.

Then there's the actual budget. Imagine that you've taken off your director's hat (budgeting for what you want) and put on your Unit Production Manager (UPM) hat (budgeting for what you need). At this stage, the budget's primary job isn't necessarily to indicate where every penny is going, but rather to give your potential investors the reassurance that you actually have a firm grasp of the production process. There it is for them to see. Your understanding of the whole process, laid out in black and white. The bottom line is obviously very important, but how you arrived at that figure is perhaps even more important.

Since the budget is such an integral and necessary element of production, you might want to hire out this process if no one in your immediate production entourage has the aptitude. Don't feel bad. Many right-brained individuals have a hard time with the budgeting process. The important thing is to have someone who will keep you focused on it through the entire production process. Small extravagances at the beginning can snowball into painful overages by the time you hit editing. The result could be, and often is, a drastic reduction in the amount of resources left to print the video to film.

Perhaps the most common method of creating a budget is by templating. Essentially you beg, borrow, or steal the most relevant current budget you can find and make the seemingly appropriate changes. The problem here is that movies are as different as people are and when you generalize a budget you are essentially "vanilla-izing" your entire project. Add to that it's a lie, not an auspicious start for a project that'll need all the good karma it can muster.

When you finally get your budget worked out, give it to someone who's done this before just to make sure you haven't missed anything. Numbers are funny things. Commas sometimes look like periods and the next thing you know you're trying to explain why the video-to-film transfer budget is only $5.00. Little mistakes like that not only make you look careless but incompetent.

A far much safer and intelligent way to create a budget is to get some good budgeting software like Turbo Budget or Movie Magic Budgeting, and a copy of Michael Wiese's book *Film and Video Budgets*. It has a wide selection of samples from various production scenarios ranging from feature film productions all the way to "film school chutzpah." It also breaks down the cost per day of every job description in both standard and nonstandard productions as well as supplying you with a comprehensive list of industry standard budget codes.

DIGITAL DIRECTING

The process of storytelling is perhaps the oldest profession, yet the inherent dynamics that constitute a great storyteller are all too often misunderstood.

Moviemakers are predisposed to the one-way narrative and, as such, need to maintain a strong visual presence in our mind's eye of the texture and pacing of the story elements. The director must also keep in mind the progression of various character arcs and how they interrelate even though subsequent scenes in a picture might be shot months apart. This supernatural persistence of vision must often be maintained for a year or more and is all too easily ravaged by drug or alcohol abuse.

In order to tell a rich and compelling story, directors need to have experienced life from both the valleys and the mountaintops. This comes with maturity. Look around at all of the truly great directors. They represent the full spectrum of the human condition yet they generally have one thing in common; maturity. You on the other hand are a brash, young Turk with fire in your loins.

Take a lot of deep breaths. The pressure and anxiety the directorial process creates can kill a career before it's had a chance to screw up on its own. Much of the pressure of directing comes from trying to fix compounded errors. You make a little mistake in casting or skimp on a location and then whenever it comes up, instead of addressing it, you aggravate the situation further by trying to "work around" it. This compounding phenomena has taken down directors and their productions, large and small.

Always nip mistakes in the bud.

After years on the set I've come to recognize many of the basic traits of bad direction. I've occasionally caught myself falling into those patterns when talking to an actor. For me, being able to identify detrimental methods of communicating with actors has been a powerful, although inexact tool.

I took a seminar from Judith Weston that dealt with acting for directors. It was based on her book *Acting For Directors*. Among the many inspirational and unusually relevant exercises that our class performed was an exercise that identified the trademarks of bad directors. Now, for the first time I actually had a quantifiable metaphor with which to measure my interaction with actors. With Judith's permission I've condensed it down, paraphrased it, and am sharing it with you.

Trademarks of Bad Directors:

Result Freaks.
"Can you make it funnier? Can you take it down a notch?"
This causes the actor/director relationship to turn into a guessing game and forces the actor into their "bag of tricks."

Delivery Doctors.
"Don't say, I love you, say I love you."
The director should be communicating the meaning of the line, not the inflection.

Process Servers.
"I think your character is very happy."
As soon as an actor tries to have a feeling on demand they look like an actor.

Emotional Mappers.
"OK, when you come through the door you're thinking that no one's home and then you hear something. You're disappointed because you wanted to be alone but you're scared because you think it may be a burglar."
Psychologizing or mapping the emotional terrain of a character is the ultimate control device generally used by egotistic directors that don't trust their actors. Aside from being long-winded and tedious, this form of direction is counterproductive in an environment where time is at a premium. The result of this literal interpretation of the script will be a performance with no through-line.

Attitude Police.
"Show me how much you hate this guy."
Forcing actors into an attitude corner is the difference between doing something and showing something. Forced attitude creates posturing which prevents the actors from listening to each other. Nothing devalues a performance more than actors that aren't paying attention to each other.

Schizo.
"He is happy but his heart is broken that she is leaving."
This pseudo-intellectualized method is intended to illustrate the complexi-
ty of the character. People are complex, they may say one thing while doing
another, but they are not actually able to do two things at once. Divergent
emotions cancel each other out and the actor ends up faking both of them.

Judgmental.
"He's an introverted geek." or *"She's a slut."*
Perhaps the most destructive device used for determining a character's
make-up. Judgment forces the actor to telegraph the character to the
audience. "I'm the good guy." "I'm the villain." A director that uses this technique eliminates suspense by showing us the end of the movie when the
character is introduced. In the end, the audience should be the ones to
make the judgments.

Good direction generates behavior in the actor. It is sensory, rather than
intellectual and objective, and specific, rather than subjective and general. It
describes experience rather than drawing conclusions about experience.

The best directors actually do very little directing, but rather guide with
questions. *"What is important about this scene?"* *"What if the character just
lost a family member?"* *"Do you feel like hitting him when he says that?"*
Howard Hawks used to say that he was merely giving the actors an attitude.
"Once they've got an attitude, then it's up to them to do the lines."

There are, of course, as many styles of directing as there are directors.

One of my favorite analogies with regards to the director's role is from
Robert Altman. I apologize in advance for any misquoting as I was at a party
when I heard him telling it and I wasn't in any shape to take notes.
Essentially he related making a movie to building a huge sandcastle. In the
beginning you're all excited about the concept of building a sand castle, so
you sit around with some other people and design the thing and plan where
and how to build it.

Everyone has a lot more opinions than you were expecting and the whole
thing starts changing so much that by the end of the process you're almost

ready to ditch the whole idea. Finally, the day comes that everyone planned on and it turns out to be a really nice day, so you go to the beach and start building the thing. With all those people trying to help it takes a lot longer to build than you thought it would.

It's getting hot, you got sand in your shorts, it's looking totally different than what you had originally envisioned, and you can't wait for the whole thing to be over. Finally, just before sunset, you finish it. People like it or they don't. A large wave comes along and washes it away and you're ready to start planning the next one.

HONING YOUR CRAFT

Unlike acting or cinematography, or nearly any other craft, directing isn't something that you can just practice on a whim.

Consider the enormous investments of time and energy that musicians, athletes, painters, and actors all dedicate to improving their abilities. Directing on the other hand, is all too often left to a last minute pang of conscience and a dog-eared copy of *Directing 101*.

Competent directing involves a number of dynamic factors that must, by their very nature, include both environmental, interpersonal, structural, and emotional components.

Directing is more guiding than bossing, more cerebral than physical, yet the vast majority of first-time directors do little if anything to actually prepare for the task ahead. Is it any wonder why the overwhelming majority of inaugural projects are so self-indulgently bad?

The first step to becoming a good director is recognizing and then establishing your style. As nearly any successful director will tell you, style doesn't just happen, it must be cultivated. The more unique and individual your particular voice or style is, the more identifiable your work will become.

Inside of you there is a voice that is composed of your innermost thoughts and feelings. The directors who have mastered the ability to listen to this voice, when all around them is clamoring for their attention, are the ones who have made their mark upon the industry.

Simply saying to yourself, "*I will listen to this voice*" will not work; not for you, not for me, not for anyone. The only way to identify the hidden uniqueness within yourself is either through extensive psychoanalysis or focused training and guidance. Personally, I prefer the latter.

If you're serious about the craft of directing there is the unparalleled level of experience that working alongside a recognized professional brings. Formal internships, and the training methodology employed by the DGA (Director's Guild of America), are proven methods for developing your craft and working toward realistic goals.

Those impatient to express themselves can find competent guidance in working schools such as The Actor's Studio in New York City, or one of my old alma maters, The American Film Institute in Los Angeles. Your nearest IFP office also has a wonderful series designed to develop your directorial skills.

There are a number of excellent workshops designed to bring out the unique voice that exists within us all. Judith Weston's most excellent "Acting For Directors" workshops in New York and Los Angeles, gets you inside the actor's mind and allows you to explore their motivations and methods. Judith's workshops and ongoing classes include support for both directors and actors, and actively involve students in the full process from concept to staging full productions.

When the television shows go on hiatus, most working directors head for exotic vacation spots to decompress from the frantic season... but not Guy Magar. He hits the road and travels the world giving his highly popular 2-day *Action/Cut Filmmaking Seminars*. If you can't catch his seminar live in New York, Boston, Miami, Chicago, Denver, Austin, San Francisco or L.A., I recommend his intensive home DVD course.

Guy's seminars are a proven resource for learning the nuts and bolts of directing as a profession and easily the best method for developing your chops outside of working your way up through the DGA program... and a hell of a lot faster.

"There is no question that digital is not only the future, but the very present as well. Besides its unimaginable impact on the world of visual effects, its most

immediate contribution has been in the democratization of filmmaking at the grassroots, no-budget level.

In the excitement of its accessibility, digital technology has clouded a basic inalienable truth: It's not the format... it's the storytelling! Regardless of what format you are recording on, the passion of filmmaking will always lie in the wondrous magic of visual storytelling... the all-encompassing craft of the extraordinary process of translating story words to story images... and that is what I fell in love with. It just happened to be on glorious celluloid during my generation."

Guy Magar

CHOPS

Once you've developed your voice, there is simply no better way to perfect your craft than to actually practice it on a regular basis.

Personally I love working with an established acting school or theatrical troop. There simply is no better way to develop your methodology than putting up scenes and rehearsing on a regular basis. Among my favorites have been the Salt City Playhouse in my home town of Syracuse, New York, and The Beverly Hills Playhouse, now in its 35th year of turning out working professionals.

My current troop includes a number of working actors and one other director that meet once a week on each other's set. Since so much of moviemaking involves waiting, we hang out in trailers and dressing rooms, working on scenes that in most instances are destined to go before a camera.

Some people cringe when they see us coming, some laugh, and some merely put more Twizzlers on the craft services table. Whatever form your pursuit of craft takes, you must take it seriously. The active quest of excellence is something that everyone in this business understands.

Directing takes work and simply deciding that you're a director won't cut it. Without a distinctive voice to your work, and the ability to utilize actors as the palette of your mind, you're merely another wannabe director standing at the back of the industry's longest line.

AUDIO

People get a little over half of their information about the world around them from their eyes. A classic study done at Yale revealed that people are influenced 55% visual (what we see), 38% vocal (the content of what we hear), and 7% verbal (how things are said).

Of course then you open the whole can of worms about the method of projection, the type of audience, and which modality they are using to take it all in. Some people are more visual, or acoustic, or kinetic in how they perceive things, but regardless of how you break it down, sound is one of the most dependable generators of emotion that the filmmaker has in their quiver.

Since all camcorders have built-in microphones, the first person to be eliminated from the low-budget production is all too often the soundman. Ooops. The less experience you have in capturing high-quality images, the more imperative it is to have a competent soundman and create an environment that is conducive to recording a good audio signal.

First thing to take into consideration is the camera's built-in microphone. Do not use it! Even if you are a lone gunman, out there shooting away on your own, don't even think about it. The first rule in recording sound is to get as close to the source as you can without getting into the camera's frame.

<<<<< Just say *NO* to on-camera microphones.

If you're a one-man band, and don't have a soundman to hold the boom, get yourself the best "mini shotgun" microphone you can afford. Attach it to your camera with a mount that has at least a little isolation to it, then get a "dead kitty" windscreen to cover the business end and leave it there.

Like every other auto function on your camcorder, the automatic volume control should be super-glued in the off position.

Generally, the farther away the microphone is from the sound source, the more noise (ambient sound) it will pick up. The reason that you occasionally see boom mikes in pictures and television shows is not because these people are clumsy, but rather because they are so focused on getting the best sound possible that they often "push the frame" in an attempt to get the mike as close as possible.

The second rule in recording sound is to record your source as loudly as possible without over-modulating. You can always turn it down in post but when you try to turn the volume up, you'll also be turning up any ambient noise that was recorded. One of the best ways to get good, dependable sound in a "lone gunman" environment is with lavaliere mikes. These tiny mikes can be hidden in clothes, behind ties, and even in hair. Since they're close to the source they generally capture a fairly good signal. They can be hooked to a transmitter for wireless transmission to a receiver attached to the camera.

When you're behind the camera you've got enough to worry about without the added demands of acquiring a good audio signal. For this reason a soundman is perhaps the most necessary addition to the small film crew.

The tiny meters and dials of the camcorder are not a viable alternative to accurate sound acquisition. This is doubly important if you're using a camera that doesn't allow for manual operation of the audio feed. It is for this reason that many, if not most, small format video productions use an external DAT recorder. When using an external recorder, be sure to slate each shot with a good crisp snap so that you can line everything up in post.

Most experienced soundmen will tell you that once you set the level for a take, don't touch it until the take is over. The other thing they'll tell you is never leave a location without getting at least a minute of "room tone." This is merely a sample of the environment that the editor can use to "glue" performances together with at a later date.

Just as the environment shapes light, it also shapes sound. A set or location with flat hard walls will bounce the sound around giving the location a "hot" or "live" sound while a location with soft furniture and objects on the wall will give a softer and less echoic (dead) sound.

One of the most serious drawbacks to tiny DV format is its inability to record a true "SMPTE" time code. I know the numbers on the camera's little

LCD screen move like time code, but the unfortunate reality is that they're only a relative numeric reference that doesn't transpose. While this problem is endemic and affects nearly every aspect of postproduction, I'm putting it here under the AUDIO heading because this is where it causes the bulk of its problems and also where the majority of the solutions lie.

Many people use an electronic Time Coded Slate (w/external time code generator) plugged directly into a DAT recorder. A snap of the slate will then give a good visual reference on the video image so the time code can be mated in post. It is very helpful if the soundman runs a channel of audio back to the camera to use as reference. This is especially useful if you're going to transfer to D-Beta for your on-line edit.

Another popular practice is to record the time code from the slate's time code generator on to one of the audio channels of their DV camcorder. This gives them a permanently attached reference signal to which they can reference their DAT.

>>>>> A time code slate is among the digital moviemaker's more essential tools. If for some reason you roll into another take without marking it, don't forget to add a tail slate at the end. Generally a small slate held upside down at the end of the scene should suffice. Make sure that your script supervisor makes note that the take was "tail slated."

GRAPHIC ESCALATION

Feature length cartoons, animations, science fiction, and other effects-heavy, budget-limited projects need special consideration. Essentially, the playing field has changed so radically that today's PC has more crunching power than ILM did back when they made *Star Wars*.

By using rather inexpensive software, on low-cost computers you've quite literally got the potential to create anything you can dream up. Perhaps the most important thing to keep in mind when embarking on an effects-laden project is upward migration. Just because your project starts out on an iMac doesn't mean that it will end up on the same platform. This is such a simple, yet important concept that I am going to mount my trusty soap box for just a bit.

My wife and I have worked on numerous movies in the past dozen years where principal elements started as rough concept on a laptop or desk top PC and ended up in multimillion dollar Inferno bays. The journey that an idea must travel, especially a unique visual concept, is a perilous one. Every time you re-cut a gem, you lose some of the original beauty.

One of the first projects we worked on together was the original pre-visu-alization for *Jurassic Park*. It consisted of an animated movie that was created in MacroMedia's Director software and rendered out in the Beta version of Apple's QuickTime (then called RoadKill). Needless to say, the project, despite its diminutive beginnings, went on to much higher resolutions.

That same scenario is replayed daily in the world of digital production where cost-effective production technology initiates more ambitious projects. By creating a system where elements of original thought and inspiration can be easily utilized by larger and more powerful production environments you are future-proofing your intellectual property and increasing your movie's potential.

Now I'm about as big a fan of Pinnacle's Commotion and Adobe's AfterEffects as you'll find anywhere. I was beta tester for both software packages back when they were far, far less stable and can probably attribute a substantial amount of my income over the years to projects and effects sequences that I've created using them. The biggest problem, however, has always been upward migration.

In numerous instances, projects started out with very limited budgets, so we'd use AfterEffects or Commotion in a desktop production environment. Usually the effects came out looking far better than the producers or the studio had imagined so they'd go out and screen the rough-cuts for distributors and end up with much better distribution. Everyone wins.

A number of years ago, Adam Rifkin, Brad Wyman, and I were sitting around on my patio trying to figure out how we could physically make *Barb Wire* for two-million dollars. Commotion, AfterEffects, and the rest of the desktop arsenal of applications played a big part in getting that movie off the ground.

We were well into physical production, and had more than a week's worth of shots in the can when the producers called from the infamous French film festival at Cannes. They'd seen a few rough cut scenes and were so impressed that they started showing them around the festival. Nothing official, just *"Hey, look at what these guys are doing with no budget."*

They ended up raising many, many millions of dollars for that movie and the first thing they did was fire Adam and bring in a hotshot music video director. Next, they added more effects and pretty soon the look started to shift from cinematic comic book (our original concept) to avant-cyber noir. *C'est la vie.* Many of the effects simply played as they had been created on the Mac, but since there was no real upward migration path, many others had to be totally redone from scratch on higher end machines. A waste of time, a waste of energy, a waste of money.

This lack of upward migration has long been a major factor in splintering the motion picture industry into the two distinct camps of high- and low-resolution. Anytime you've got a point of quantifiable separation, you're going to see technological effetism rear its ugly head.

TA-DA!

Combustion2 from Discreet Logic runs equally well on Mac, Windows, or Linux machines, uses Adobe After Effects plugins, and costs about the same as comparable desktop applications after you've purchased a suite of plug-ins to put them on equal footings. Essentially it's the fully endowed, younger brother of the multi-million dollar Discreet Logic Inferno, which is the backbone of the high-end effects world. The cool thing is that everything you create in Combustion, like masks, chroma-keys, rotoscoping and such, ports directly upward into the big machines.

As much as I hate to learn new software applications, I sat down and learned this one. My wife, who is an Inferno artist with movies like *Godzilla, Armageddon, Mission Impossible II,* and *Vertical Limit* under her belt, was an instant convert. Combustion is a good addition for anyone considering a future in high-end video or film production. Does it replace AfterEffects or Commotion? No! The three applications create a solid foundation on which the bulk of contemporary motion picture production is founded.

<<<<< While countless other applications vie for their share of the emerging market, Adobe AfterEffects continues to dominate the contemporary digital cinema desktop.

HOKUSAI'S REVENGE

The Digital tsunami that swept over the motion picture industry left in its backwash a business that is fundamentally changed. Every methodology that we've come to embrace has had to adapt not only to a new digital toolset, but to an inherent reinvention of postproduction methodology.

When the digital desktop first schmoozed its way into the film industry, it was all about the box. What the computer could do, how dependable and how fast was it? These days, a box is pretty much a box. Whether it has a partially eaten fruit on it or a few emblazoned letters, they all do basically the same things. Like formula race cars, underneath the colorful shells, they all run around the same tracks at the essentially the same speeds.

The specialized leading edge of digital postproduction is now defined by third party, sub-applications called plugins.

DUELING FOR HEMISPHERES

There are essentially two distinct worlds in motion-graphic postproduction and depending on which side of your brain is more active, you'll generally develop an affinity for 2D or 3D.

Two dimensional (2D) artistry basically includes various combinations of COMPOSITING, ROTOSCOPING, and RETOUCHING.

COMPOSITING involves combining two or more images and can be as simple as placing the weatherman over his animated maps or as complex as scenes with numerous layers and graphic elements. We recently re-created The Battle of Actium for the Discovery Channel. The battle took place off the coast of Greece in 31BC between the Navy's of Antony and Octavian. The master shot included 700+ ships, each with five hundred rowers manning huge wooden oars, while several hundred little CG Legionaries hurled arrows, spears, and flaming balls of fire at each other. The shot required almost two thousand layers containing more than a quarter million elements.

ROTOSCOPING is the process of frame by frame manipulation of an image, to add or eliminate a graphic component. Year after year, one of the most often requested visual effects we perform is the removal of blemishes from famous faces. As you can imagine, it is a process that is not taken lightly.

RETOUCHING involves a number of graphic tricks that essentially enhance the look of the image. Very often this includes removing wires and gear that is used to suspend and protect actors and stunt people, as well as removing the inevitable scratch or two that has long been the bane of this industry.

Three dimensional (3D) methodology includes creating virtual sets and characters, as well as a growing number of effects such as digital explosions, clouds, and atmosphere.

VIRTUAL SETS were first introduced in the late '80s and are basically sets that are built in a computer, into which your live characters can be composited. What started out as a novel way to cut production expenses has turned into an increasingly popular production alternative.

The inevitable follow-up to virtual sets was of course, VIRTUAL ACTORS. Perhaps the most famous virtual actors to date are the dinosaurs in *Jurassic Park* but there have been quite literally thousands of digital actors walk across our screens since then. From the Captain and crew of the *Titanic* in James Cameron's epic tale to the legions of warriors in George Lucas' latest *Star Wars* installment, the number of virtual actors continue to expand as they continue to get closer and closer to the camera.

<<<<< The more sophisticated digital technology becomes, the more it blurs the lines between what we perceive as real and what is real.

And what would a blockbuster be without explosions? Digital effects such as explosions, fog, rain, and smoke are very often grouped into a category called VOLU-METRICS because they take up true 3D space rather than being represented as a flat surface. As the computer's camera moves into a volumetric effect such as a cloud of smoke, the scene will darken progressively and visibility will decrease until the camera comes out the other side.

The ever-expanding digital tool set is giving filmmakers with limited resources the ability to compete with big budget productions. When partnered with the new generation of cinematic quality digital cameras, the true power of digital production is unleashed.

UNCLE GEORGE

In his self-imposed exile from the Hollywood mainstream, George Lucas has developed a cinematic methodology that many are adopting. By combining Hi-Definition acquisition with a powerful suite of digital tools, his talented team of acolytes is defining the future of motion picture production.

I recently shot my own movie using a scaled down version of Uncle George's methodology and a fistful of the latest plugins. In addition to cutting the actual production time by almost 80%, the cost savings were absolutely enormous. Like George, I shot with a Hi-Definition camera and recorded to a D5 HD recorder via the camera's Serial Digital port.

My picture is called *Mid-Century* and it takes place in the year 2045. Computers have evolved into their own civilization which has built a ring around the Earth from material they've mined from the moon. It combines live action with computer generated environments and all but two of the 47 scenes were shot on a chroma key stage. The main difference between my movie and Uncle George's is that mine cost four zeros less.

To illustrate the dynamic power and range of the filmmaker's digital toolset, I'd like to use one of the scenes from my movie that takes place on the ring that surrounds the earth. The shot takes place as the leader of the computer race (played by Faye Dunaway) is driving an aging Bill Gates (played by John Glover) to the central processor in a JetCar.

Obviously, when you're lucky enough to get a veteran actor to be in your little independent movie, you've got to be ready to make certain concessions. When you've got a number of veteran actors in your movie, you're going to make a lot of them. True to form there were a number of unavoidable schedule conflicts with the JetCar scene; John with his television series *Smallville* and a play in New York, and Faye with the motion picture, *El Padrino*. The only way to get the two of them together was in postproduction.

Since Faye and John are both consummate actors, I wasn't worried about getting their performances to match. What I was concerned with was getting consistent lighting and pulling clean mattes.

Having done a substantial amount of chroma key work, I learned long ago to shoot blondes on blue and everyone else on green. Since John's character goes through a number of different make-up induced aging looks, we shot his JetCar elements against green screen at the same time he was scheduled for other scenes with that particular make-up. Three weeks later we shot Faye's performance against a bluescreen.

>>>>> John Glover on green and Faye Dunaway on blue Chroma Key.

The scene elements were later captured into a Mac using a CineWaveHD system and then edited in Apple's FinalCut Pro using garbage mattes for alignment. Once their relative positions were established and the audio was sync'd we used the Automatic Duck plugin to export the elements into Adobe AfterEffects where the scene was reconstructed in separate layers.

The two main chroma key plugins that are used most extensively in cinematic postproduction are the Pinnacle Primatte and the AdvantEdge plugin from Ultimatte. Since they are both based on slightly different three dimensional colorspaces you'll need to do your own testing to figure out which one works best for your particular situation.

<<<<< Ultimatte's
AdvantEdge sets
the bar for professional
chroma key work.

The original tests for *Mid-Century* were all keyed using the Primatte process, but once we started pulling Hi-Def matts we switched to the AdvantEdge in conjunction with Pinnacle's Composite Wizzard suite of plug-ins. Both Primatte and AdvantEdge plugins allow for a number of parameters that are key frame-able over the length of the shot and are remarkably more accurate than the real-time equipment that comps your local weatherman against his cartoon maps.

Having shot John on green and Faye on blue, and even though we used the same lighting instruments for both, there was a noticeable hue shift caused by the proximity of the chroma key set.

>>>>> Color Finesse
brings ultra-high end
production tools to
the desktop.

The ColorFinesse plugin has taken much of the guesswork out of balancing shots and is one of the most sophisticated color matching systems this side of a Da Vinci. Unlike the majority of color timing modules found in many applications, ColorFinesse lets you put up two windows simultaneously so that you can actually "match" your color timing. Sounds like a simple thing but anyone who's timed something shot in different environments will really appreciate this plugin's easy-to-use interface.

Due to the way that Hi-Definition constructs its image, you'd be hard-pressed to find a DP that wouldn't be inclined to throw a bit of light diffusion on the lens when shooting adults. The problem incurred when shooting elements on chroma key is that any filtration that you use on the lens is going to interfere with your ability to pull a clean matte in post.

55MM is a unique set of plugins from Digital Film Tools that simulate popular optical glass filters as well as specialized lenses. They work equally well in all of the conventional motion graphic applications and allow you to add equivalent amounts of filtration to a scene after you've pulled your matte. In this case we added the equivalent of a 1/4 ProMist Black to the actor's comp layer.

Once the shots were aligned, mattes were pulled, filtration added, and everything was color timed, the scene was rendered out as a Hi-Def QuickTime with an alpha channel.

<<<<< The individual performances were brought together in a single QuickTime movie. The Alpha channel (shown here) is usually invisible.

So this is where we switch hemispheres and enter into a 3D world.

I've worked as Visual Effects Supervisor on a dozen motion pictures since the turn of the century and I continually rediscover that the single worst place to make an effects-heavy motion picture is in L.A. Even though there's a good deal of talent here, it's all quite expensive and there's very little interest in working on anything that isn't destined to become an extravagant blockbuster.

For me, the true power of the Internet is in its ability to create associations that would not normally occur. With motion picture postproduction, the ability to collaborate with talented artists, regardless of where they live, proves to be an invaluable resource time and time again. The postproduction team for *Mid-Century* is comprised of artists living in Italy, France, Germany, U.K., Spain, Australia, and Brazil.

The JetCar scene involved components from a number of these artists. While Adam Benton and I shuttled ring designs back and forth between the U.K. and L.A., and David DellaRocca sent environmental comps from France, Spain's Cristobal Vila had designed a vehicle that was a rather natural extension of existing design trends.

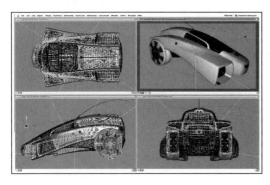

<<<<< The JetCar in ElectricImage's Universe application.

While I enjoy science fiction, I prefer the more realistic genera of speculative fiction where the characters and devices adhere to the basic precepts of Newtonian physics. I was look-ing for a vehicle that looked essentially like a mid-century Lexus and Cristobal's design nailed it.

The world of 3D is essentially made up of virtual surfaces called Polygons and Nurbs. These computer-generated surfaces can be combined to rep-resent things as big as planets or as small as a particle of smoke. Using six square polygons you can create a cube, with ten million of them you can create a dinosaur. Whatever the relative size or shape, without a substan-tial amount of craftsmanship, these essential building blocks of computer geometry will generally end up looking like unspectacular blobs of plastic.

For a more realistic look, 3D rendering applications use a process called tex-ture mapping which essentially allows you to align and paste a picture or a movie onto a three dimensional object. If you paste a picture of a brick onto a 3D model of an elongated cube, you will have made a rudimentary 3D brick. If the picture of the brick had an Alpha channel that looked some-thing like a frame of video noise, and you used that "invisible" channel of Alpha information as a Bump Map, then your 3D brick would appear to have dimensional texture and be far more realistic.

>>>>> The difference between "good" and "photo-real" is often in the use of the Alpha channel.

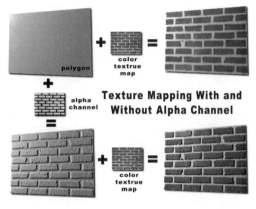

Texture Mapping With and Without Alpha Channel

Car finishes, however, are a tricky affair. In real life, the more expensive the car, generally the more unique and complex the finish is. Materials such as metals and transparent surfaces also have unique characteristics that involve some very spooky math called shaders. There are a number of different types of shaders but they are all essentially small mathematical formulas that can be adjusted to create a wide range of surface treatments or looks. Once you've got the various parameters of your shader "dialed in," it will automatically replicate itself over the surface of an infinitely large or oddly shaped object like a planet or a car or a wisp of smoke.

There are a number of excellent plugins for all of the leading 3D applications that extend the range of realism into areas that would not normally be addressed in a popular desktop application. I was fortunate to interest Cristobal Vila, who is one of my favorite designers in this project. He designed a wonderful vehicle that was a natural extension of existing design trends and since his preference was to use ElectricImage's Universe (*www.electricimage.com*), we standardized 3D postproduction around it. Universe comes with a respectable assortment of surface shaders but I wanted a very specific "Lexus" look and feel.

>>>>> The KonKeptone, Mforge interface can be daunting but the results are spectacular.

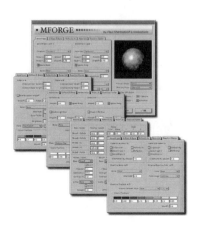

We used the Konkeptoine (*www.konkep-toine.com*) M-Forge Material Shader plugins which manipulate optical characteristics to achieve true photo-realism. The resulting finish rendered out looking like something off of a contemporary show room floor; exactly what I was looking for.

The model of the ring was mapped using a combination of conventional picture-based textures that I had created in Adobe Photoshop and a custom corrosion shader created with the TripleDTools (*www.tripledtools.com*) aFraktal plugin. The corrosion shader is capable of creating a wide range of deteriorated looks which can be layered on top of existing texture maps.

We needed an endless horizon of random clouds that were substantial enough to generate turbulence as the speeding JetCar sailed past them. The atmosphere and clouds of the ring environment were created using a combination of the Konkeptoine zFog plugin and the TripleD PowerParticles plugin which offers an amazing amount of control over the behavior of emitted particles.

Like shaders, particles are tiny units of code that can be adjusted to emulate a wide range of organic properties such as smoke, fire, clouds, sparks, water, and hair. There are controls for things like decay time which allows a cluster of smoke particles to gradually dissipate, or randomness which can make a tight stream of water turn into a spray. If you marveled at the fur of the monsters in Pixar's *Monsters, Inc.* or the motion of the grass in PDI/DreamWork's *Shrek*, then you were enjoying particle systems that were wrangled by true masters.

The Hi-Definition QuickTime of Faye and John was then texture mapped to a polygon that was positioned inside the JetCar model using a setting that causes the black areas of the sequence's Alpha layer to render transparently.

Everything was put into motion and two days, four applications, twelve plugins, and three-thousand five-hundred and eighty-six frames later a small "bing" coming from my office alerted me to the fact that the scene had finished rendering.

<<<<< The secret of one of the greatest "magic tricks" in visual effects.

Once all of the scene elements were rendered and edited back together they were given a unifying thematic signature (A.K.A. look) using the Look Suite of the extremely powerful MagicBullet (*http://www.toolfarm.com*) plugin by San Francisco's Orphanage. I used the *Matrix*-like Neo pre-set for scenes that took place in the unprotected areas of a toxic earth, and the oversaturated richness of the Epic pre-set for scenes on the Ring.

As important as a good computer and a solid suite of master applications are for the digital moviemaker, the true power of contemporary postproduction is echoed in the quiver of plugins that you use. While this brief example only deals with a single shot in an ultra-low budget movie, I feel that it represents the emerging trends that this book lays out.

The Digital Desktop is a subject that is so vast that it would take a very thick book to do it justice. That book is called *Creating Motion Graphics Production* and was written by my good friends Trish and Chris Meyer (*http://www.cybmotion.com*).

EDITING

In the late 1980s, we started seeing the first wave of nonlinear editing systems. EditDroid, LightWorks, Avid, and others started attacking the status quo. For a hundred years, editors had been handling their film with such unchanging mechanical tools as the Steenbeck, the Moviola, and the Kem. Tons of equipment, some of it fifty years old or more, constantly churning out Hollywood's gross national product. Most, if not all, saw this digital invasion as an affront to the craft of editing.

The vast majority of the old school of editors never did adapt and slowly slipped into retirement as a new generation of faster, more efficient editors took over the industry. In the end, it may be the director who tells the story but it's the editor who translates it.

The old guard, with their lifetimes of "hands-on" craft experience were being replaced in an instant by brash young film students with several years of theory under their belts. The industry itself buckled under the blow as the tide of independent films began to swell.

The laws of film elitism require that every self-professed film lover proclaim the virtues of low-budget, independent cinema while bemoaning the dismal plight of the big-budget, studio blockbusters. Well, big budget or small, there is no other single element of the production process that so codifies the final product as being good or bad as editing.

Good editing can elevate mediocre directing and barely competent cine-matography far beyond its humble birthright. Of course it also works the other way around.

Sometimes it seems as though I've owned and used every major non-linear edit system that there ever was including a prototype laserdisc based EditDroid (1987), PC based EMC2 (1989), 486 based LightWorks (1991), Macintosh-based Avid Media Composer (off and on from 1990 to present), and the most bulletproof system that I've ever owned, the Media100xr.

Occasionally I'll be working on a large project with traditional film editors who have just switched to non-linear. In those instances the system of choice is always one of the flavors of Avid because that is the metaphor the motion picture industry uses to make movies.

Being an old Mac guy at heart, I've used Apple's FinalCutPro since it first came out. While it provides a wonderful entree into the world of miniDV video production, it doesn't have the upward migration path of a program such as Avid's DV-Xpress. Now keep in mind that this is coming from a rather hardcore Mac guy who also has a long and well-documented grudge with Avid.

You can make all the arguments you want but when it comes right down to the bottom line, Avid is <u>the</u> industry standard. In an industry as fickle as this, you need all the standards you can get your hands on.

Without the capacity to transpose your work directly up to a conventional motion picture edit environment, you're just another videographer with some expensive toys and an opinion that is based on marketing hype.

If Apple spent as much time getting to know the craft of this industry as they do the investment potential of the companies they buy, they'd realize that editors, especially independent editors, are a migratory species. Indie editors might sit at three or four different stations during a single week.

One of my biggest problems with FCP is that it isn't portable. If you've upgraded since the first version like I have, then you know what an unbearable pain in the ass it is to install. Not only do you need to pander to different operating systems, but different versions of QuickTime and entirely different activation codes as well. My best time for installing FCP is a little over three hours. Best time with Avid Xpress is 16 minutes.

>>>>> The Avid Dongle
hangs amid a few
of its kin.

The other thing I like about Avid Xpress is that it uses a USB Security Key (dongle). All you need to do is sit down at a system with the software on it, plug in your dongle, and you're up and running. This may not sound like a big thing, but it is. First, it keeps people from messing around with your edit when you're not there and secondly, it prevents piracy. I hate piracy in any form. It denotes weak charac-ter, poor morals, and incurs bad karma for your project. 'Nuff said...

XpressDV-(above) / Apple FinalCutPro-(below)

>>>>> Avid's XpressDV
and Apple's FinalCutPro
interfaces.

If you've already purchased FCP, don't sweat it. It's a fine environment for putting together something to show your capabilities and after all... that is the biggest market segment by far. Apple is not a foolish company. While they may not fully understand the professional market, they do understand the consumer.

As I sit on the patio, writing this chapter, my own movie is being edited on a CineWaveHD system inside my house using FCP. Since *Mid-Century* was shot on HD, and the vast majority of desktop HD systems currently use FCP as the editing interface *du jour*, that is what we're using.

My editor is Arash Ayrom, who I originally met while we were both working on David Lynch's Academy Award nominated motion picture *Mulholland Drive*. Although primarily an Avid editor, Arash has learned the FCP interface protocol out of necessity, as have many professional editors.

Having spent an equal amount of time working on independent movies with both large and small budgets, Arash's opinion is particularly relevant to the state of the industry. So... on my way to the fridge, I stuck my head into the production room and asked him to jot down what he felt were the significant differences between the Avid and FinalCut applications.

Ten minutes after I arrived back on the patio with a glass of ice tea, Arash walked out, handed me a sheet of paper, and then went back to editing.

ARASH'S WISH-LIST FOR FCP (as of version 3.0.2)
1.) Customizable keyboard.
2.) Gang function between Viewer and Canvas.
3.) Multi-cam support.
4.) Ability to load sequences into Viewer, look at the timeline, and then cut into Canvas and preserve edits.
5.) Changing names of clips in browser doesn't affect clips in the Timeline.
6.) Icons in the timeline to indicate effects.
7.) Time Code overlay should be moveable (not in center of picture).
8.) The ability to work natively with key numbers.

Arash adds: "*If and when you get a traditional motion picture funded, the studio or distribution company will most likely insist that you hire a professional editor. Like most people, you'll find that the basics you learned from using FCP will give you a good vocabulary for communicating with your editor... who will of course, be using an Avid."*

NLE AS AN ACQUISITION ENVIRONMENT

OK, bear with me on this. As you probably surmised from Chapter One, I'm a long-time fan of direct-to-disk recording. Back in the late '80s it was a real pain in the ass, but now there are just so many cool tools to work with that I thought I'd add a little bit on this unique aspect of production.

I often use block camera's for visual effects work and for capturing elements that require a unique POV or time base. Since they don't have any complex recording mechanism or viewing system, they make unusually cost effective alternatives to conventional HD acquisition.

<<<<< The Ikegami HDL-40 is one of my favorite block cameras and when combined with AJAs 10-bit KonaHD video board, create a great combination for desktop resolution.

Matt Dillon's directorial debut (*City of Ghosts*), is an incredible effort from a first time director, and it was a great experience to work with someone who is so passionate and knowledgeable about the moviemaking process. Matt shot his movie in Cambodia on 35mm film and it captures the gritty essence of that steamy environment.

Due to the rapidly changing weather, there were several shots where we needed to insert drifting fog banks to match shots taken earlier in the day. Rather than fire up an entire location package, I snapped a CanonHD lens on to an Ikegami HDL-40 block camera and fed it into my AJA KonaHD system via the SDI connector. We drifted some liquid nitrogen over a black 4 x 4 and using the on-screen monitor in Adobe Premiere, captured the elements directly into the computer.

One of the great things about plugging a camera directly into a computer is that you can use programs like Premiere as an intervolometer to not only capture continuous sequences but time-lapse and stop-motion sequences as well.

In conventional cinematography the intervolometer is a step motor that advances the film a single frame and then triggers the camera to expose it. You've no doubt seen those shots of clouds sailing across the sky (1 frame per minute) or flowers blooming (6 frames per hour) or buildings being built (4 frames per day) or seasons changing (eight frames per month)... all intervolometer. Premiere has a cool little control window that is easy to use and bulletproof... two of my favorite features.

>>>>> Adobe Premiere's time-lapse/ stop-frame control window.

Then there's the stop-motion and puppet motion work such as Tim Burton's *The Nightmare Before Christmas*, which was actually directed by Henry Selick who went on to direct *James and the Giant Peach* and then *Monkeybone* (which my wife did quite a bit of work on). Unlike the time-lapse intervolometer system that takes a frame automatically every Nth second, the stop motion capabilities of Premiere capture a frame every time you hit the space bar.

Put a fertile mind together with these kinds of tools and something strange is always going to happen. Among my favorites are damn near anything Nick Park (*Wallace and Gromit*) does and, of course, the meister of the unusual, Terry Gilliam (*Monty Python, Jabberwocky, Time Bandits, Brazil, Adventures of Baron Munchausen, Brazil, The Fisher King, Brazil, Twelve Monkeys, Brazil, Fear and Loathing in Las Vegas, Twelve Monkeys...* and of course... *Brazil*).

CARE AND FEEDING OF VIDEO

While the editing process is where your story comes together, in digital moviemaking it is also the stage of production where you stand the greatest chance of doing the most damage to your resolution. Image management is the name of the game here. The care you take in the editing process will be reflected up on the screen.

If you've been shooting in DigiBeta, DVCPRO/50, or MPEG/IMX you'll want to transfer your footage via SDI. If you've got the capability to digitize a component signal then do a test using the same footage captured both ways, put it through the same hoops as your project and then compare. If you've got a system that is capable of using one of the new high bandpass FireWire type transfer methods, be sure to test it against a conventional SDI signal. Don't believe numbers or marketing hype, test it yourself!

If you've shot your project on one of the flavors of miniDV, the simplest solution for maintaining resolution is to bump your selected DV "takes" up to D-Beta, MPEG/IMX, or DVCPRO/50 and then sync in your DAT audio. This gives you a far more robust environment for editing as well as more channels of audio for mixing, and of course, SMPTE time code.

This methodology increases the cost of your production a bit, but the gain in accuracy and convenience will be its own reward. When you do finally get around to printing your movie to film, or projecting digitally, the D-Beta format will give you a far more stable and more widely accepted delivery mechanism since most printers and commercial projectors don't accept the miniDV format.

The System

Get the biggest monitor you can, better yet, get a couple of 'em. Like any good work environment, the surface area of your desktop has a lot to do with how easy it is to keep track of things. By the time you get into editing, the name of the game is data management. A sizable workspace goes a long way toward knowing where everything is.

Storage is one of those things you can never have enough of, especially if you're planning on printing or mastering from your edit system's output. If you're editing at a really low compression ratio (2:1), the space that each frame takes up is going to be much greater than at higher ratios (50:1).

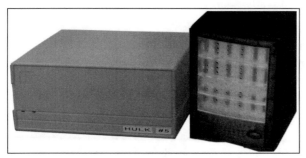

<<<<< I bought the 1Gb drive on the left in 1989 for $6,000. It transferred data at a blinding 3Mb per second. I just bought the 1Tb drive on the right (HUGE MediaVault) for half that much and it transfers data at 200 Mb per second. Don'tcha just love Moore's Law?

Don't count on storing your entire movie at low compression ratio within your system unless you've got more than a hundred Gigabytes.

Get yourself a good orthopedic chair. You're going to be spending weeks in this thing, make them as pleasurable as possible.

The eleven-hour workday is fine for moving light stands and set pieces around, but no one can be creative on a continuous eleven-hour day work cycle. Physical exhaustion is much easier to recover from than mental exhaustion.

After working a hard ten hour day you might be physically spent but after a good night's sleep you'll usually be up and about, ready for another hard day. Exhaust yourself mentally and it might take a week to recover. Digital production schedules should revolve around eight hour days. Run three shifts if you have to crank out the work, but make sure that you give your people an opportunity to recover.

Rule-of-Thumb

Nonlinear systems all follow the basic rule-of-thumb, digitize your selects, build bins for each scene, you'll never have enough storage, you'll never have enough time, and Coke and pizza are your best friends. Oh yeah, and once you've got it calibrated, don't touch the damn monitor!

The Work Environment

How you configure your edit system is up to you. The vast majority of people get a table and simply start piling equipment onto it. I've spent a good many years sitting among computers and production equipment, and personally, the thrill is gone. I'm tired of the persistent whine of the drives and fans and I'm tired of the techno-clutter. My preferred environment is to sit out on my porch with my TiBook and shuttle render commands to the big computers via my AirPort.

Today, just about every new desktop computer comes equipped with some sort of non-linear system already installed. One of the coolest mini-systems is the Sony VAIO® C1MW PictureBook™ Series Notebook. It is an 867MHz screamer running Windows® XP Professional with a build in camera, iLINK® (IEEE 1394), 384MB of RAM, 30GB hard drive and a 1024 x 480 screen and the whole thing fits in a jacket pocket. We're talking about a very convenient video sketchbook that you can use anywhere.

I've got a kid that works for me that does amazing things with FireWire and Adobe Premiere. It all comes down to what works for you and fits within your budget. There's always a way to work around resolution issues as long as you can identify them.

WHERE TO START?

There are certain aspects of conventional production methodology that don't really change because of innovation. One such thing is "Tone & Bars" in video and the counter in film.

Black at 00:58:00:00, then Bars and Tone from 00:58:30:00 to 00:59:30:00, then black to 00:59:40:00, then slate (includes the film's name, the production company and date. You'll

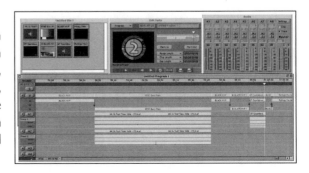

later come back and add the running time) to 00:59:50:00 where you'll insert your countdown numbers and a beep at the top of each second from 10 to 2. At the end of the "2" you go black until 01:00:00:00 (one hour) where the program begins. Any creativity or liberties taken at this point will not only screw up every professional that comes in contact with your movie but it will also make you look like a clueless dork.

Fade up from black...

SCORING YOUR EPIC

So you finally got to the end of your edit and now it's time to add the score. This is how you subliminally tell the audience how you want them to feel about each scene and character. The thematic underscore creates mood and texture. A scene underscored with violins and trumpets can cause emotions to swell with majestic expressiveness, while a lone oboe can escort your audience into an almost cathartic empathy with your characters.

In the standard Hollywood fare we all-too-often see every gesture and nuance underscored with dramatic themes. The audience never gets a chance to make up their own minds or breathe. On the other end of the scale is the small budget production that is forced to use "canned music." Often the emotion and theme don't match or the timing is off.

In these instances, it is often better to lay an audio reference track down and edit the scene to it. As blasphemous as this may sound, a good sound track has a pacing to it that is based on thousands of years of refinement. By editing your scene to that evolving thematic correlate, your scene takes on a tempo and pace that not only merges it with the musical underscore but also conforms it to an established tempo.

8 ▷ CAST 'N' CREW

*"The cinema offers this miraculous double feature:
you tell a story and while you are doing so you are living
another one yourself, an adventure with people as
extraordinary as those in the film you are making."*
Federico Fellini

As much as you might like to think of yourself as the lone desperado out there shooting away, it's almost impossible to create anything of lasting value in a vacuum. The people who buy into your graphic hallucination are trusting you to take care of them. It's not just a legal obligation, but a moral one as well.

There are a lot of shortcuts that can save you time and money. Low-budget moviemaking involves a seemingly endless re-negotiation of your bottom line. Accommodations are invariably made, things are done without, but I've yet to meet a successful filmmaker that didn't take the well-being of his cast and crew very seriously.

I'm not a big fan of clubs, especially when they're exclusionary. Even so, I recently shot my own movie under full Industry/SAG contract; not because I'm a flag-waving union type guy, but because I respect my cast and crew.

Making a movie is a hard job, and dangerous, too. By working under industry guidelines and regulations, my cast and crew was covered by workman's comp (insurance), and their retirement funds were paid into. Now trust me on this, I didn't pay out any exorbitant salaries, and working with SAG is nearly as hard as making the movie... maybe harder, but the important thing is that my people were protected. Nothing else in the entire production process is that important.

More than anything else; more than resolution, more than budget, more than box office gross; it is your concern for your cast and crew that determines your professionalism.

... So I guess that this is as good a time as ever to bring up the topic of the DGA. Yes, it's a dinosaur. Yes, it's exclusionary. Yes, it is expensive to join.

I'm sure as an indie filmmaker, the DGA is about the last thing on your mind, but here's my thinking on this.

This book is about turning your hobby into a profession. As a professional moviemaker you've got considerations that the hobbyist doesn't need to bother themselves with; PROTECTIONS, CONNECTIONS, and CLOUT.

As a director on a low-budget film you are in a very vulnerable position. Something goes wrong, you could be paying for it for the rest of your life.

As a professional moviemaker, you're probably in need of some legal and financial protection as well. While organizations such as the IFP are a tremendous assist in getting your career off of the ground, once you're off and running, the playing field changes rapidly.

Since you're probably not punching in nine-to-five at the office, you'll need a health plan, maybe even a nice little pension plan. No, you aren't immortal.

With the vast majority of low-budget, independent features, the director is seldom working for a salary. If the movie does well, he's promised a piece of the action. Cable television and DVD distribution have created a highly profitable distribution channel for independent work, but these are all large corporations that only see the bottom line. You need some way to track the money that is due you and then have enough clout to collect. To do that you'll need the playground bully on your side.

Contrary to popular belief, the guild has long been a resource with open doors for the independent moviemaker. Now, with many of the old guard passing on into retirement, the guild has been forced to reevaluate its position.

The DGA Independent Director's Committee has sculpted out a unique package of support for the independent that offers the same essential pro-tections enjoyed by the big guys.

The really cool thing about the "new" DGA is that the vast majority of the filmmakers I hold in high regard are part of their new Indie thing. John Waters, John Sayles, Mary Lambert, Wayne Wang...

The golden days of the film industry are giving way to the pixelated vision of a digital future. Proximity to Hollywood is not a concern. On the contrary, production seems to be making a concerted effort to get as far away as possible. I just think that it's kind of cool, when the dinosaurs come down to graze with the rest of us cattle.

THE AUTEUR

The word Auteur gets bantered around a lot these days. One person who can do it all. People try to hang that moniker on me from time to time and it always makes me cringe. I've been a cameraman my whole life and I've had the good fortune to shoot for some of the greatest directors in the business; but when it came time to make my own movie, I got someone else to shoot it. Why? Because I have a number of very talented and well-respected actors in my project. They were all familiar with my work and reputation in the industry. They trusted me to make them look good, not only physically as the camera sees them but professionally as the audience sees them.

There is no possible way that you can do justice to great actors by both shooting and directing them. Moviemaking is a collaborative process and just because you can do every job in the entire manufacturing process, doesn't mean that you should do them at the same time.

Of course there's Robert Rodriguez, who gets as close to being an auteur as anyone I know. His book, *Rebel Without a Crew*, is perhaps the perfect counterpoint to this one since we both possess similar skill-sets, are both proficient cinematographers, can write our way out of a wet paper bag, and both know our way around a digital postproduction environment.

Robert and I were standing at the Valet (this is Hollywood after all), following an interesting lunch where we were discussing the methodology of his upcoming production of *Spy Kids 2*. As we waited for our cars to arrive, he pulled out his wallet and showed me his rather impressive array of guild membership cards. WGA, DGA... the whole enchilada.

Robert takes great pride in the fact that he is a bona fide, soup-to-nuts film-maker and, in my experience, he is as close as it gets to being the exception to the rule. Having seen him work, I can tell you that his secret is to surround himself with consummate professionals and then orchestrate his production like a battle plan out of Sun Tzu's *Art of War*.

But hey... you don't have a cadre of highly gifted artisans to surround yourself with, and the last time you read the *Art of War* was... well, never. Your best chance of success is to weed out the most brutally honest and excruciatingly practical production methodology that you can find.

You'll need to look deep into the mirror of reality and scrutinize your natural proclivities. Be on the lookout for people who you feel possess your missing traits and then plead with them to buy into your little machination. These people are your partners, confidants, collaborators, and could very well be your key to success.

Since they also possess skill-sets that are markedly different than your own, they will also be an unending source of blinding insight as well as consummate frustration. The idea is to never have more than one or two slashes (writer/producer/director) between your job descriptions at any one time. Those who bite off too big a chunk, always seem to choke on it.

It is good to have people who you admire, but there is a fine line between admiration and emulation. Just as the latest Nike sneakers won't really make you fly through the air like Michael Jordan, a Canon XL1 and the latest version of Apple's FinalCutPro won't turn you into Robert Rodriguez either.

There is a vast and fundamental difference between advertising mythos and reality. You step over that line without comparable talents and you're just another chalk outline on the Boulevard of dreams.

NO MAN IS AN ISLAND

Moviemaking is a process that involves alternative points of view. In addition to sage organizational and financial counsel, a healthy dose of dissension is one of the more important ingredients that a good producer brings.

Controversy stimulates creativity and without it you become stagnant. No matter how blindingly brilliant you think your idea is, no matter how proficient you think you are at the craft of cinematic one way narrative, without an experienced "second opinion," your project stands a very good chance of becoming little more than self-indulgent drivel.

Not just the curse of emerging moviemakers, the discount bins are full of direct-to-video flops from people who should simply have known better. Arrogance, insolence, you can call it what you will, but the filmmaker who refuses to seek out alternative points of view is captain of a sinking ship.

Many of the grandest failures are simply credited to psychological or emotional problems when in fact the problem is more often than not physiological in origin. Many of the various jobs in the moviemaking process require a variety of both right and left hemisphere functions. It is very difficult to transition from the mindset of budgetary concerns to the mindset of writing a line of dialogue or setting a shot.

The most successful people always seem to surround themselves with those who possess an alternative point of view and the chutzpah to express it.

A FORMULA FOR SUCCESS

Just because you've got a limited budget doesn't mean that you need to limit your resources. The knee-jerk reaction of most people starting out on their first cinematic venture is to put a crew together from friends and family.

There are so many physiological peccadilloes involved with this approach that it isn't even worthy of a gratuitous acknowledgment. By using friends you're merely repurposing whatever little social group manifestation preexisted. Social groups are usually quite democratic, moviemaking is not.

By making a movie with your friends you'll constantly be striving to maintain the group dynamic... except of course, this time you're the king. Well it doesn't work that way for a number of reasons.

By upsetting a preexisting group dynamic you force an inherent restructuring that negates your chance of a stable production environment. Since you probably won't be using top notch actors, you're going to need all the stability you can muster.

Perhaps most importantly, the chances are slim to nonexistent that your little group of friends contains all of the talents that are necessary to fully engage a successful manufacturing campaign.

By actively seeking out excellence in all aspects of the craft you must go outside your immediate group of friends. Again, a resource such as IFP is invaluable in assembling a team that actually has a chance at creating a successful product.

Try to limit the number of hats you wear and look for people who are passionate about developing their craft.

The writer that rejects the cliché and creates characters that constantly evolve and engage the audience's deepest, unresolved emotions will always find more than their fair share of success.

The director that allows the actor be in the moment, thinking real thoughts and feeling real feelings right in front of us will connect the audience in a way that will seem like magic.

The cinematographer that uses his light to paint the spectrum of emotions across the palette of the human face will bring life and vitality to his characters.

The producer who makes good choices, picks good people, and then gets out of their way so that they can tell their story, will be financially rewarded.

What are your goals and objectives? What inspires you? Scrutinize your motives. Do you have a passion for story telling? Are you drawn to celebrity? Are you merely fascinated by the technology? Do you love working with other talented, passionate people towards a collective goal, or are you just looking for a good way to get laid?

Let's face it, directing is one of the only professions where you're treated like a god. People scurry about to do your bidding and the power you wield, if only in your limited kingdom, is as close as most mortals come to omnipotence.

Many successful actors are quite simply people in search of a personality. A vast majority of industry personnel embrace the production crew as a surrogate family while others seem to be here merely because they've proven themselves unqualified to do anything else.

As many people as there are in this glorious industry, there are an equal number of motivations. The secret is not in following your dreams but rather in following your proclivities.

Like a great painting by a true master, the cinema combines a duality that spans the spectrum of the human condition. From the greedy lawyers to the gregarious gaffers and grips, this industry embodies the most robust assortment of characters found anywhere. The secret lies in finding your natural place within the process.

GET A GRIP

First thing to do is ask yourself what you see yourself doing? What are your goals and objectives? Sure it's your idea and probably even your script, but are you really the best person to direct or shoot it? Maybe since you have the "Big Picture" the project would be far more successful if you acted as Executive Producer or let someone else take a pass at that "gem" of a script.

It's great if you enjoy making movies but if your project doesn't make money, or you don't pay back the people who invested in your project, your future as a movie maker is going to be severely limited.

There are a dozen major job descriptions in the conventional motion picture manufacturing process and they are each responsible for dozens of departments operating under them. Each of these departments breaks down and branches out to tens if not hundreds more job titles given the size of the budget.

On projects with severely limited budgets many of these jobs can be combined, allowing a single person to wear multiple hats. The problems start when, in the name of budgetary limitations, one of these jobs is eliminated rather than absorbed. The resulting hole in your organization can sink your project before its even had a chance to leave the dock.

THE PROCESS

Starting from the point of view of a conventional, moderately budgeted, 35mm motion picture production and continuing on down to the ultra-low budget "lone wolf" video project, we'll take a look at what the various jobs do and why they're each so important.

There are numerous ways to break down the motion picture hierarchy. Studio Boss, Executive Producer, Director, Writer, and so on in a linear fashion. The problem is that the organization of a motion picture isn't linear and not all people are around for the entire duration.

A writer is actively involved in the start of a project, many times even before a director has been attached. The editor, who in many ways has the final word, may not even know of the project until principal photography has been finished. But, generally the writer hangs around on the periphery, sometimes contractually obligated to generate the occasional script fix, and editors generally cruise into the dailies just to get an idea of what's going on.

The production process can also be broken down into the distinct stages of DEVELOPMENT, PREPRODUCTION, PRODUCTION, POSTPRODUC-TION and DISTRIBUTION. Various job functions crossover through all five stages while some deal with only one or two stages in the production process.

DEVELOPMENT — This is the period in which the initial concept, whether for a motion picture or television show, is conceptualized, written, and pitched, though not necessarily in that order. You could find yourself pitching a hairball concept or a full-blown script. You could be pitching for the $500 you need to bail your cameraman out of jail or twenty-million dollars to make your next science fiction extravaganza. Once you've convinced someone to back your cinematic venture you've got to let all the good people who just anted up to have their way with you. Don't take it personally, it's just they way they do it in this industry.

PREPRODUCTION — You've got your money, the scabs are healing up nicely and you're slamming together cast and crew, trying desperately to find a production facility out of the country so you can get away from all these studio creeps. This is when the project takes on its timbre as the cast and crew becomes the woof and weave of the story's tapestry. Mistakes and shortcuts here will quite literally, haunt you till the day you die.

PRODUCTION — "Lights, Camera, Action!" Once you're rolling the sheer inertia of the process begins to sink in. The train has pulled out of the station and it's a whole lot longer than you imagined. Every decision that you've made up to this point is now following you down the track and will continue to do so until you utter the final "Cut, it's a wrap."

POSTPRODUCTION — A lot of production people look at this as their time to come up for a breath of fresh air. It is technically the end of the initial manufacturing process. If you're a director or other heavily vested individual, you're swimming for the surface like everyone else but just before you break through, the editor, who's got this really big lung full of fresh air, grabs you by the ankles and drags you back down.

If the production process could be described as running around a cactus patch in bare feet, trying to stomp out small fires, the postproduction process could be described as an endless, featureless exercise in cave dwelling. Every mistake you've made, every bit of coverage you didn't get, every time you said "We'll fix it in post," this is when they all come back to haunt you.

And your loyal cast and crew? They've all gone on lovely vacations, hanging out on beaches, and sipping Margaritas. And you? You're sucking down two-day-old coffee in a building that should have been condemned at the last turn of the century, trying to figure out a polite way to ask your editor to increase his personal hygiene regime to twice a week.

DISTRIBUTION — Damn, just when all the wounds had healed from the development process, here come a whole new herd of bison intent on having their way with you. They're called distributors, syndicators, and network executives, and every one of them thinks you've got a purdy mouth. If you're really lucky, and the distributors like your movie, these beasts will set your movie up for exhibition, and if you're really, really lucky the audiences won't hate it.

Then one day the check clears the bank, you're out on the promo circuit, and all you can think about is get'n back in there and doin' it all over again.

I guess I should apologize for my cavalier and somewhat jaded view of the time-honored process. Those who have yet to make their first sojourn into the bowels of the Hollywood machine might find my observations rather crude. Hey, write your own book.

WHO DOES WHAT

In the most typical industry parlance there is a dividing line of job functions in the production process. It is called, quite simply, THE LINE. You're either above it or below it. I like to think of all of the people above-the-line as the people who don't get their hands dirty, while the people below-the-line are the ones who actually make the movie. So, above the line you've got all the producers, writers, the director, and the actors, while below the line hover all of the production staff and assistants to everyone above the line.

The basic rule of thumb is that the Producer hires everyone above the line while the UPM (Unit Production Manager) hires every one below the line. Think of a Production Manager as the below-the-line producer, or in military terms, the staff sergeant. Simply put, they run the show. The job is one of the hardest, most important, and least appreciated because it is a full time battle to maintain a creative atmosphere in an environment that all too easily gets bogged down in technical minutia.

There is a growing trend to call Production Managers, Associate Producers, which to me is somewhat akin to calling Da Vinci a paint slinger. But hey, I guess when you're standing at a bar, trying to impress the hot blonde that just walked in, it sounds a lot cooler to say you're a Producer than a Unit Production Manager.

So basically the UPM takes the script and develops the first budget that anyone really pays any attention to. He also figures out how many days the project should take to shoot and between the two factors, Time and Money, calculates the Production Value. Basically the UPM negotiates a formula as old as production. Price, Quality, or Speed — pick any two.

The Director's Guild of America takes a much more succinct view of the UPMs functions essentially stating:

"The Unit Production Manager, under the supervision of the Employer, is required to coordinate, facilitate, and oversee the preparation of the production unit or units assigned to him, all off-set logistics, day to day production decisions, locations, budget schedules and personnel."

Of all the people involved in each of the five distinct processes of production, the UPM is one of the most important job functions. In many instances, a good UPM is far more important than a competent director. Second in importance to the UPM is the 1st Assistant Director who actually does all the paperwork that keeps the production humming along.

There are two things a production runs on, vast amounts of paperwork and junk food. In my years of production experience, I can't remember a craft services table that didn't have a half-empty canister of Twizzlers sitting on it. But I digress.

So the First is basically responsible for breakdowns and preparing the strip-board, the shooting schedules, day-out-of-day schedules, cast availability, call sheets, weather reports, and is occasionally required to direct background scenes and supervise and direct crowd control.

While the First is doing all this work the Line Producer is busy dealing with emergencies and trying to keep the show running while also trying to take credit for everything the UPM does.

A good Director is essentially "an allower." He comes on the set every day and allows everyone to do his or her job. More often than not, he's had little, if anything to do with the script and almost nothing to do with securing financing, other than lending the credibility or infamy of his name to the process. Hopefully the Director is an inherently good storyteller and is capable of guiding the collective consciousness of the audience.

Directors are essentially the keepers of the metronome by which the process evolves. It is their responsibility to translate the script into visual terms — and this my friend is no small matter. Hopefully the Producers hired a good Casting Director who picked good Actors that personify the roles. Then all that is left is for the Director to put them in the right places so they can do what they were hired to do.

Of utmost importance to the look and feel of the movie is the Director of Photography (DP). For many years it was the Cinematographer who ran the production. Only when the ASC (American Society of Cinematographers) went up against the far superior cunning of the DGA (Directors Guild of America) did the Director emerge as the on-set boss.

For the Director it can be, and sometimes is, their first day on the job, while the Cinematographer, more with film than video, needs to have a lifetime of experience behind them. The Director of Photography relies on his staff of Gaffers and Electricians to move lights and direct and modify the beams they throw. The Best Boy assists the Gaffer in setting up the lights while the Electricians make all the necessary electrical connections and maintain the power supply.

One of the more notoriously gregarious members of the production crew is the Grip. Basically, anything, other than lights, that needs to be moved, one of these guys "grip" it and move it. They are the handy man of the set, building scaffolding, placing props, and creating unique devices to assist in various shots. If the camera is set on a dolly then it is the Dolly Grip that physically moves it.

In film productions and higher end video productions the audio is recorded separately from the image. The Sound Recordist (Sound Man even if they're female) and his or her Boom Operator are responsible for recording not only the spoken sounds of the actors, but also a catalogue of ambient "room" sounds that will be used later by the editorial staff.

The Script Supervisor is essentially the Director's brain. Rarely, if ever, are the scenes in a movie shot in sequential order. It is the Script Supervisor who is responsible for making sure that everything from clothes and hairdos to the position of the dead body matches the shot they did at another time. They are also responsible for making sure that the scenes have been shot from all the necessary angles that the script calls for.

Second Unit does stunts, effects shots, crowd scenes, battle scenes, and generally shoots all the plates for later effects shots if there isn't a dedicated effects unit on the show.

At the very bottom of the heap are the lowest paid employees, the PAs (Production Assistants), otherwise known as gophers (go for this, go for that). Their job is to direct traffic, control access to the set, and go for stuff.

So that's a rather basic, albeit tongue-in-cheek, overview of the essential structure of your basic motion picture. Figure an average ten million-dollar project will have a couple hundred people running around between several stages and locations. But hey, you don't have ten million dollars. That's why you're reading this book.

So now we gotta figure out how you can cram all those job descriptions into three or four people. First thing you've got to do is figure out who the most important people are. Simple: Director, Unit Production Manager, Cinematographer, Grip... and here's how we're going to combine the jobs.

DEVELOPMENT — Like the slimy caterpillar that is destined to evolve into a beautiful butterfly, the UPM starts out as an Executive Producer. He is like an organ grinder who, along with his trained monkey (Cinematographer/Director), raises the money and develops the script. The Executive Producer/UPM or the Cinematographer/Director in many instances is also the Writer.

PREPRODUCTION — Congratulations, you've got your money, so now the Executive Producer starts to metamorphose into the UPM, looking for cheap, or better yet, free locations and an individual to actually take respon- sibility for doing the physical work a.k.a. (Grip/Gaffer/PA). Meanwhile the Cinematographer/Director gets involved in casting.

PRODUCTION — Once you're rolling, the Executive Producer/UPM assumes the Script Supervisor's position while the Cinematographer/Director arranges actors and along with the Grip/Gaffer/PA/Sound Man sets the lights and then finally shoots the scenes. Someone's wife or girlfriend usually gets to be make-up/wardrobe/craft services, don't forget the Twizzlers.

POSTPRODUCTION — The Cinematographer/Director now becomes the Editor because they're the only one who has been able to follow the erratic sequences thus far. The Executive Producer/UPM/Script Supervisor becomes the Script Supervisor/Assistant Editor and helps keep track of where the various shots and elements are. The Grip/Gaffer/PA becomes a PA/Producer/WebMaster and develops potential distribution channels while fending off actors and vendors looking for their money.

DISTRIBUTION — Hopefully the PA/Producer/WebMaster has generated some significant interest and lined up some really good festivals as the three of you head off into the sunset with your hard-earned show and a half-empty canister of Twizzlers.

The cast and crew is the true equity of a production. They are the woof and weave of the tapestry you've spun. The degree to which you coordinate their efforts and protect their interests is the cornerstone of your professionalism.

9 DIGITAL CINEMATOGRAPHY

"There is no such thing as a digital cinematographer.
We're all cinematographers."
Steven Poster ASC

I started my somewhat eclectic career in cinema as an assistant to Academy Award winning cinematographer James Wong Howe (*Hud, Rose Tattoo, Molly Maguires*). Mr. Howe's acerbic wit and rough mannerisms made him an interesting person to work for. He died in the middle of shooting *Funny Lady* with Barbara Streisand and James Caan (talk about lighting the difficult two shot).

Before his death I often took him to an acupuncturist out in the San Fernando Valley. As we were sitting there one day waiting for his appointment, the chiropractor from the adjoining office came bursting into the waiting room with a gurney full of what was then, state-of-the-art video equipment. He proceeded to play his grainy, jittery, B&W home video for us until Mr. Howe turned to me and asked. *"Scotty, you know why video always looks so crappy?"* Well, I proceeded to ramble on about resolution and sample rates until he interrupted me. *"Video,"* he said. *"Always looks so crappy 'cause there's so many crappy people shooting it."* May he rest in peace.

Although harsh, he was actually quite correct in his observations. The most unfortunate aspect of digital cinematography is that it generally ends up looking like home video. If you don't particularly want your project to end up looking "crappy," then treat your video camera as if it were a film camera and treat your shots as though you were acquiring on film.

THE LOOK

During the filming of *Mulholland Drive*, David Lynch was looking for a small form-factor digital camera to experiment with. I recommended the Sony PD-150 because of its image quality and versatility when used in DVCAM mode.

One of the great things about some of the newer DV cameras is their wide latitude for calibration. By using a good camera chart such as the DSC Lab's CamAlign, and the software Waveform Monitor included in many software NLE systems, you can tweak a camera's gamma curve, histogram, and color density range to create a substantial number of different looks.

By actually opening up the camera (since this invalidates the warranty I can't even answer e-mail that asks for instructions to do this), I calibrated the PD-150 that he'd purchased to a denser, more film-like profile.

A few months later we were prepping for the worldwide inaugural commercial for the Sony PlayStation2. It was a huge project that would eventually become one of the more heavily viewed commercials of the century, playing in well over a hundred countries including China, Japan, Europe, and the southern continents. David says that he's so happy with the look that he's getting from the PD-150 that he wants me to shoot the commercial with it.

>>>>> The author tries to get the feel of the tiny camera. It took a lot of advanced *Tweak-ology* to get the PD-150 to play nice within the conventional production environment.

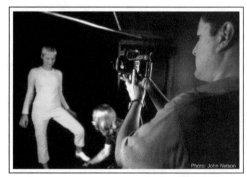

Photo: John Nelson

David's view of the emerging digital toolset takes a uniquely artistic view. *"It doesn't really matter what way you work, or what medium you work in, it's all about ideas. Every story, every idea, wants to be told a certain way. Now, with digital cameras, the really great thing about them is the amount of control you have afterwards to fiddle around and start experimenting and get even more ideas."*

The PD-150 is a great little camera but the field of view is unusually narrow so we fitted ours with a Century Precision Optics wide angle adapter over which we layered a number of neutral density filters. The short stack of NDs gave us an equivalent rating of around 100 ASA. With all of the pyro and hard slashing lights, it was crucial to ending up with detail in the highlights.

By making these small formats work for the picture you not only eliminate many of the visual clues that people generally associate with home video but you force yourself to actually light the scene. The other factor in the "video look" is, of course, mass.

DYNAMIC MOTION

Film cameras are generally bulky, heavy affairs. When they move, it is generally with a plodding massiveness that belies their inertia. Video camcorders on the other hand are light, flimsy affairs that we can fling around with mindless abandon.

Go rent your top ten favorite movies, brew a big pot of coffee and get yourself a yellow pad. Now watch all ten movies and make a note of every time the camera flits around or makes any movement that could in any way be construed as coming from an object weighing in at under thirty pounds.

Lightweight camcorders were designed for home video use. If you want your image to move like it came from a film camera, create an environment that causes your tiny camcorder to move like a real film camera. If you're going to use a tripod, get a big one with a large fluid head. Get something that was built to hold a fifty-pound camera and it will give you moves that echo that massive environment.

For handheld shots go get yourself a ten pound weight at the local sporting goods store, or better yet get someone to machine something cool for you and hook that little, flimsy camcorder to it and leave it there. It will give your shots a massiveness and inertial quality that is nearly impossible with a camcorder.

>>>>> For the PS2 commercial we built a number of custom mounts that not only gave the tiny PD-150 a more massive feel, but also allowed it to be aimed and positioned with greater control.

"While there are definite benefits to the simplification that digital offers, I think that there are still a few critical tools that need to be developed and refined," adds David. *"These small cameras don't move cinematically, they're light and flimsy. We need a really nice little Steadicam type device and we need to see more tools like the rigs we made for this commercial, little stabilizers, little dollies and cranes, to make them real smooth and cinematic. Then there's the obvious tools that filmmakers need like follow focus, and more mechanical interaction."*

GETTING THAT CINEMATIC LOOK

I'm not talking about the software filters here, we'll get to them later. I'm talking about the collective characteristics of the image that tell the audience whether they're watching a quality production or another crappy video. The camera is the tool by which we record the story we are telling. The more professionally it is recorded, the more inherent perceived quality our production will have.

While both film and video record light reflected off of objects, they do it in different ways. Film is its own recording mechanism and storage medium while video's image must be encoded, transposed, and recorded to video tape, hard disk, or RAM. Digital video is quite finite in its inherent form while film possesses an almost infinite spectrum of attributes.

To get video to look cinematic we must develop methodologies that emulate the essential nuance of that medium. If we compare a single frame of 35mm film stock to a broadcast quality video frame, we will discover four main areas of difference.

First is the resolved size of the image. While an NTSC video frame has essentially 349,920 pixels (720 × 486), a frame of film is easily capable of resolving 12,582,912 pixels (4096 × 3072). Even the high-end of HD can only muster 1/6th as many picture elements and at far less colorspace.

The amount of color that a medium records is called the colorspace or color gamut. Film can display over 800 million colors while the best uncompressed video can barely maintain a color gamut of 256 colors for each of its three component colors. Red=256, Green=256, and Blue=256 which, when cubed, gives us 16.7 million colors. For every color that video can display, film can display 48.

As we will discuss later in the chapter, film has a much higher contrast ratio (dynamic latitude) than video and can record more than six times the range of illumination. This gives film far more depth and detail as highlights roll off gently into denser regions. The same scene on video would generate solid blotches of black or white.

Digital formats retain strong contrast all the way out to the resolution limit while film formats start losing contrast at higher resolutions and have progressively lower contrast as you go out to the limit. Of course, the resolution of film also degrades with every photochemical duplication from camera negative to release print. In contrast, you could theoretically employ a digital cinema postproduction chain that maintains original image quality at least as far as the projector. (With a decent three-CRT home theater projector, you could enjoy the full, original image quality right up on the screen.)

My object is not to talk you out of using digital acquisition, but rather to help you understand that video is a limited medium, so extreme care must be taken to protect what resolution the format is capable of resolving.

The following suggestions will help you keep your video image from looking like video. Whether or not you can tell a good story, well that's up to you.

TAKE STOCK IN YOUR IMAGE

I'm sure it goes without saying that you should only use new, high-grade, name brand videotape. Never reuse or tape-over anything, and keep it as dry and cool as possible. The tiny DV format tapes are far more delicate than you might imagine, especially after they have been recorded to.

>>>>> Do you ever get the feeling that there's a guy in a suit, sitting behind a big desk somewhere, and he's laughing his ass off?

Remember that no matter how small they make the tape, or how expensive it becomes, it is still just rust glued on to plastic. However desperately we want to believe that this is the glorious digital age, we've got to remember that the vast majority of digital marvels are still composed of moving parts. Make dubs of your masters immediately and only use the masters for transfer or final on-line. 'Nuff said.

Motion Artifacts

The motion artifacts of video are unique and tell an audience that they are watching video even after you've printed to film. If you shot your movie on a PAL system, the artifacts will be far less noticeable as having originated on video but they'll still be annoying. Bright objects moving horizontally across the frame and fast camera pans are the worst. Serious testing is in order if you're considering such movements.

Image Stabilization

While we're on the topic. If you use a camera that has image stabilization, never turn it on. This is a feature best relegated to tipsy wedding photographers and harried vacationers. If you can't hold your camera still, put it on a tripod and cut down on the caffeine.

Image stabilization in consumer camcorders essentially works by fixing on an area of high-contrast and then stretching the image and taking just the middle part. The decrease in resolution, and sharpness, is unacceptable in professional video, much less in video that is destined to be projected or printed on film.

NIX THE ZOOM

One of the biggest tip-offs that you're watching video is a zoom. DON'T ZOOM! DON'T EVER ZOOM! It doesn't matter whether or not you think a zoom will enhance the end result, you are wrong! Go back and look at your top ten movies again. You can probably use the same sheet on your yellow pad. Not a "dolly" or a "truck" or a "push" where the camera actually moves closer to the subject, I'm talking zoom. After viewing all ten of your favorite movies please notice how nice and clean your yellow pad is.

Zooms are for weddings and home video. Filmmakers, on the other hand, generally use a very expensive set of prime lenses or at least the metaphor. A "prime" is a lens of fixed focal length. In DP lingo it refers to the distance between the optical center of the lens and the film plane, when the lens is focused at infinity (endless point in space, not the car). To the videographer it means that you frame the shot using the zoom function selecting a setting between "wide" and "telephoto" and then leave it there as you make your shot.

If you need to get the actor's face to fill the scene, get up off your ass and physically move closer. The object is to move the camera. A camera move gives a scene dynamics and a greater sense of presence. It helps develop a point of view and establishes the environment in which you're telling the story. Yes, there are professional zoom lenses but they are generally used as a rapidly accessible set of prime lenses.

While we're on the topic of lenses, I'd like to offer up an observation. The tendency with small video camcorders is to get too close to the subject. They're small and unobtrusive, almost ubiquitous in contemporary society. Add to this the high number of people who are using a camera mounted microphone and it's probably safe to say that this is one of the bigger factors in the "video" look.

The problem with shooting someone from a short distance is that you'll generally need to use a rather wide lens that has an angle of view in excess of 90 degrees. People tend to look goofy when shot with wide-angle "short" lenses. I call it the Jim Varney effect, and while the late comedian made a career out of it, the look leaves a bit to be desired on your leading lady.

>>>>>> In addition to being an unusually good person, the late Jim Varney made a very good living by knowing how to use cinematography to enhance his characterizations. That's Jim on the left.

A lens that has an angle of view in the 10 degree range will generally put you at least 12 feet away from the subject and will generally give you a far better sense of the person's character. Test this as often as it takes till you get the feel.

AUTO EXPOSURE IS FOR CAR ADS

This is simple; at least it should be. Pick an exposure that gives you a relatively short depth of field and then turn off your auto exposure and tape your exposure ring in place. If you need more light... bring in the equipment. You need less light, learn how to cut (reduce) the light. Cinematography is all about controlling light physically, <u>not automatically</u>. There simply is no other factor that will elevate the perceived value of your production more than following this paragraph.

CHOOSING A CAMERA

Automatic Anything is Bad. First thing you need to look for in the selection of an appropriate digital video camcorder is whether or not you can override the automatic functions. Auto focus, auto iris, auto white balance, these functions are created for amateur home videoists, not digital moviemakers.

If you can't override the auto functions of your camera stop here, put the book down and go do something else because anything you shoot is going to look bad and drag us all down. The unmistakable shift as the auto-focus searches for something to lock onto, or the nauseating displacement in depth of field as the auto-iris corrects for changes in brightness, these are all the unmistakable signature of cheap video and lazy people and indicate that whatever follows should not be taken seriously.

MATTE BOX

The camera is a system designed to collect and control a stream of reflected light within the limits of its designated recording specifications. Perhaps the most practical and significant step towards controlling light is the matte box light shade. It serves a dual purpose, as its name would suggest, of shading the forward lens element from stray shafts of light while also allowing you a mechanism for attaching a variety of filters. You'd be hard pressed to find a professional film or video camera that didn't sport one of these most basic tools of the trade.

<<<<< A good matte box is an indispensable addition to a quality acquisition system.

The sorry attempt for a shade that accompanied your camcorder doesn't count and whether you construct one yourself out of cardboard or spring for one of those custom, after market jobs, there is little you can do to improve the quality of the image more. To be effective, the shade should extend at least six inches from the front element and be solid enough so that it doesn't wiggle around.

To make sure the matte box's occlusion is as close to the image edge as possible without impinging, put your finger at the centers of the four sides and move it in toward the center until it shows up in the viewfinder. Your finger should be just short of the first joint. Any less and you run the chance of the matte box cutting into the image, any more and you won't get the full light shading benefits.

GAIN

Most cameras have a gain switch that increases the camera's sensitivity in low light situations. When you increase the gain, you add noise to the image, which in some instances looks a bit like the grain found in a fast film emulsion. Many people use the gain setting as a short cut to lighting. Don't!

True, a little noise is the fastest way to add a cinematic nuance to your video image, but there are far better ways to do this in post. What you lose by boosting gain in the acquisition stage is resolution, colorspace, and the ability to control the amount of grain you end up with in your final print. What might seem like teeny-tiny little specks of grain on your video monitor will look like a full-on blizzard when projected. Once it's in your image, it's almost impossible to get out. A drop of super glue is the best thing you can do to your gain switch. That way you'll never be tempted to use it.

VIDEO LEVELS

On the other end of the scale is the problem of too much light. When shooting video that will later be printed to film you should avoid shooting in direct sunlight when possible. The contrast ratio generated by direct sunlight is far greater than most video cameras can handle and the resulting image problems are only worsened in the printing process.

Most professional video cameras have a mechanism known as the zebra indicator which lets the operator know if there are areas of illumination within the scene that exceed the camera's ability to record it. Wherever the brightness exceeds the pre-set level, the zebra indicator superimposes a striped pattern over the area.

The zebra is generally based on a setting of 80-95 IRE (Institute of Radio Engineers). Think of 0 IRE as total black and 100 IRE as total white, indicating the maximum amount of voltage that the system can handle. While film can quite often record these values, NTSC video considers black at 7.5 IRE units (usually called the pedestal in postproduction and setup in the field), and white at 80-95 IRE. If you can set your zebra indicator to start clipping at 70-75 IRE you will be able to maintain detail in the brightest areas of your projected image. If you push it into the 90-95 IRE level, the brightest areas of your image will be little more than splotches of light with little or no image information in them.

<<<<< The clouds in this shot are too hot to handle and display the "Zebra" pattern to warn of clipping.

At the lower end of the contrast problem are the blacks. Just as the high-intensity whites will have a tendency to blow out when printed to film, so too will the blacks have a tendency to crush and go all black. The human eye is really the culprit here. We look at a scene and can make out the detail in the shadows just fine. Several months later we're sitting in a dark screening room arguing with our account executive about the huge black swaths that hide the subtle actions and details that we worked so hard to create.

Just because you can see it with the human eye, don't believe it. Just because you can still make it out on the video monitor, don't believe it. If you've got something going on in the shadows that you want the audience to share, make sure that information makes it to the screen by giving it far more illumination than you'd normally think it needs. A black that weighs in around 9 IRE will give you very pleasant, uncrushed shadows by the time you get to the screen.

By keeping a close eye on the contrast ratios that you're creating within your scenes, you should hopefully arrive at the film printer with a slightly flat looking video master and just slightly punchier if your goal is digital projection. Of course you've tested all this beforehand, right?

A Waveform Monitor should always be the final arbitrator of the lighting values in your video image. It determines what is broadcast quality, printable, or projectable by measuring the actual voltages of the video image and is often the first indication that your image is destined to have problems within your chosen distribution mechanism.

>>>>> Rack mounted or digital desktop, big production or small, on location or on the set, there is nothing like a calibrated signal to assure you of the best possible image.

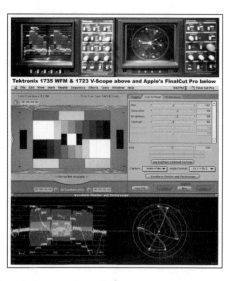

Tektronix 1735 WFM & 1723 V-Scope above and Apple's FinalCut Pro below

The WFM measures the level of the video signal as voltage and is capable of representing the image visually in several forms. The most common use being to monitor the pedestal and peak white levels of the video image.

Many software applications and non-linear edit platforms also have built-in signal diagnostics. These slightly more sophisticated systems generally include a Vectorscope (V-scope), in addition to the obligatory Waveform Monitor (WFM), which is helpful in determining the color timing of your video signal.

There is so much craft involved in reading and calibrating your acquisition system that I'm including a separate chapter, written by David Corely who many, including myself, consider to be the meister of professional calibration. It can be found in the reference section at the back of this book.

HD
COMP
SDI
RS-232
FIRE WIRE (IEEE 1394)
RGB

<<<<< Add-on converters like the Miranda DVC-800 give you a wide choice of flavors to pump into your system.

LATITUDE

Motion picture film is able to record a significantly greater range of light intensity than video. While the average motion picture film stock can generally accommodate at least a ten-stop range (Kodak figures film at 1000:1 contrast ratio) in the brightness of a scene, prosumer video is only good for a fraction of that if it's lucky (Kodak figures video at 150:1 contrast ratio). A really good, professional camcorder like a D-Beta or DVCPRO50 may get as much as seven stops, but it is still in a limited gray scale resolution. The method with which the video industry calculates a particular camera's response to light is expressed in terms of range and graphically represented by the response curve.

In his paper, *"Sony HDCAM Exposure Latitude, Issues of Dynamic Range,"* renowned industry expert Larry Thorpe (V.P. Sony Broadcast), illustrated how the HDW-F900 has an exposure latitude of 10.5 stops in 60i mode which equals a dynamic range of 2500:1, and latitude in 24p mode which is s 9.5 F-stops. This can be captured on HDCAM tape at 8 bits if overex-

posed peak white signals are carefully set to the 100 IRE level... Now aren't you glad you read those other chapters first?

KODAK 5248 ASA 100 FILM STOCK

SONY DSR-500WS DVCAM

The human eye can perceive an enormous range in the levels of brightness. Standing inside a house at night our eyes can make out details both within the brightly-lighted interior of the house as well as in its dark and shadowy exterior. A fast motion picture film would struggle with a high-contrast lighting environment like this, while any video format would fail miserably.

Film is not only more forgiving with high-contrast ratios, but also handles the way the extreme values of white and black are handled. While video essentially clips the values that exceed its limits, film has a far more forgiving nature. At the brightest and darkest ends of the scale of illumination, film eases the values into all white or all black. This is called the "soft shoulder."

In an attempt to soften the abrupt clip levels of video, the knee compression circuit, or soft clip, was devised. While it really doesn't do that much for the blacks, it has the capacity to noticeably extend the exposure range by emulating the soft shoulder of film. Many cameras have circuitry that reduces contrast by averaging the signals. While this often creates better looking video, it isn't recommended for video destined for film due to the amount of information that is discarded in the equation.

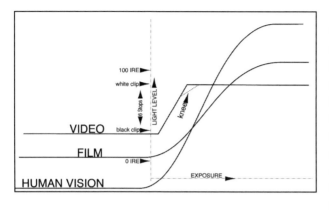

<<<<< In many cameras the angle of the knee compression circuit can be adjusted and lengthened to give even greater exposure range. With careful calibration, the range of a high-quality camera can be expanded almost two *f* stops.

LENSES

Unfortunately there is no such thing as a perfect lens, they all suffer from varying degrees of chromatic aberration, diffraction, slight variances in the index of refraction, and low tolerance manufacturing anomalies. Generally a glass lens is far superior to a resin one, and a coated lens is always superior to an uncoated one. The more elements (individual lenses) a system has, the greater the resolving power and accuracy. The essential quality of a lens can be expressed in terms of F-stop or T-factor.

The quality of cinematic lenses like a nice Cooke Prime or the always-popular Panaflex, is far, far, far superior to that of any prosumer camcorder. There is an unsubstantiated rumor that the video camera manufacturers actually de-engineer the camcorder lenses so that they don't compete with their far more expensive ENG (Electronic News Gathering) systems. Comparing them side by side generates a compelling argument for these rumors since the CCDs are often quite similar.

So there you are, starting out with inferior glass, or plastic, as the case may be. Compounding the deficiencies in light gathering, focus, and image sharpness is the fact that virtually all camcorders come with zoom lenses which further degrades the already insubstantial image quality.

By adapting standard cinematic methodologies to the digital video metaphor we will begin to create an ambiance, if not the actual resolution, of studio quality fare. By looking at how the camcorder handles light we can work around its limitations and get a step nearer to creating that truly epic film-like look.

Exposure is the calculation of light intensity over time. Or, Exposure = Intensity x Time. Every increase or decrease in time or intensity will inversely affect the other in equal proportion. If you double the amount of light but decrease the amount of time by half, the exposure remains the same.

The aperture controls the amount of light that is allowed to pass through a lens. It is regulated by the iris, which looks and operates similarly to the iris in our own eyes. When shooting in low light situations the iris opens up to allow more light to fall on to the CCDs. Similarly, a well-lit page of type is far easier to read than a poorly lit one.

The amount of opening of the iris is expressed as an F stop which is a mathematical equivalent calculated by dividing the focal length by the effective diameter of the lens that is in use at that particular setting. A lower F stop opens up the aperture, allowing in more light and shortening the depth of field. With a wide open aperture an object that is in focus at five feet will have a "field of focus" extending only a few feet or even inches towards and away from the lens.

As the lens is "stopped down" and the iris is closed tighter, the amount of light hitting the CCDs is greatly reduced and the field of focus is extended. The same object that is in focus at five feet may have a field of focus that extends from just a few inches in front of the lens on out to infinity.

>>>>> The wider the iris, the more light hits the CCD, and the shorter the depth of field becomes.

The vast majority of camcorders don't have F stop indicators on their lenses, and in most cases attenuate the luminance value of the initial video signal to give an electrically arrived at correlate F stop value. The F stop is usually displayed in the viewfinder window next to the shutter speed.

Lighting ratios are what define character in a monocular world and the single best way to determine your ratios is with a light meter. Nothing will give you consistently better composition and exposures. Failing that, you've got to become familiar with the manual control of aperture and shutter speed.

Shutter

The other way the lens/camera regulates light is the shutter. Film cameras have a physical shutter that cuts off the flow of light while the next frame of film is dragged forward. The standard motion picture shutter consists of a spinning disk with an opening of a specified angle that rotates at the frame rate of the film. A shutter that has an opening of 180 would be open half the time. Since the standard frame rate of cinema is 24 fps and the shutter is open half the time, the shutter speed would be 1/48th of a second. This is generally rounded off to 1/50th of a second in most film cameras.

<<<<< This illustrates a 90-degree shutter, which would transpose to 1/100 second exposure.

Video CCDs, on the other hand, generate a steady stream of image/data. Since there are two fields to every frame, and NTSC operates at 30 fps, most NTSC video cameras shoot at a shutter speed of 1/60 second. Since PAL runs at 25 fps it shoots at 1/50. The baseline objective is to use a shutter speed that is twice as fast as your frame rate.

Many decent quality video cameras have an electronic shutter which will be able to give you shutter speeds from 1/4 second up to 1/10,000 second. Even though the camera is recording at 1/60 or 1/50 of a second, by setting the shutter at a lower rate, say 1/15 second, you start to develop a "look" that many people feel echoes the cinematic nuance of film. I personally find this effect quite disturbing, but am putting it out there so that you have it in your quiver. Once you enter the realm of frame rate experimentation, testing becomes imperative.

You can also use the shutter to control the amount of light without changing your F stop or adding neutral density filters. Each consecutive exposure time is cutting down or increasing the amount of light entering the camera by one F stop, which means that it is effectively halving or doubling the exposure. Don't go above 1/250 second without doing some tests to see if you like the strobing effect that it creates.

As I mentioned before, the object is to find an F stop that allows you to create depth in your compositions (start with an F/4) and then use that stop to shoot your entire scene.

THE SECRET OF NEUTRAL DENSITY

Since you've now got your trusty matte box hooked up to your camcorder you can easily attach neutral density filters to it. These are plain gray filters that absorb light of all colors in equal amount. Think of them as sunglasses for your camera. They are used to control the quantity of light that enters the lens, not the quality. You will need a small collection of these relatively inexpensive filters before you start shooting.

While you can spend hundreds of dollars on a really nice Tiffen glass set, for camcorder use a decent cut gelatin set is quite sufficient. Basically a ND 0.1 will allow 80% of the light through which would increase your exposure by 1/3 F stop. The ND 0.6 reduces transmission by 25%, which is an even two F stop increase. At the top of the practical collection would be the ND 0.9, which would result in a three F stop increase, or 87% reduction in the amount of light entering the camera.

What we are trying to do here is stabilize and reduce the "low light" sensitivity of the camcorder so that it begins to echo the light handling characteristics of a conventional film camera. By throwing an ND over the lens we are forcing the scene to be lit just the same way you would be forced to light a conventional film set. Once you get your mind around this concept, and accept that it will entail far more work than simply turning on your automatic camcorder and shooting away, you will start to generate some truly cinematic shots.

POLARIZING FILTER

Since light bounces around in all directions along its axis, the reflections that it creates in windows, water, and glass lenses often create an impenetrable barrier. A polarizing filter is an essential accessory that can reduce or eliminate these reflections. In exterior shots it can darken the sky and create far more dramatic clouds than you'd generally find.

In the most simplistic of terms, when light strikes a reflective surface like glass or water, it becomes polarized and only bounces in one direction. Think of a polarizing filter as two pieces of glass or plastic with some microscopic venetian blinds laminated in between. What these micro-blinds do is essentially filter out all of the random light and allow only the parallel-polarized light to pass. The object is not to eliminate all of the reflection but rather to reduce it to a point where it becomes a suggestion of reflectivity.

Polarizing filters are also used for penetrating haze and in many cases make a good ND filter. While not as constant as a conventional ND, a good polarizer is generally good for a filter factor of ND 0.2 or 1 1/2 F stops. When shooting trees and foliage, a polarizing filter can raise the color saturation of leaves and shiny surfaces significantly by reducing their surface specularity.

Finding the Sweet Spot

You've got to experiment with your system to find its particular sweet spot. Short of buying a light meter, you'll need to buy, build, or steal some test charts. You'll need these for the rest of your illustrious career so plan on spending a little time or money on 'em. Everyone's got their favorites, but since I transition between the worlds of film and video on a daily basis, I feel that the DSC Laboratories system (*www.dsclabs.com*) is of particular relevance to the digital video-for-film community.

>>>>> Since the last edition of this book was released, I've worked on more than a dozen motion pictures, two music videos, twenty five commercials, and fifteen television shows. None of them started without a chart, and in all but one instance, the chart was the DSC CamAlign.

Go outside on a bright sunny day and shoot a few seconds of a person standing in full sunlight utilizing all of the automatic functions of your spiffy new camcorder. Next, set up the 85% gray card in the same location and angle it so that sunlight is falling fully upon it. Now, turn off the auto functions of your camcorder. You will probably need to read the instruction manual of your particular camcorder to see how to override the auto-iris and auto-focus functions. The F stop equivalent on camcorders is generally displayed in a small LCD window within the viewfinder and has a tiny button or dial for adjustment.

The idea is to place various densities of ND filters over your lens until you arrive a good average setting that you can shoot your entire production at. I like F8 for masters because it gives me a nice depth of field, not too deep, not too shallow, and it is almost smack in the middle of any professional lens, which gives you plenty of room to move. For tight shots or a nice intimate two shot, an F4 throws the background out a bit and gives a nice isolating effect to the actor's dialogue. Using combinations of the ND 0.2 will also match the transmission index of most polarizing filters and allow you to regulate your exposure while maintaining your F stop.

<<<<< Get to know the personality of a good set of lenses. It is something that will stick with you for the rest of your career.

Once you're locked in to a nice solid F8, have someone step in front of your gray card (you can use the blank gray page in the Color Plate section of this book). With the auto-focus feature on your camcorder disabled, perform a manual focus using the highlight in their eye as a point of focus. It is often helpful to zoom into the eye, focus, and then zoom back out and re-frame the shot. This is the only time that you're allowed to use the zoom!

The sharpest setting for most lenses is generally 1 1/2 to 2 stops down from the widest aperture while the sharpest resolved image is obtained with the greatest depth of field using the smallest aperture. The method we're working with here should give us the best of both worlds.

Once you've got a good recording of your subject in full light, rig a white bed sheet, or better yet a section of a white army surplus parachute above them so that the sunlight is diffused, shoot a few seconds more of your subject. Next, get a bright white surface at least several feet square and position it to the side and slightly below the eye line of your subject. Make sure the surface is bouncing light back toward the subject's face. Record a few seconds of this. As simplistic as this exercise sounds, when you view the resulting images on a video monitor you should notice a far more crafted look in the later shots than in your original one.

Keep in mind that unless you're shooting a documentary that you shouldn't obsess about shooting the "reality" of the scene. You're telling a story and manipulating the viewer's perceptions. Take liberties with reality if it helps you convey the mood or intent of the scene... it's your tale to tell.

CAMERA PLACEMENT

Just because you see life at eye level, don't confine the camera there. In addition to being boring, eye level shots make your movie feel like a documentary. This is not life, but rather a synthetically manufactured, alternate reality that hopefully contains all the elements that your audience's lives don't. The placement of the camera is one of the most important acts in moviemaking. It is your statement of what the scene represents and of how the audience is supposed to view this particular situation.

Camera placement tells your audience how they're supposed to view the shot or scene. A low shot of a standing person gives a sense of power and control. During the shooting of *Citizen Kane*, Orson Welles wanted a low shot looking up at actor Joseph Cotten. He had such a clear understanding of the power of camera placement that he had them jackhammer a hole in the studio floor to put the camera in.

Of course, I've always wondered why he didn't just shoot off of a mirror lying on the floor and then flop the shot as an optical... but then, I guess the story about jackhammering the studio floor is more interesting.

Just as the Steadicam dramatically opened up the sense of presence for conventional 35mm motion pictures, a new generation of "motion engineering" devices designed for digital cameras is emerging. From those little custom devices in the tiny ads in the back of your favorite industry rag to the new generation of body mounted stabilizers, the tools to get an engaging shot are there. All you've got to do is use them.

<<<<< One of the new generation of motion machines, the Weaver Steadman arm saves enormous wear-and-tear on your camera operators while giving your shots an unmistakably professional look.

For *Mid-Century* we used a hybrid dolly from Chapman/Leonard, outfitted with a double-axis boom arm and a lightweight three axis fluid head from Weaver Steadman. My good friend and DP, Joe Di Gennaro points out: "No matter where the actors settled into position, I could 'slide right in' to an over-the-shoulder shot. There was never a need to stop the action because an actor was 'upstaging' his partner. Our rig gave us practically the same flexibility and look of a Steadicam, without having to wear myself out by being strapped into a vest with an articulating arm all day."

Since the camera was completely neutral, it could "float" it anywhere from six inches off the floor to a height of seven feet, and tilt from straight up to straight down.

Look at the opening shots of *Forrest Gump*, or last shot of *Moulin Rouge*. They have a magically majestic movement far beyond anything humanly probable. They are masterfully dynamic. They draw us into the story and pull us out of our Newtonian reality.

Theater-going is not a democratic process. It's not supposed to be. You've got the sofa spuds that like to sit way back so the whole screen is close to the same size as their beloved television tube. You've got the sensation junkies who inhabit the first few rows, looking more for visceral interaction than insightful characters, and then you've got your audience. Me, I like twelfth row center. That's where the Director of Photography shoots for and whoever is sitting in that seat is essentially looking through the viewfinder.

MULTIPLE CAMERAS

Obviously, if you're shooting HD, you've probably got your budget stretched thin and you've only got the one unit. Chances are good that you've been through this before so you probably know how to keep your performances and exposures in the same groove so everything cuts in post.

For those who find themselves shooting with a less expensive format, consider getting two cameras, set one on a tripod and hand hold the other so one's over the shoulder and one's on the face for the close-up. There, you just saved a lot of time and energy. Heck, get three cameras. The more coverage you get now, the more choices you'll have later.

After you develop a rhythm with your actors you'll find that the first take's almost always the one with the magic. Generally you'd shoot a couple more takes then come around for the close-up or the two shot and do the series all over again.

But chances are, you're not using seasoned actors. They probably don't know how to modulate their performances. They probably don't have the slightest understanding of recreating the same performance you just shot from the side when you come around for the close-up. These mismatches in the flow of the performance might not look like much on the set, but by the time you get into editing they won't cut. Even if you do recognize the problem, the more you shoot, the more it'll just keep getting muddier and muddier and you'll never get back the magic of that first take.

In conventional film production the whole process is so convoluted with DPs and their crews, loading, cleaning, checking, and logging each shot that hardly anyone ever uses multiple cameras. But hey, you're not using film. Cheapest thing you've got is videotape. Burn it up, baby! By using multiple cameras you can cut the on set time nearly in half. Since the actors know there are several angles being shot at once they will want to put more effort into the portrayal.

And while we're on the topic of burning video, don't be foolish enough to try to save money by not running the tape a bit before and after takes. Heads and tails are very important. Just because you pressed the little red button doesn't mean that you're recording. Do it like the pros and let the tape get up to speed. Sure video starts up a lot faster than film, but it's always better to have a little extra than not enough.

SET-UPS

All things being equal you should figure on an efficient production crew getting at least thirty to forty exterior set-ups a day. Interiors generally slow you down a bit because of the lighting. If they don't slow you down then you're not taking enough time lighting the scene.

INTERIORS

I personally like interiors, while perhaps the majority doesn't. I especially like sound stages where everything is designed for the process of getting the shot. Interiors allow you a much greater control over continuity. When you're done shooting for the day simply shut off the lights and lock up. Next morning everything's in the same place, the lights are all the same value, the actor's marks are still where you left them. Don't have enough budget for a sound stage? Rent an old warehouse for a month or two. It not only gives you a place to build your sets but you can rig huge stationary soft boxes that can be used throughout your entire production.

Several years ago we shot *Barb Wire* in the old Hughes Helicopter factory out in Playa Del Rey. Funkiest old building you ever saw but it gave the cast and crew a home base to work out of as well as an inexpensive location for the movie's production. The look of the movie actually took on much of the look of the building. Many of the props were merely re-purposed materials we found lying around. It's not just funky, small budget projects that use old hangars and warehouses either. During the same time we were in production, *Independence Day* was in preproduction in the even funkier adjacent building.

One of the big secrets to lighting a scene is to have plenty of room to move the lights and camera around. The more control you have over the light, the more control you have over the audience's perception of the scene. Bare bulbs focused directly at your actors create a harsh environment and amplify the agony or torment that they may be experiencing while a collection of soft, diffused light sources create an atmosphere of peace and tranquility. When you're setting your lights, don't forget to turn the house lights off!

WRANGLING THE BEAM

The actual type of light you use isn't nearly as important as how you control it, so rather than get involved in describing all the various flavors of lighting instruments available to the filmmaker, we'll look at some cost efficient methods of wrangling the beam. Consider renting or buying a small lighting kit, nothing bigger than 1K with several small focusable lights, a couple larger spots, and a few soft lights such as Kino Flos or Chimeras.

There are essentially two main types of "key" light. Raw sun and artificial light.

The "key" light is the main source used to light the subject, while the "fill" light generally comes from an angle close to the camera and is responsible for "filling in" and softening some of the shadows caused by the key light. The intensity of the key in proportion to the "fill light" determines the mood of the scene. A "high key" lighting set-up creates a bright scene with a lot of highlights while a "low key" scene has a much higher ratio of lighting and creates a much darker and visually more contrasting scene.

The basic rule of thumb states that the ratio of key light plus fill light should be 2:1 for prosumer video formats or as much as 3:1 in professional systems with higher resolving power. It's a good idea not to exceed 4:1 unless you're going for a particular look.

Just about any introductory book on lighting will tout the "Three Point" lighting system. Don't. Problem is, light rarely if ever, falls in this configuration. While it remains a popular photographic (still image) metaphor where you're creating a representation, in motion imaging the light must echo the environment.

The essence of good lighting is to initiate light from the general directions of the world you have created. Filter it, shape it, tint it, modify it, but the bottom line is that it needs to be MOTIVATED. It needs to have a reason for being there and it needs to come from the same general direction of that motivation.

In *Mid-Century* there is a scene where John Glover and David Guzzone are on a people mover that is hanging about a mile over the floor of a giant ring that encircles the earth. Since the entire scene was shot on green screen, we needed to echo what would be the natural distribution of light, in that hypothetical situation.

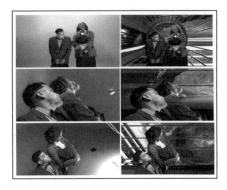

<<<<< John Glover
and David Guzzone checking
out the virtual scenery.

Since it is daytime on the surface of the
Earth, the MOTIVATED light would be
the sun, which is coming from below.
The actors need to be composited into
a shot where they are being illuminated
primarily from above by the reflected
light of the Earth, and secondarily by the reflection of the Earth's soft light
from the floor and walls of the Earth Ring.

Although the bulk of *Mid-Century* was photographed in a studio, we had
only a limited amount of lighting equipment at our disposal:

(1) Arriflex 1.2K HMI Par light
(1) Arriflex 400 watt HMI Pocket Par (with a "Chinese lantern" style Chimera)
(3) Arriflex IK tungsten fresnels
(2) Arriflex 650 watt tungsten fresnels (with small, Video-Pro Chimeras)
(3) Arriflex 300 watt tungsten fresnels
(3) Arriflex 150 watt tungsten fresnels
(3) Source Four Ellipsoidal spotlights with gobo patterns
(2) 2K tungsten softlights

Since we had many shots that involved various unique lighting signatures,
and a tiny crew, Joe Di Gennaro devised an ingenious method of wrangling
our light, which he explains:

*"One of the easiest ways I know to maintain flexibility in lighting is to incorporate
a dimmer system instead of relying on the traditional approach of using nets
and scrims to control the light intensity. My standard choice is a pair of 100
amp 'twelve packs' containing 1.2K dimmers and another 100 amp 'six pack'
of 2K dimmers. Although I have built my own system from the guts of an old
AV studio, many film and theatrical lighting rental companies offer these items,
which can be controlled by either a silicon rectifier panel, or with software driven
by a laptop computer.*

>>>>>   Play that funky music
white boy. Few things
are more valuable to
a low-budget production
than a good Director
of Photography with a few
tricks up his sleeve.

SCR (silicon rectifier) dimmers only work with tungsten lighting, however. I was very pleased to discover that our Arriflex HMI lights had flicker-free, 'dimmable' ballasts, so I could control the intensity of the HMI lighting with the same flexibility as the tungsten; with the simple turn of a dial, instead of having to load the unit with scrims, etc.

When using a dimmer with tungsten light, the reduction in voltage causes a shift in the color temperature. I tend to use this otherwise adverse effect to my advantage, incorporating the various colors of light in the design. Instead of adding Amber (CTO) gel to a light for a warm effect, I will choose a slightly over-sized unit, and bring it 'down' on the dimmer, which will reduce the color temperature and shed a warmer light on the subject. With my dimmers wired into the studio's power supply, I felt confident that we could stay 'light on our feet' with regard to lighting."

METERING THE SCENE

Let's say the first check cleared the bank and you're on a shopping binge. Consider saving a few hundred bucks by getting a camcorder with a few less bells and whistles and then take the extra coin and buy yourself a nice light

meter. I know the trend is to light from a monitor but there is simply no toy, ahem, excuse me, piece of professional production equipment that you can purchase that will give you consistently better looking images than a good meter. Falling short of that, learn to take readings with your camera.

<<<<<   Short of a good eye or a
Waveform Monitor, a light meter is your
best tool for getting a good exposure.

Photo: John Nelson

It's not all that hard really once you get used to it. The trick is to get used to it before you start shooting your movie. Have someone hold the gray card up to get the correct exposure for your actor's face and read the F stop off of the indicator on your particular camera. CCDs are nothing more than extremely dense clusters of teeny-tiny light meters. Another rule-of-thumb says to stop down 1/2 stop for Caucasians, and open up 1/2 stop for darker skin.

For those who wish to expand their knowledge and craftsmanship, I've included a brief tutorial on the care and feeding of your light meter in the Reference section of this book.

Once you've got the scene and your actor metered, have the actor or the "stand in" stand in, and get up close and meter the darkest and then the lightest portions of the face. If the darker side of the face reads one stop higher than the bright side of the face then you are at the recommended lighting ratio (2:1) for video that is to be printed to film. Always keep in mind that you're going to gain contrast when you print to film.

If you are planning to project digitally, or if you're shooting for broadcast, you can generally push your contrast ratio to 3:1. Of course you're going to test this first, right? Some women are better at makeup than others, which is one of the reasons that you want the same person to do all of your makeup for everyone who steps in front of your camera. A problem comes when you settle in on a specific ratio and the actor has actually created or enhanced their own facial features using makeup. The compounding effect is generally quite tragic.

If you do get to the final edit and determine that the shot is too flat you can always boost the contrast but if you shot it too contrasty to start with, you're stuck with it.

RAW SUN

The main advantage of sunlight over artificial light is that it is free, covers your entire scene, and is quite easy to manipulate. The wide assortment of devices used for controlling and directing sunlight are generally far less expensive and easier to use than other forms of illumination. While direct sunlight can be harsh in a filmed environment, in a video environment it's downright severe.

The intensity of the sun's illumination isn't the only problem that it causes. It moves. Steadily and continuously the sun sweeps across the sky all day long. Shots you took in the morning sun won't always cut into shots at the same location later in the day.

If, like every one else in the industry, you look at your dailies in the order shot, rather than sequentially, you probably won't see the problems until weeks or months later in editing. It is extremely noticeable when you spend several hours shooting someone's dialogue and then come around to shoot the other person's dialogue after lunch.

When you go back for reactions on the first actor you could have a gap of three or four hours. That amount of time span creates an enormous gap of believability. The audience may not know what's wrong but they'll know something's not right. While they've stopped to figure out what the problem is, they aren't following your story.

Perhaps the oldest and most widely-used accommodation for mellowing out direct sunlight is cloud cover. Often called "god's silk," cloud cover generates a mellow, diffuse light that records well on film or video. With film, this is generally all you need, but with video you should also introduce a bit of "fill" to keep your subject from going flat.

>>>>> Noted British cinematographer, Geoff Boyle, contemplates the lighting re-calc as he waits for the talent to arrive on set. More important than the source of your light is how you control it. These simple tools allow you to diffuse, cut, bounce, and generally mold the light to do your bidding. Now if it was only as simple with the talent.

Fill panels are generally part of the gaffer's kit but it's always good to have a couple of your own laying around. The two most common varieties are foam core art board, which can be picked up at any art store, and the more professional (and more costly) spring-loaded "hoops." The hoops generally have one side white and the other either metallic silver or gold.

When you don't have good cloud cover, or the clouds are small and sporadic, it's time to pull out the diffusion panel. You can buy these large panels of translucent material ready-made or make them yourself out of some PVC pipe and an old Army surplus parachute. The difference between a shot in direct sunlight and one done in diffuse light is quite dramatic as you've seen if you followed directions earlier on.

THE SPECTRUM OF LIGHT

The other problem with sunlight is that it changes color throughout the day. This is generally something that you can't see with the human eye unless it's sunset or sunrise. Imagine that you're shooting in a huge domed filter that is red at both horizons, bright yellow at the 45s and white "dead top center." Generally these types of color density shifts are taken care of in the color timing stage of a film's production. With digital video this means that you've got to add another very time-consuming step to the processing of your images.

ARTIFICIAL LIGHT

Basically, light looks white to the human eye. That's because we have a mechanism in our brain that actually corrects for color shifts in the environment around us. It's actually rather unnerving when you realize how inaccurate the human eye is at determining color. Ever notice someone's window from outside at night when they're watching TV. It has an intense blue glow to it while the window right next to it may have a reddish cast and the one next to that golden.

From the street our brain will actually see the broad variations in color generated by various lighting mechanisms because we don't have a specific color reference to lock on. If we were to walk into that house and into the room with the television in it, everything would appear quite normal. Our brain knows the inherent color scheme of the environment and corrects accordingly. As we move from room to room, the same location that we saw generating a reddish hue will also seem normal as will the room with the golden cast.

With film we must constantly monitor the "color temperature" of lights. Many lights actually change color over time as the elements warm up. Corrective filters must then be added to get the various lights to match. There are two main film types which are balanced to the light source frequencies of Tungsten (codeB at 3,200/K) and Daylight (codeD at 5,600/K). Scenes lit with sunlight will appear normal when using a camera white balanced for daylight while scenes lit with 3,200/K studio lights will appear normal when shot on a camera white balanced for tungsten.

If you were using studio lights to enhance an outdoor scene that was using the sun as the key light, you would need to put blue gels over the lights to balance their color temperature. If you're shooting inside, using studio lights as your key, then you would need to put orange gels over the windows to balance the natural sunlight coming in the windows. Many cinematographers in this situation will choose to shoot a daylight film and correct the key lights to daylight or use a lighting source such as the neon KinoFlo.

In many instances you will find that various lights have different color temperatures. It is a good idea to actually videotape all of the locations that you plan on using at night, prior to starting production. Different lights will require "gels" to balance their color temperature. A fluorescent light next to an incandescent table light may create a noticeable and unwanted effect.

While there are tuned and tinted bulbs that can be placed in conventional sockets, the most common practice is to wrap fluorescent tubes with gels. Within a fixture it is also possible to have several neon tubes each generating a wide range of color temperatures from pink to bilious green. Needless to say, lighting is better done prior to the non-gaff crew and actors arrival.

WHITE BALANCE

Unlike the human eye, the CCD is stupid. It translates what it is fed into electrical current and those are encoded into a video signal. Video has an entirely different method for dealing with color temperature. It's called "white balance" and it's basically a modulator that shifts the frequency of the entire video signal up or down to accommodate for the ambient color of the environment.

On most prosumer camcorders the white balance is an automatic gizmo. Find out how to disable the auto functions and keep it off! Hopefully, your camera will have the capacity to take a white balance through the lens, if not, consider another camera.

Manually setting the white balance is actually quite simple and consists of placing a white board or piece of paper at the point at which your principals will be standing and then focusing the camera at the target. Once the target fills the viewfinder hit the white balance button and the color reference of the camera will shift to accept your lighting setup as white. If you want to add some colored filters to the scene for effect, do it after you've taken the white balance or your filtered light will be balanced out.

COLOR TEMPERATURE

Color is expressed in terms of Color Temperature and essentially ranges for out purposes between the 1,500/K of a candle flame up to the 30,000/K of a crystal clear, high-altitude northern sky. The most relevant color temperatures that film and video makers deal with are:

60-watt household bulb @ 2,800/K
Film Studio lights @ 3,200/K
Photoflood lights @ 3,400/K
Sunset in Los Angeles @ 3,000 to 4,500/K
Noon summer sunlight @ 5,400/K
HMI @ 5,600/K
Blue sky light @ 10,000/K

THE QUALITY OF LIGHT

Light controls every aspect of what we do and the care that we take with it will either enhance or detract from perceived value of our final product. We are storytellers and we tell our stories with light and sound. Take away the light and all you've got is a radio show. We paint with light. It gives depth and presence to the scene and it creates mood. In order to paint with light you first need to see it in all of its nuance and spectrum.

The quality of light that is used in film production is developed and controlled by a small army of people who have spent the bulk of their lives refining methods and techniques for diffusing, redirecting, and creating moods within the visual spectrum of illumination. There are hundreds of lighting systems from the enormous HMIs to the tiny Inky Dinks, incandescent, luminescent and strobe, each offering its own particular palette of luminance.

Modern video technology creates a recording environment that can shoot in a wide range of brightness values but has far less sensitivity than film. This doesn't mean that it records more colors or subtle shades than film, but rather it is capable of recording a much wider range of light intensities.

Some video cameras are capable of shooting in situations where the human eye is even incapable of seeing. This gross latitude, (that's "gross" as in encompassing) that is inherent in the digital video environment is one of the primary reasons that video always looks so non-dimensional.

One of the most unfortunate hallmarks of digitally acquired image is that it all too often looks quite flat. The need to dimensionalize your scene and pull the characters away from the background is perhaps the most essential of elements that go into your look.

Dimension is not a naturally occurring component of acquisition formats with great latitude, so a substantial amount of craft must be used. Craft is the key word here, and as with any other form of expression, it requires work.

PAINTING WITH LIGHT

Spend a little time browsing the paintings of the masters. Their whole world was tied up in the quality of light. Look at the way they handle shadow and form. By using light to define regions within the compositional framing of the shot we can create an enhanced perception of depth and dimension. Look at the shadows. Are they hard or soft? Do they fall off rapidly or continue on? What angle are they coming from? What color is the light that caused them? The quality of light is often best described by the shadows it casts and the first step towards "seeing light" is in recognizing the importance of shadow.

As I've said before, lighting ratios are what define character in a monocular world.

Just getting the right balance of light to illuminate your scene is only the start. Light is the essence of the scene. It creates the mood and atmosphere of the environment as well as helping to develop the character of the actor. A well-lit scene is often a combination of direct, diffused, and bounced light sources.

One of the goals of good lighting is to separate your actors from the background without resorting to making them brighter than the environment.

By using a slightly warmer color temperature (orange/CTO) in the background, your character will come off of the screen with more dynamics, and by using a cooler background temperature (blue/CTB) they will create a warmer, more intimate sensation with their performance. In addition to creating a context and mood, using different color temperatures gives your scene dimension and keeps your actors from becoming part of the scenery.

A small direct light source directly above the camera (eye light) gives life to the actor's eyes while a direct intermediate spot directed at the back of the actor's head (hair light) helps to separate them from the background. A broad diffuse or bounced light source behind the camera can keep light from direct sources like the sun from creating deep shadows around the eyes and is, in itself, essentially non-directional.

One of the best exercises for lighting the human face is to put a couple of those realistic Halloween character masks on a couple wig dummies and then practice with various lighting setups. For adding a really high-quality look to close-ups, try putting a strong, highly diffused light source above and slightly forward and to the side of the face. Take care to "cut" the light so that it doesn't hit the lens.

Since light falls off at a square of the distance, the soft contrast ratio that this setup creates is quite attractive, especially when shot with a medium long lens. As foolish as this exercise may sound, by the time you've figured out how to get that rubber mask to look good you'll be ready for the big time.

PERSONAL STYLE

Lighting style is particular to the individual. Some cinematographers like to pull out every light they have access to and then fiddle with them for hours.

I've worked with people like this and it is a costly and frustrating affair for every one involved. I've also worked with DPs who can do amazing things with very few lights. One strong beam can be redirected and shaped into incredible environments by people who can actually "see light." I won't explain this but I will guarantee that you'll fully understand when you get it.

Before learning to visualize light as volume, many people are amazed at how flat their images look when they finally see them projected. While our eyes view the set and actors in stereo we are dealing with an essentially monocular system of recording and display. A quick and easy solution is to look at a scene through only one eye before you shoot it. A viewing filter will enable you to see contrast ratios and lighting balances much clearer.

LIGHTING THE SCENE

When shooting dramatic scenes, it is a major transgression to impose technical limitations on an actor. In order for a performer to appear sincere, he/she must feel comfortable. In order to maintain that level of comfort, an actor should feel free to be a bit spontaneous and not be "nailed down" to a rehearsed choreography.

In one particular scene between John Glover and Terry Hanauer, I staged a blocking rehearsal on the set, then, as our trusty gaffer, grip, and best boy, Chris Buchakjian, began to light the scene under Joe's direction, Terry and John went back to the "green room" to rehearse.

>>>>> Once you are on a hot set, theory becomes a lot less important than good methodology.

Photo:Elyse Couvillion

If Joe had taken the blocking rehearsal as gospel, I would have been hard pressed to accommodate John when he returned to the set for the take, asking: *"What if, after my entrance and before crossing to the chair, I sat down on these steps for a few moments, can I do that?"* It gave me great pleasure to say *"No problem, John. Move wherever you like!"*

Joe adds: "*I always try to light a 'scene' as opposed to a shot. To accomplish this, I will routinely use a 'large source' lighting technique. Large source does not necessarily mean high wattage. In this case, my major light source (my key light) was only a 1.2K Arri HMI PAR, affixed with the widest lens and placed at a distance of approximately twenty feet from the actors. By placing an 8 foot square piece of grid cloth, stretched on a frame, midway between the actors and the lighting unit, the light source becomes the entire surface of the diffusion material, spreading an even light intensity to the entire set.*

This allowed John and Terry unlimited movement within an area of about ten square feet, without any noticeable change in exposure. If I had used smaller lighting units, closer to the action, I would have had difficulty, not just with maintaining exposure, but I would have run the risk of crowding the actors' movements with equipment. Employing this relatively common piece of grip hardware allowed me to light with 'broad strokes,' creating an attractive, yet highly flexible lighting design."

<<<<< Good lighting principals allow the scenes to evolve more spontaneously.

VOLUME DYNAMICS EXERCISE

As an exercise in the subtle dynamics involved in lighting, rig a light a few feet above you as you sit in front of a mirror. Rig some method of focusing the light (aluminum foil barn doors) straight down so that it creates a pool of light a few feet wide on floor and then put a dark towel on the floor where the light hits so that there is little reflected light.

Turn off all other lights and sit under the beam while looking at your reflection in the mirror. Notice the harsh manner in which your face is illuminated. Now, cup your hands as if you were scooping up a handful of water and slowly bring them up under your face. Notice how the deep shadows under your nose and eyes are disappearing and the almost luminescent quality that this organically diffuse, reflected source brings to your face.

Play with light. Experiment with it, bounce it, cut it, and figure out ways to diffuse it and learn how to make it do your bidding. Sit to the side of the beam and use white paper or cardboard to light your face using only reflected light. Notice how much softer and controllable the results are. As imperative as good lighting is to the conventional film production, it is even more important to video-to-film productions.

When you finally learn to "see light" you will truly become a cinematographer. Factors like resolution and platform will become less important to you than the quality of illumination. People who don't share your passion will muse at your predisposition to tweak your shots and fiddle with the lights. To them it will seem excessive. In the end, long after the inconvenience of your efforts is forgotten, there will be a recording of dimension and persona that will underscore everything you've done.

10 :·:· DISTRIBUTION

*"The past went that-a-way. When faced with a totally
new situation, we tend always to attach ourselves to the objects,
to the flavor of the most recent past. We look at
the present through a rear-view mirror. We march backwards into
the future. Suburbia lives imaginatively in Bonanza-land."*
Marshall McLuhan (1911-1980)

McLuhan believed that books were responsible for isolating society
because they were best read in private, while emerging electronic media
(he died before the Internet) would soon connect the world globally
("global village") and re-tribalize the human race.

True to his vision, new technologies come screaming toward us, ready-to-eat,
flash-frozen in handy-dandy family-packs that overthrow the old regime of time
and space. Distribution, once a neatly wound concept, has become unraveled.
You created a product, you took it to market, but now the question becomes,
which market? What product?

Unlike book publishing, motion picture distribution below the studio level is
something that lacks any standardization. This lack of fixed methodology
causes vast clouds of misdirection to drift through the industry like a burrito
fart in a movie theater. Even the basic tenants of distribution are changing
daily as whiffs of new release strategies arrive unannounced.

Distribution is such a complex cloud of odoriferous gas that there is no way
that a single opinion, experience, method, approach, or point of view could
ever be relevant to someone who was being engulfed in another experience.

There is also no way of talking about distribution without putting it in the
context of the person who is expressing their views. What works as a viable
distribution strategy for one person might be total suicide for another. Only
by getting the overall picture of how the various options and methods work
for different people can you ever hope to develop your own strategy.

I have my own views, my own approaches, but they are based on people I
know, opportunities that I've cultivated over twenty years in this business,

and the type of content that I create. There is no way that my distribution methodology is relevant to say... some young hotshot moviemaker in Missoula, Montana.

When I go to a major festival, I already know a hundred people including a majority of the acquisitions executives for the various distributors. My experience is different. When I want someone to see my stuff, I just get on the phone and ask them to take a look.

Since this book is geared toward professionals, I am assuming that you will be making a marketable product that echoes excellence in everything from script to edit. As a professional you need to look past all the special interest hype that surrounds this industry and examine the playing field of distribution with as realistic a view as possible. I don't have any cute Top Ten list for distribution. It just doesn't work that way in the real world.

I started working on this chapter by talking to the heads of the hallowed bastions of independent film distribution. What I ended up with was little more than sanitized corporate spew, as superficial as their metaphor-laden catalogues of aesthetically vacuous content. If I was to render down the essence of more than a dozen interviews the results would sound something like... *"Contemporary independent distribution is entirely based on high-quality concept and creation... of course it doesn't hurt to have a couple big names in your project either."* Maybe I'm just obtuse, but I got the feeling that these people have been reading each other's press clippings for waaaaay too long.

Next I called a number of well-known directors and producers and asked them for a few bits of wisdom. Zip-zilch-nada... just a bunch of well-organized, self-aggrandizing babble and I figure that the readers of this book have already been subjected to enough of that... OK, so I'm not that well-organized.

After talking to more than a hundred people, the opinions I found most relevant, original, articulate, and enlightening were those of Producer Gill Holland, Director Todd Verow, Distributor Marc Halperin, and Internet Impresario John Halecky. While they all have massive experience in the independent world of production and distribution, they all come at it from entirely different directions and with entirely different objectives and motivations.

I have enormous respect for each of these people and although their goals and methodologies may differ dramatically from your own, or my own for that matter, anyone with the capacity for original thought should be able to piece together a viable game plan after reading the rest of this chapter.

I've removed my dialogue from the following conversations so that I could devote more page space to what they were saying. I've also made a few cuts here and there and done just a tad of rearranging, but I've endeavored to maintain the essence and context of the original discussions in their original voice.

GILL HOLLAND

I first met Gill Holland at Sundance. He's one of those people who is always at the right parties, at the right time, and knows who the right people are to talk to. Being a rather casual guy, he might seem like just another avant filmmaker looking for the next trend. Those thinking that would be wrong.

Gill has produced more than twenty independent features since his very successful, 1997 release of *Hurricane* which was directed by Morgan Freeman. Even though Gill's record of accomplishments is rather extensive in the independent filmmaking world, I prefer to think of him as the man who brought us *Greg The Bunny*.

>>>>> Gill Holland.

"*Greg The Bunny started on Public Access Cable. A couple guys shot it on miniDV in their room in the East Village, they didn't even want to be on screen which I guess is why they started using puppets. They were doing four or five shows a year with basically no cost so we cut what they had into a four-minute pitch for IFC, and then later shot the IFC show on an XLI. We cut a four-minute trailer out of that and used it to pitch Fox who thought that it was cool and let us make it into a real show, which ended up shooting in HD 24P.*

Impact of Digital

Everyone thought that once miniDV got out of the mainstream, where it is now, that there was going to be this huge digital rush on Sundance. Over the years Sundance gets between six and nine hundred submissions. Sixteen for competition and sixteen for American Spectrum so basically two out of... (you do the math). There's probably another 50% that get made where the timing isn't right for Sundance. So figure that there's maybe 1,200 showable Indie features made a year.

The industry was expecting all these thousands and thousands of Indie films but it just isn't going to happen. There's only so many people who actually have the initiative and the cheerleading and managerial skills to get enough people to work on a movie to get it finished. I think the vast majority of people get all geared up and then end up shooting for a day or two only to discover that the process really isn't all that much fun.

Of the thirty-two films that got accepted to Sundance this year, almost half of them already had distributors. Miramax, HBO, New Line, Fine Line, easily twelve of the movies in competition were already distributed. Five got TV deals, a couple got acquisition deals, so you're really talking about 1% of Indie films getting any distribution.

One of the more unfortunate aspects of the Indie market is that film festivals have become rampant for a couple reasons. First is the consolidation caused by the majors buying up the Mom & Pop theaters, so there are fewer truly independent movie screens. Marketing groups put up film festivals in towns that have lost their independent theaters in an attempt to meet the residual demand. Once a year, people can see independent films for a week, and it fills the appetite.

The problem for the filmmaker is that most festivals don't pay rental fees. The ones that do generally don't end up paying for more than a few of the projects screened because the filmmakers don't know to ask for them. You're basically giving your film away just to feed your need for gratification. Festivals have become the de facto distribution alternative for movies that don't get real distribution.

If you're looking to get your movie seen, and to maybe do a little Q&A with the audience, well then there are a lot of choices out there. But if you're looking to get distribution there's only four or five festivals in this country worth going to. New York, Telluride, South by Southwest, AFI, and, of course, Sundance.

Unless there is significant distributor presence, agency presence, industry presence, or press coverage that's going to give you quotes you can use on your video box, it's not worth going. They show your movie four or five times in an 800-seat theater where they charge $2.00 a head to see your movie and most of them won't even pay your air fare.

If it's a small festival, and you don't think that there will be much press or many connections, ask for the rental or don't even bother going. Of course there's a lot of people and that's the only thing they can get so they get to show their movie, and get the warm feeling of being a filmmaker.

I made four movies last year for $100,000 dollars total. We shot them with a PD150, edited on a G4, and you can get to a nice rough cut to submit to festivals for $25,000. Figure on letting the distributor pay for the blow up to film if they want.

The cool thing about shooting with DV is that you don't need Arnold Schwarzenegger to get a green light. You can green light yourself. You can cast the people next door, make discoveries, and experiment for almost no money. It offers novice moviemakers a chance to find their voice without needing to crawl out from under extensive financial obligations. Since there are fewer capital risks the DV moviemaker can take more creative risks.

I'm simply amazed that more people don't just go out and practice.

When Hollywood makes a fifty-million dollar movie, it's got to appeal to so many people in order to turn a profit that they can't afford to take any risks. That's why you almost never have the emotional connection to the blockbusters. It's more visceral, edge-of-your-seat kind of content.

Pitching

Filmmaking is pitching. You need three basic versions. The elevator pitch which is 20 second version, and then the cocktail party pitch which is your two-minute pitch, and then you have your fifteen-minute studio pitch. They should all be ready to go all the time because you never know when that golden opportunity will arise. A good concept and good phone voice will get you amazing things in Hollywood because people are desperate for material.

If you start out with good material, and you know it cold, and you've got a really tight presentation — but not so tight that you can't respond to their concerns — then you're in good shape. Just keep up your enthusiasm and don't let an occasional question or interruption throw you. Very often it's more important to illustrate the tone of your project than the actual scene beats.

Sometimes you're in a pitch and you get the feeling that you're just not connecting. It's always nice to have something else in the pipes that you can switch to. Of course you don't want to come off like a used car salesman, but if what you are pitching is starting to stink up the room, I don't think anyone minds if you throw something else out there.

Of course there is no life without death. There is no pitching without rejection. At every point in your project there are people telling you, "No, I'm not giving you money," "No, I'm not going to be in your movie," "No, you can't use my location." It becomes a battle of persistence.

Some movies have karma and they're just not meant to happen. It took me a while to realize that.

Distribution

Most acquisitions executives won't even take the time to screen your picture if it doesn't have a name attached. Foreign is heavily predisposed to American movies with names and since foreign is such an important part of the deal, you've really got to ask yourself if there is a salable aspect of your movie.

There's more money in foreign today than there was even a few years ago. It was about 50/50 for years but now it's more like 60 foreign, 40 domestic. The independent domestic distributors just don't have any money. I'm sure companies like Strand have never paid more than a hundred grand for a movie. There just aren't that many successful independent distribution companies left out there. So if you're going to make an edgy, topical movie with unknown actors, you'd better make it inexpensively.

The days of being a festival sweetheart and then getting theatrical release are just about over. I think Blockbuster bought more movies at Sundance this year than anyone else. Theatrical used to be the Holy Grail. People were driven by the need to see their names on the marquee. Now the industry seems to be getting more realistic — show me the money.

This recent documentary I had called Dear Jessie — ran through the festival circuit, played in fifty cities, then sold to HBO and was nominated for an Emmy. More people saw it the first day it played on HBO than in all fifty cities and film festivals combined.

As a moviemaker you want people to see your work. The decision becomes, do I take a twenty grand advance and get the guaranteed ten city release, or do I take a hundred grand and have a premiere on cable. If it's your money and you want to experience the theatrical aspect of this industry, then take the twenty grand. If it's other people's money then you have a moral and financial obligation to take the larger sum. Either way you win, either way you're a moviemaker.

DV

Before this whole wave of DV moviemaking started we had a trend where independent films were getting so much better technically that the separation between the Indies and the majors were little more than a difference in points of view. Since the visual difference was becoming negligible, it took longer to tell if the movie didn't have a story or if the story it told was distributable. But now, no one's making movies on 35mm, they're all shooting DV, so the poor spatial quality is a given and now you have to figure out in the first five minutes if the story is any good.

We're seeing a trend of established Hollywood directors and actors getting into a three week, run-and-gun DV shoots — sometimes it's just about the work. Sometimes there's something more honest about it. Let's face it, I doubt that Soderbergh saw much financial return on Full Frontal, but I don't think it was about that. I think it had more to do with him getting back to his roots for a few beats before picking up the studio banner once more.

Any time you get to work in this industry is a good thing but everyone seems to be preoccupied with being a director. I hear people complaining all the time that there are so few women directors, but 50% of line producers, script supervisors, and editors are women. Just getting paid to work in a creative field is a minor miracle.

It seems to me that the movies that are getting picked up and are actually making money are the ones that were made for under $100,000 or over $1,200,000. Either the films are made with names that can guarantee foreign, *video, and the like, or the films that are made without names but are really good and get bought for more than they were made for.*

The problem now is that you can make a film so cheaply that you get a film like Tadpole *that only cost $300,000 — somehow they got Sigourney Weaver — of course that movie is going to make money. But if you don't know big name actors, then you'd better have an intensely unique and dynamic story. If I had $21,000,000 to make a movie, I'd hire Julia Roberts for $20,000,000 and make the movie for $1,000,000.*

INDIE VS. ART

The word "independent" has been so co-opted that it doesn't mean anything anymore. I think we're going to need to start calling it guerrilla filmmaking. The word independent has become a fashion statement because independent filmmaking as a movement has already won.

Back in 2001, Hollywood released American Beauty, Being John Malkovich, *and a dozen other independent movies — they just happen to have stars. So in a way, the Indies have become part of the mainstream and the former Indie distributors have been consolidated by the majors.*

I think that a good amount of Indie moviemakers are driven by the urge to express themselves artistically. Art is meant to be shared. If the only people that want to show your film is a little festival out in the middle of nowhere — go show it — you'll get a warm feeling. Maybe it will inspire you to do better on your next project."

TODD VEROW

Todd's blatant disregard for resolution and cinematic virtue embody a wide range of maladies from the nauseating shifts of cheap auto focus to the grainy sub-world of PXL-Vision. There is hardly a Todd Verow film that doesn't contain nearly every cinematic foible that this book rails against so you can no doubt understand my quandary when I tell you that Todd Verow is one of my favorite independent moviemakers.

With a dozen critically-acclaimed short and feature length movies to his credit, Todd has established himself as a bona fide fixture in contemporary digital cinema. His style is edgy and dark, and more often than not spends far more time basking in the dark recesses of our repressed subconscious than most are comfortable with.

I've talked with Todd at length about his motivations and methodologies and what follows is as close as I can get you to the other side of the industry.

<<<<<   Todd Verow.

Technology

"For me, story and performance are more important than the recording medium. I like the intimacy that the small camcorders provide because they allow me to be the only crew member but I find it a bit disturbing how so many DV filmmakers are becoming obsessed with all the technical stuff.

Personally, I prefer systems that are simple and not all full of features that you'll never use. There's a lot of stuff that gets in the way of filmmaking. Sometimes it seems like manufacturers add features to cameras and software to compete with other manufacturers rather than to help the moviemaker tell their story as simply as possible. I use a little Canon miniDV camera and edit on Adobe Premiere. Simple, clean, easy to use.

It seems as though technology is being used as a replacement for content. So many people are making movies as something to do with the latest gadgets rather than asking themselves what it is they want to say, and how do they want to say it.

I know you (the author) are really into manually controlling everything, but I feel as though by using the microphone on the camera, and by using available light and the automatic functions that I'm creating more of a sense of believability. The image and sound haven't been processed and cultivated in the classic style. There's a rough edge to it, just like life. I'm trying to get back to a more real way of filmmaking.

I like the Dogma concept but I disagree with their rules. I just don't like rules.

Style

Little Shots Of Happiness (1997) started out as an experiment where I created a character and then worked with the actress (Bonnie Dickenson) to develop situations which were then shot documentary-style. The result is a fictional narrative where actors play characters, but instead of the standard fictional recording, they are shot documentary-style which has a greater sense of reality.

Eventually I started working with larger numbers of actors and even scripting things a bit here and there, although the majority of my work was still improvisational and rooted in documenting a performance.

The problem with a lot of independent filmmakers is that commercial success is their primary goal. You've got to dumb down your work and get stars attached because that's all that really matters to a distributor. Although I don't feel actively defiant, I'm just not interested in making that kind of movie.

One of the more significant benefits of this style of production is that I've developed a better ear for dialogue because I've been working with actors who were able to improvise. I think that it's made me a much better script writer. So now I've got a couple scripts that I want to get made with a little bigger budget.

The problem with bigger budgets is that you've now got investors, and so integrity becomes an issue. I don't think I'd want to get involved in anything that was controlled by someone else or that I couldn't just walk away from and make myself.

We as filmmakers need to take our power back and realize that it's enough if you're successful on your own terms. If I was dealing with a studio I'd still need final cut, because it's my movie, my vision. I need to have creative control because that is what the process is really about.

The people who are true to their vision always seem to appreciate being part of the process more than the ones who kick out an endless string of commercial content.

Of course bigger budgets would most likely entail using higher resolution formats like HD or film, but I wouldn't give up using the smaller formats. The thing I like about DV is that it allows you learn about how to compose shots. It's not just about shooting cheaply, it's about being able to shoot a lot of footage and experiment with different interesting things which you can then apply to higher resolution and more expensive formats.

The important thing about the digital revolution is that it has forced filmmakers to realize that they don't have to shoot things in a conventional way. Experimentation is good, so even though I plan on venturing off into the world of bigger budget production and perhaps more narrative projects, I see my DV projects getting even more experimental.

Distribution

Forget about distribution, it is always going to be a problem so why worry about it. Show your movie anywhere you can. I still submit to the festivals, but they're becoming more like commercial distributors. They're looking for stars and popular themes. So we show up wherever we can, and have a good time, and get the audience response. That's what it's really about; getting it in front of an audience.

Successful distribution doesn't have to be about filling up a huge theater. When the Sex Pistols started playing, thirty or forty people showed up and they still had a good time. Anytime you've got people getting into what you've created you are enjoying a fair measure of success.

Festivals seem to have all become quite bland. It seems as though most of the more regional ones just show stuff that played at Sundance or Cannes instead of digging through the growing piles of submissions to find something new and different.

Thousands of people have only seen my movies on the Internet. It's not my preferred method of distribution, but hey, the numbers are there. I think that people understand the bandwidth issues and make accommodations.

My principal advice for emerging filmmakers would be not to worry about distribution and just focus on making something unique and fresh. Something different, something experimental. If everyone followed the same rules, the future of this industry would be pretty bleak.

Moviemaking is a life, it is a total commitment like the priesthood. Ask yourself why you are making films. Go to the source of the art form of moviemaking and investigate the underground because that is where the true history is. That is the part of the industry that it is diverse and inspiring. The unifying theme is that if you have a good story, and the talent to tell it, you can't go wrong."

MARC HALPERIN

I hooked up with Marc Halperin over a couple beers at an industry get-together in Burbank. He is a twenty-six-year veteran of the motion picture industry and was hired by Universal to handle the national distribution and exhibition of their Classics division almost eighteen years ago. Since then, Marc has served as the General Sales Manager for both Miramax Film Corporation and FineLine Features. More recently, Marc has formed his own company (Magic Lamp Releasing) that specializes in the distribution of independent films.

There are a number of "Marc Halperin" types in the world of independent distribution, but there is only one Marc Halperin.

<<<<< Marc Halperin.

"In the '80s and '90s we had a phenomena that we called Dentist Movies. They were the largest resource out there with available money and you had groups of them pooling together and forming Subchapter-S corporations to go out and make a movie. We had to look at hundreds of those projects each year.

Today, because of tax shelter laws, that aspect of the industry has pretty much disappeared. As bad as the Dentist Movie clutter was, today's miniDV clutter is much worse. At least with the dentists you had a well-educated group that understood the basics of telling a good story.

The much hyped broadband marketplace was intended to relieve some of the DV clutter but it never showed up. Now we've got this huge traffic jam of content that we've got to sift through to find the one or two gems a year. Even if you find something that has some inherent value to it, there really isn't a well-established venue to show it.

There are a few digital-equipped theaters but the companies like Mad Stone and Magnolia who originally talked about getting into the digital theater business still haven't stepped up to the plate. We still don't have readily accessible theaters that you can download your movie to. I talk to these guys on a weekly basis and there still isn't any definitive date as to when these facilities will even go into operation.

One of the biggest problems is that the quality low-resolution digital content that was supposed to drive the industry never showed up. There's a lot of DV content out there, just not anything that people really want to see.s

There are a number of people who are working on satellite down link venues that go into colleges and bars to show movies, but that's probably three to five years away. On the high-end you've got companies like Hughes that have the capabilities to stream cinema quality image but again, where's the quality content?

The only hope that grass roots moviemakers have is to make something that is just so damn fresh, and so well told, that it's going to jump through the cracks. If you look at projects like Tadpole as a case study, the reason that it worked was only because they were able to get major stars. If it didn't have people like Bebe Neuwirth and Sigourney Weaver in it, the movie would have gone nowhere. Even with truly great performances by name actors, the movie didn't do nearly as well as it would have had it been made conventionally.

Even when you look at movies like Full Frontal, which was just filled with huge names, it's so brutal to watch that you only have to look at the numbers it pulled to see the writing on the wall. This was the best example of why not to shoot on DV that I've ever seen.

The good thing about Full Frontal is that it polarized the distribution sector and washed away the notion of ever trying to distribute anything shot with those little camcorders. Steven did the industry a big service by giving us a quantifiable standard that stands in the face of all the media hype.

I know that there's a trend to say that it's all about the story and that if you've got a good story to tell, the method with which you tell it doesn't really matter. Well, I think we've seen an end to that myth. The presentation format is important, the audience does care about resolution. If the hottest director in Hollywood, using the hottest actors in Hollywood can't pull it off — then forget about it.

There is a lot of delusion in the market now. Lots of ads from computer companies and camcorder manufacturers. They have a vested interest in promoting the delusion, but the reality, the truth is that these little DV environments are an excellent way to make a calling card that you can show to investors. Hopefully if you really do have a knack, it will show. Then you can raise enough money to go out and do it the right way.

Internet

The Internet is especially good for this early stage of a moviemaker's career in that they can build a following, and then start building industry awareness not only for their movie but also for themselves as a moviemaker. Look at Blair Witch. Not much of a movie really, but the people who made it put a really great Web campaign together. They built an online community and then kept them coming back with diaries, and commentary, and compelling reasons for people to want to know what happens next.

They also made sure that the Sundance people were aware of their campaign and saw it coming well before the festival's selection process began. I really don't think that the project would have even been selected if the filmmakers hadn't done their homework. You look at that movie with a critical eye and it falls apart very quickly.

But the filmmakers were smart. They understood the market well enough to launch their campaign in the summer when schools were out so that every teacher in America didn't use it as a lesson plan to illustrate the difference between fact and fiction — documentary and movies. If the kids who comprised the vast bulk of the audience were in school, the myth that this was a real occurrence would have disappeared in 72 hours. Since there was no mechanism to dispel the myth, the web buzz grew to create a truly unique success story.

The movie was a hit before it was screened. Very original idea. That whole 'mock-umentary' thing was an undeveloped category. Now every wannabe moviemaker is trying to copy their concept, but that was a one time deal. We won't be seeing any more Blair Witch-type projects because they marketed that thing so well that they sucked all of the marrow out of the category.

By the time Artisan stepped in, the movie had already developed enormous inertia, the online community had already spread the word and basically all that Artisan had to do was keep the website from crashing. Of course they took all the credit for the movie's success, but the inertia was already there long before they ever knew about it. All they had to do was stay out of the way.

Festivals

Festivals are great but you've got to make sure that you're in the right one. There are at least several festivals every week somewhere in the country, never mind the world. Most of them are neighborhood festivals that don't mean anything to the distribution community. To go in and win awards at four or five festivals that no one has ever heard of doesn't really do you any good.

Bottom line is, how many films get purchased out of the festival's lineup. Sundance and Cannes are consistently very high while a festival like the new Tribeca festival in New York only had one sale that I know of this year. Very often it's not the best films that get bought but rather the most hyped.

If you can get into a prestigious festival, Sundance, Cannes, Toronto are your tops and then South by Southwest, New York, San Francisco, Chicago, Seattle, and L.A. after that... if you can go in and make some waves, then you've got something to show for your efforts but it's still only a festival.

The important thing is to get a deal. A distribution deal on the movie you're show-ing, a production deal to remake it under studio auspices or a financing deal to make your next movie. It's not about festivals, it's about the deal.

We were recently at Sundance with the people from Palm Pictures who we do the distribution for. We went after Sex And Lucia after seeing it screened and put together the entire marketing and distribution plan for it. The movie was shot in Spain using 24P HD and the full theatrical experience is there.

They used real cinematic quality cameras that were shot by pros, using conventional production methodology. There's just no comparison to someone running around with a tiny camcorder on their shoulder using available light.

Obviously we're not going to get wide distribution because we don't have any big names in it... but it's a great story with terrific acting and it looks really big up on the screen. We've got it booked into all the major art houses all around the country and expect to do a million dollars with it by Labor Day with 32 prints. (Author's note: They exceeded their goal by a considerable amount.)

But we're focused on independent distribution, we know how it works, how much you can realistically expect a film to return. In an auction environment like a festival, too many people overpay for a film that never does any business, and that is generally the history of Sundance. If you look at the last ten years, 90% of the films that came out of there went down in flames. Movies like The Castle, Soup, Happy, Texas... *good movies, but what happened to them? There was a four or five year stretch where every film that came out of there tanked at the box office. It was just disastrous.*

The market is so driven by names that you just can't get around it. If you've only got a million dollars, go out and get names to work for a piece of the action. Give them your million dollars to sweeten the deal and then make your movie on your credit card. If you can shoot on film — do it. If you can shoot on Hi-Def — do it. If you put together a top notch cast with top quality production crew and a perfect script and are able to keep the inertia of the original magic, then you've got a solid shot at success. Less than that, you've got less of a chance.

The medium that you shoot with doesn't really matter as long as it is pleasant to watch. If you could get miniDV to look good on the big screen, it would be a viable medium — but you can't. The hottest guy in town already proved it, and some kid from Alabama armed with a tiny camcorder and FinalCutPro is not going to prove him wrong.

A good-looking movie with a great cast, great story, told well... if you don't have the basic ingredients, you don't stand a chance."

JOHN HALACKY

Despite his rather conventional "filmmaker" roots, John has parleyed himself into a decidedly non-conventional arena. Fresh out of film school, he worked his way through one of Hollywood's most powerful talent agencies, eventually ending up in the feature films development division of Paramount Studios along with John Goldsmith and Sherry Lansing. He later moved on to Warner Brothers' feature film division where he was an acquisition executive for several years before joining iFilm in 2000. John has played a pivotal role in iFilm's major restructuring, a role that helped iFilm emerge as the leader in online distribution.

<<<<< John Halacky.

"iFilm survived the dot-com craze, but not without a few battle wounds and lessons learned. The whole concept of making a bundle off of Internet distribution came and went in less than a year. It was all wrapped up in speculative investments and more than a little smoke and mirrors. There were a lot of people who all had these great ideas about mass distribution of all the new content that was supposed to come streaming out of the digital frontier. It never showed up. A few people here and there made a lot of money but a whole lot more lost it.

If moviemakers are still under the impression that they're going to make a bundle off of Internet distribution, well... it just isn't going to happen. The money isn't there to support it and the Internet audience is quite simply more interested in punchy little one-liners.

What the Internet does offer is the ability to stream your style to a global market. Kind of like a video business card. You make something easy to watch, fun and interesting, you'll be amazed at what happens. We have a number of films that have had over a million views. That's a million people, all over the world that now know that filmmaker's style. Compared to the film festival route it is not only more cost-effective and more efficient but also more global.

The hottest short we're running right now is called 405. It's a quick little piece about a jumbo jet landing on a freeway and it's a little over four minutes long. Short, funny, with an interesting little edge. At last count it has logged a little over four million views. While it wasn't used as an income generator, it did get the guys that made it quite a bit of work with established production houses.

So while the get-rich-quick schemes and distribution hype that surrounded the Internet a few years ago has faded away, they left in their wake a wealth of opportunity for people who are looking for a way into the industry. If you want to get the word out on your film, you want people to see what you've got to offer, you want to raise awareness for your project... the Internet is a gold mine.

Mike Mitchell's short film Herd *went to feature and was remade as* Deuce Bigalow: Male Gigolo *the same year it went up on iFilm. Mike went on to direct* Greg The Bunny *and a number of features. We constantly get calls from agents and managers looking for the next hot filmmaker.*

At iFilm we generally set up filmmakers with a link back to their home page where they can have press releases, reviews, and contact information. With over ten thousand pieces of content on the site, we're starting to amass a rather significant number of success stories for our filmmakers. The object is to complete the loop by giving a filmmaker a venue as well as the channels and tools to take their project to the next level.

We've had a number of filmmakers who have released their long form movies through the site and are quite happy with the results. While I don't really think that sitting in front of a computer screen for an hour and a half is as interesting as sitting in front of a television, and especially not as interesting as the full theatrical experience, it really comes down to content. There is quite simply cutting edge content that is available online that you just can't see anywhere else.

In general the comedies that are under ten minutes do so much better than the longer dramatic pieces. This is unfortunate because we have a number of Academy Award nominated shorts on our site but the venue market just isn't fully matured. So if I was to venture a formula for success on the Internet it would be, quirky, funny, cute, and under ten minutes. We have had a number of very successful long form movies. Rupert Wainwright's The Sadness Of Sex *has over a half-million views and continues to get extremely good numbers. We broke it into ten segments for easy viewing and the response seems to be quite positive.*

As streaming technology improves, as the images get bigger, we are seeing more activity on the more dramatic pieces. The next time the Internet realizes a noticeable bump in bandpass, I think that we'll see it begin to encroach on network and cable programming... significantly. Of course there's the point at which the computer monitor and the television become indistinguishable. I don't think that point is very far away.

The main misunderstandings come where people try to fit their content into the online template. It doesn't work that way. The Internet is a medium unto itself. It requires an entirely different set of artistic, creative, and production standards. Things that work on a theater screen don't necessarily work in the restraints of streaming video. And it works the other way around, too.

You can still do a feature on the Internet, but you need to shoot it differently, edit it differently, and script it differently. The pacing for someone sitting back in a dark theater with a hundred or so other people is entirely different than you'd use for someone leaning into a computer monitor. Humor and emotional themes need to be constructed differently. Swish pans and nonstop action are all great up on the theater screen but they cause compression artifacting on the computer screen. Internet movies also seem to do better with fewer characters.

The entire process from concept to audience reaction is a whole lot faster. Resolution takes time. The subtle nuance of cinematic artistry takes time. At this point they are somewhat squandered on the Internet. Set it up, and pay it off. Similar to the sitcom formula without the character development. If you just want to rack up huge numbers, shorter and funnier always works for the Net.

The Internet is evolving not only as an alternative distribution mechanism, but also as an alternative style. Look at the similarities between the successful content of the Internet and the early Indie movement.

I'm sure that the "Internet Look" will migrate, we're already seeing a number of success stories. Anything good, in any venue is going to bubble to the top. So there's several thousand people shooting stuff for the Internet, and they all think that they're going to get famous overnight. Obviously the odds are stacked against them, but regardless of the numbers there's always going to be a few *individuals that bubble to the top because they have something original to say, and say it in a unique way. It drastically shortens the cycle, increases the potential to be discovered, and is a total renovation of the convention.*

Before the Internet you needed to make lots of VHS dubs and send them off to people in the hopes that they'd watch it and then do something good for you. Now, we put up a movie on our site, the filmmaker sends out the URL and tells people to watch. So much easier, so much faster. And since we track the numbers, you know how many views you're getting.

One of the more significant ramifications of this methodology is that it gives you access to agents and acquisition people who can't legally look at unsolicited material. But if you put it on the Net, and say "Hey, take a look at my link" it's already out there, well, the legal liabilities are greatly decreased. If they look at it and hate it they can forget that they ever saw it. On the other hand, they might see something in it that they like and can then contact the filmmaker and start the dance through appropriate channels. Perhaps more than any other value that the Internet offers the conventional filmmaker is the opportunity to pitch your work to more people.

The other benefit for the filmmaker is that they get instant feedback. Usually a lot more than they might want. The conventional feedback loop is based on test screenings and the results are usually biased by the people who solicited the audience and a number of other factors. You've also got the tendency of viewers wanting to be polite. With the Internet you are getting feedback from a broad demographic that is international is scope, and more inclined to give it to you straight.

Obviously with the anonymity that the Internet offers, and the fact that it is open to the world, you're going to get the obligatory idiot who posts negative reviews just because they can. A veteran filmmaker who creates a bold or unique experiment is probably going to get flamed by a twelve-year-old kid who only understands bathroom humor. That's what people with limited vocabulary and limited capacity do, they flame. Unfortunately, the more unsuccessful a person is, the more time they have to float around the Internet imposing their misery on other people.

Those people are everywhere and after a while you learn to filter them out. What you do end up with are some really great criticisms, and critiques that are probably a lot more realistic than anything you'll get from your family, friends, or business associates. Between the rants and the raves, quite often lies feedback to the true visceral reaction to your work.

As a filmmaker myself, I can tell you that truly unbiased critique is one of the hardest commodities to come by. The Net offers a unique way to find your groove and define your style. You see what works and what doesn't, maybe you modify your methodology, maybe you don't. But at least you have a point of reference, a greater understanding of how your voice fits into the chorus of the industry."

11 ⠢ PRINTING TO FILM

*"When you see HD on HD it looks like HD
because it is HD. When you see HD on Film
it looks like Film because it is Film."*
Sean Fariburn SOC

This entire book is dedicated to squeezing the absolute optimum resolution, colorspace, and density out of your chosen video system. From the initial choice of camera through production and postproduction, everything you do effects the amount and quality of information that the film recorder has to work with.

Perhaps the most misunderstood and most mystifying aspect of video for film is the actual process that up-converts the video image and then prints it to film. Just as there are numerous flavors of compression, so are there a number of methods of up-converting the video image to a higher integer of data. This process is often called "up-rezzing," but there is no way to actually increase the amount of resolution you've ended up with after the production process.

You can tweak the colors, increase contrast, increase the number of pixels that represent the frame, but you can't increase the resolution. What you got is what you got. Live with it.

The most important consideration in the printing of your digital movie is your motivation. Why do you feel that you need to print your picture to film? Is it just to say that you've produced a "film," or are there other factors at work?

Since the last edition of this book hit the shelves, festivals have made enormous accommodations with respect to the digital moviemaker. The era of celluloid effetism that subjected the Indie filmmaker to a $20,000 admission fee has evolved to the point where even festivals like Sundance and Cannes have very respectable digital venues.

But hey, let's say that for whatever reasons, you've decided to print your digital epic to film. Let us kneel down at the altar of technogogary and pray for guidance.

I know that there is the odd Post house that will print directly from DV format, but the only reason that I can imagine for doing it is if you edited linearly within a DV native edit suite, never re-compressing, and never used any other methodology whatsoever for storing or moving the signal around. Barring that unusual scenario, mastering back to a DV format, a format that has a significant 5:1 compression ratio, could be considered resolution suicide.

The vast majority of DV moviemakers use some form of non-linear edit system. Most of those systems have the capability to sample in and record out in Y, R-Y, B-Y, why would you ever want to re-compress your video at a whopping 5:1 ratio on the last leg of its very painful journey?

A lot of people think that if they master back to the same format that they originally digitized from that it will magically make things better. It won't. Compression causes a compounding degradation of the video image. In many instances it is far worse than the degradation caused by successive generations of analog copies.

If you've got a Fire Wire (IEEE1394) or iLINK equipped camera and an edit system that can accept and edit in the native compression scheme of that specific camera, you can forgo two very painful steps in the degradation of your image. Even though you may be able to Fire Wire directly into your computer doesn't mean that the compressors that enable your non-linear system's transitions and effects are compatible or non-degratory. Sony DV is different than Panasonic DV, which differs from Canon DV, then you've got various flavors of DV within the various manufacturers.

Don't get sucked into this "Digital is Forever" fallacy. Digital is a delicate mélange of ones and zeros. Like dropping a hand grenade in the middle of some neo-Nazi marching battalion, compression drastically messes with their formation. Every time you re-compress you're compounding the deficit of the original compression. It's not simple math.

The most widely accepted method is to feed your finished edit out to D-Beta or HD for transport to the printer. From the time the first photons of your image hit the CCD, the voltage potential that it described has been sampled, compressed, resampled and recompressed, and then resampled and up-converted. At least using D-Beta the re-compression from the edit system's native format was only 2:1 instead of miniDVs 5:1.

One important and almost always overlooked aspect of transposing from DV to D-Beta is that they are both compressed formats. MiniDV at 5:1 must be resampled and recompressed to D-Beta's 2:1 compression ratio. Not a really big deal if you're going to use your nonlinear system as an off-line edit and then take your EDL (Edit Decision List) to an on-line, D-Beta edit facility for creating your final edit.

When in a position where I need to print to film from something that has come out of a nonlinear edit environment, the data files are left on the disk which is then delivered to the printer. By going back out to video, any video, it would only be compressing and reprocessing the images one more time.

Perhaps the most positive aspect of the video-to-film process is that the movie often takes on a saturation and richness that the digital version never had. Many people are amazed at the depth and texture that the transfer process has created and the almost subliminal enhancement of quality that the addition of grain adds. The flip side is a noticeable loss of sharpness, which can be catastrophic if you've already lost significant sharpness due to poor lenses or multiple compressions.

Color Correction

Color correction is critical to obtaining a good balance in your film transfer. Any variations in the hue, saturation, or value of your color will only be intensified in the transfer process. Obviously, it's going to be a heck of a lot cheaper to do the color correction while you're still in the digital realm of the on-line environment. Use the highest quality broadcast monitor that you can get your hands on. Go out and rent a really good one just for color correction process if you don't already have one hooked to your edit system.

Once you've got a color corrected master it's time to head to the printer. Hopefully you've done a lot of tests and know the various shortcomings of all of the choices available to you.

Transfer Options

Various video-to-film processes create different looks as well as having different effects on your budget. Kinescope, the process of filming a monitor, is by far the least expensive method for transferring your movie. General prices run between $150 - $300 per minute for 35mm transfer and half that for 16mm.

CRT Film Recorders, like the Solitaire and the Celco, are perhaps the most common method of transferring digital images to film. They basically work by breaking the video frame into separate Red, Green, and Blue images. A very high-intensity black-and-white cathode ray tube then scribes each line of luminance individually for each of the three value frames in the image. When the red channel is being printed, a red filter actually swings into place as the cathode ray exposes each line individually.

For a 2,000-line resolution image it makes 2,000 passes. Then the blue filter swings into place and the process starts again after which the green filter swings into place and the process once again transpires. After all three filters have been used, the film and the video both advance one frame and the process starts all over for the next digital image.

Back before printing computer images to film was readily an accessible service, I owned my own Solitaire film recorder and printed directly off of the hard disk. Not only was this cruel and unusual punishment for friends, family, and neighbors, (they're loud and obnoxious devices) but every desktop jockey in the country was bugging me to do a test for them.

No matter how attractive the concept of owning your own film recorder may appear (you can usually buy a used one for the cost of a good transfer) don't do it! The time and money you waste on tweaking, film development hassles, and a seemingly endless list of woes will far overshadow and eliminate any potential savings you may incur.

>>>>> In the early days of digital production everybody was a technical engineer. The film printer is behind my right knee.

Prices for a 35mm, CRT print can range from $200 per minute all the way up to $1,000pm depending on quantity of work and what the market will bare in your location. Figure on working out a deal for around $450 per minute for a long form transfer.

One of the most popular methods of printing digital video to film is a direct digital transfer done with a laser recorder such as the ARRILASER. The color palette is rich and full, the contrast is balanced, but the super fine intermediate stock that laser printers use doesn't have the texture of a good camera stock.

HD-originated material often does better on a Celco type machine where you can print to a camera stock and instantly pick up much of the nuance of film-originated material. HD images that were originally acquired on film stock and then telecine'd to data files usually don't need the added grain so a Laser type printer using an intermediate stock usually does the trick. Two entirely different methodologies need two entirely different image profiles.

If you want your digital movie to look like film then print it to a good camera stock using a CRT. If you want it to look like rich video then print it to intermediate stock using a laser.

I print lots of HD to film and I've narrowed my choices down to two. E-Film in Hollywood for laser work and DigitalMagic in Burbank for CRT work. You've got to do your own tests to figure out who to trust your work with, but I've done my tests and I'm happy with my results.

Bill Fightner is the CTO of E-Film and has helped more than a few digital filmmakers out of their binary rut. His views on printing digitally acquired content to film are the definitive word as far as many filmmakers, including myself are concerned.

"Both camera stock and intermediate stock have the potential to make your HD look stunningly cinematic. While printing HD to a camera stock guarantees you the addition of grain and the cinematic nuance of commonly used film types, the intermediate stocks from both Kodak and Fuji offer a slightly wider range of colors. In some instances, the colors in your HD data stream might simply not be available in a camera stock.

If you want to map the colors that the camera sees over the full color gamut of film, you can maintain the gammas so that the gray scales match and then highly saturated colors should map out to match the color profiles on the film stream. In this case, the methodology of shooting WISIWIG (what I see is what I get) for the monitor would need to be amended because you'll actually get more color back from the film than you see on the monitor."

What this means with regard to factory preset on most high-end production cameras and all HD cameras is that the knee point is set between 95 to 98. Because of the greater latitude of film the clip point can be moved to 106. Many of the newer cameras generate 20 or more samples between 100 and 105 compared to about five samples with the older cameras. Since there are more samples in the knee, the roll off of the densities will more closely match the film's soft shoulder.

The decision of which method to use must obviously be weighted against the potential recoupment of your movie. Is it quite simply good enough to warrant a further investment of $50,000 for a full-blown, 35mm, digital print, or would a nice $6,000 Kinescope, 16mm print serve your purposes just as well.

Your success or failure in this area will be almost entirely dependent on the quality of the final resolution that you end up with and how methodically you researched all of your available options. If you're making a movie in Kansas, and the only film printer for a thousand miles is in Kansas City, get yourself on a bus and either go to New York City or head west to L.A. Hang out and investigate every option that you have.

Talk to other filmmakers, scout the on-line resources. Any shortcuts or wrong turns taken here will haunt you every time you project your movie.

12 › LOW-REZ

"Empty pockets never held anyone back,
only empty hearts and empty heads."
Dr. Norman Vincent Peale

Despite my best efforts to persuade you otherwise, you've made up your mind to shoot your movie in miniDV and that's all there is to it. I will assume that this is your first or second project so let's work with it. There are essentially so many variations that it would be impossible to cover them all, so let's pick a common scenario and then you can make adjustments with regards to your own production.

First and foremost...

... DON'T LEVERAGE YOUR ASS ON YOUR FIRST SEVERAL PROJECTS...

... especially something shot on miniDV! The chances that you could recoup your investment are nonexistent.

Is it worth mortgaging your house for? No Way! Is it worth going out on a limb for? You bet! Is it worth paying 21% in credit card interest fees for years to come? Probably not! Is it worth working your ass of to earn the extra money? Without a doubt! If you've got the fever, and nothing in this book so far has talked you out of it, then the Doctor says, "Make your Damn Movie!"

My advice is to raise the money to make your first couple of movies. This does two things. First, it makes you appreciate the investment, and secondly it tests the true measure of your commitment. Don't have enough motivation to earn and save the money? Hmmmm. Your chances of success are much less.

I have a reader that delivered pizza to finance his movie. He had a 1,500 pizza budget. There was a group of high school girls that washed almost 500 cars to make theirs. A high school teacher had each class do a different scene of his movie. After two years, he's only half done, but still on track.

One of the most significant benefits of having written the first edition of this book is that I've become aware of hundreds of projects that used it as a guide. Needless to say, the revisions in this edition are in no small part, driven by their experiences.

GAME PLAN

Figure out a production timeline and then stick to it. One of the most important elements of success is to have a set of specific goals that you can articulate. Now, everyone that joins your little crew knows where they're going and when they need to be there. Goals give focus and deadlines give the whole production a pace. In a large production this is a natural byproduct of the budget and scheduling but smaller productions all too often wither away from tomorrow-itis. Create an intelligent schedule and then stick to it because a goal without a deadline is only a wish.

Get a Recycler magazine from the closest metropolitan city and do the bulk of your shopping from it. You should be able to pick up a good used, FireWire-equipped miniDV camcorder for $500. The important thing here is to shoot everything in 16×9 aspect ratio so you're going to look for a camera that actually uses a 16×9 imaging chip. Since your choices here are severely limited, your next best option would be to get a camera that stretches the conventional 4×3 (Panasonic, Cannon) image rather than one that crops the top and bottom of the 4×3 (JVC, Sony). Total: $500.

For a simple option you could check out one of the several reputable used equipment dealers like B+H photo in NYC (*bhphotovideo.com*). They are more expensive than buying out of the Recycler but then you've got a camera that is backed by a substantial and reputable company.

Next look around for a used Mac or better yet, a used G4 with at least 256Mb of RAM and the largest monitor you can find. The Mac should cost under $600 and hopefully comes with Apple's Final Cut or Adobe Premiere 5.0 or higher. You could look for a FireWire enabled PC but by the time you got everything up to speed it would probably cost more than the Mac. Use your own judgment.

FireWire is going to give you about 4 1/2 minutes of audio and video per gigabyte, so figure on picking up around 80 Gb of FireWire drives so you'll have room to move around. Sometimes you can find really good deals on drives but you never know where they've been so it's not a bad idea just to bite the bullet and get some new ones. Figure on spending around three hundred dollars.

Pick up the best used, mini-shotgun microphone you can find for around $100 and you've just slammed together your entire digital production environment for well under $2,000.

The bad news is that since this system is built around the 4:1:1 miniDV format, you're starting out at 5:1 compression ratio with greatly reduced colorspace. The good news is that it won't get any worse. The FireWire accommodates the DVs 3.6Mb second data rate with room to spare and the DV-friendly FinalCutPro edit software is transparent to the final image.

EQUIPMENT

Foam core reflectors from the art store and a white Army surplus parachute are the two most important elements of your outdoor shooting package. For interior shots consider bouncing sunlight into the room from reflectors (aluminum foil covered foam core) located outside in direct sunlight. Once you start with lights you've gotten into an area that costs money.

Many rental houses carry inexpensive lighting kits like the Lowel DP light kit that are quite versatile. Just remember that you're trying to achieve a film look so you're using the ND filters, right? Total: $100 per week rental × 3weeks = $300.

Almost as important as the lights themselves are the tools to bounce, diffuse, and cut the actual beams. Again, foam core with reflective surfaces as well as black. A good hardware store will have spring clamps that look somewhat like large clothespins. Get a dozen of these as well as a few rolls of double-sided foam tape and several rolls of duct tape. Since you're a filmmaker, you should always call it grip tape once you're out of the hardware store. Total: $100.

PRODUCTION

Drive your production or it will drive you. Hopefully, you've gathered a few friends around to help with the actual shoot, and you've even got a few

actors from the local school or workshop to work for free. If they are professional actors you've made a deal to pay them a deferred SAG salary if the
film gets distribution. The important thing to work on here is not so much
the technical aspects of the production but rather the social skills involved in
keeping everyone happy and focused. More than any other aspect of no-
budget production, teamwork and a congenial environment will lead to a
successful shoot. Total: Tape stock $100, Food: $100, Slush: $100.

Often overlooked in micro productions is the obligatory wrap party. I
know that you're short on funds but there is simply no better way to say
thank you to all the people who put up with your sniveling insecurities and
unreasonable demands. Beer, wine, pizza, and a bottle of good tequila.
Total: $250.

POSTPRODUCTION

In the past half-dozen years, there has been more misinformation, more
hype, and more boldface misrepresentation about postproduction than perhaps any other aspect of production.

Post is theoretically where all of the pieces come together. It is where you
assemble your story. Now that nearly every personal computer comes with
an editing application and FireWire ports, it has also become a commodity.

If you're a Mac-only person then your choice of editing software applications
is rather limited and Apple's FinalCutPro is about as good as it's going to get.
Although I rail against it quite often, FCP is really not a bad program and it
seems to be getting better with every release.

The important thing to realize here is that FCP is a primarily a video editor
while Avid is primarily a film editor. Yes, you can add some special software
to your FCP system and make it work as a cinematic editor, but then you're
taking the family sedan off-road.

Avid Xpress (XpressDV) works equally well on Mac or PC computers and
has the added benefit of building your professional vocabulary. The other
thing I like about Xpress is that the same dongle works with both Mac and
PC versions.

Often overlooked in the midst of all the hype is Adobe Premiere. Perhaps the first desktop video editor, Premiere offers the added bonus of being a very good visual effects and graphics package as well. Anyone thinking of putting together a desktop system for postproduction could do far worse than start here.

>>>>> Premiere works equally well on Mac or PC systems, has the most robust digitizing system and one of the easiest-to-learn editing paradigms in the industry. More than a few independent moviemakers have left the buggy world of high-end, dedicated systems for the bulletproof dependability of Adobe Premiere.

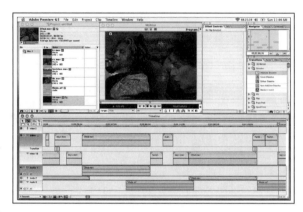

If you're new to desktop production, the encumbrance of learning a number of different applications can take a healthy bite out of your schedule. Premiere offers a single solution with a well-written interface and powerful application to back it up.

EDITING

Since DV only needs about 18GB for 90 minutes and you've got room to spare, you can forget off-line editing all together. Just sit your butt down and get it done. Either you've got the ability or you'd better know someone who does. Fortunately I do.

If you plan on using the Internet for distribution then that's about it for expenses. You've kicked out your movie for a little over $3,000. Congratulations!

FESTIVAL FERVOR

When I wrote the first edition of this book there were only a couple of festivals that were screening digitally so I included a whole bit about how you could print to film cheaply. Now, almost all festivals have some accommodation to screen digitally so I've pulled that section.

Of course there is the caveat that you really do enhance the perceived value of your movie by projecting it on film so if you've got a hankering you can download the "Printing to film on the cheap" segment from my website at: *www.pixelmonger.com/printtofilm*.

So now you've got your movie "in the can" and you're perusing the lists of film festivals. Yer buds at IFP can come in handy here, needless to say, there's more than a few of'em who've been through the process more than once.

In addition to being a very well-respected film editor in both the independent and studio sectors of this industry, Arash Ayrom has spent quite a bit of time in the festival trenches. Having associations with a number of major festivals, as well as serving as a programmer for the L.A. Film Festival for five years in a row, Arash has a very well-honed point of view that anyone intent on hitting the circuit would do well to heed.

"On average, we got about 500 or so film submissions a year. In a good year, maybe 5% of these were decent. The rest were dreck of the very worst sort. Often imitative of some genre or popular film, they would come at us in waves. One year was the Tarantino wannabes. Another year was Romantic Comedy Hell. Gangster films are very popular, but usually quite terrible. The introduction of DV only made it worse.

My point is that if you are going to make a film, do it because you really have some sort of brilliant idea in your head, not because you think you can do what some other filmmaker who met with success did. This is also true of all the elements that go into your film. The cinematography should work towards advancing your film, not showing that you can do what they did in The Matrix 2.

Your actors should be cast because they are good, not recognizable. And, of course, work with a real editor, not some guy who happens to have the latest copy of FinalCutPro Pro on his laptop. The editor is your last saving grace, especially if you shoot a less than perfect film (which means, everyone).

Having said this, if you are shooting DV and cutting on FCP, and employing other low-budget techniques, make sure you are organized before you start! This means that you should involve everyone in the process. Make good storyboards. Show them to your DP and editor and then listen to what they have to say. Your DP will determine the look of your movie, and your editor is the person who will actually tell your story, their opinions are not only relevant, but essential.

Everyone involved in your project should have final copies of the script. Your shot list should be approved by both your DP and your editor, and it should be organized so that you know which shots are essential and which are optional. Coverage is vital! Sound is vital! Use good microphones and a good sound recordist.

Although you can make a digital movie for much less money than a film, follow the process and methodologies established by the legions of filmmakers before you. Make use of the experience of others to make sure your process is viable and that all of the disparate technologies will work together.

A final warning: Do NOT blindly follow the recommendations of hardware or software manufacturers! Just because a company says its editing software will work with hi-def footage doesn't mean it will. Ask around, take time to look at online forums, ask questions, and don't buy into the hype."

BUZZ BUILDING

Now is the time to really turn up the effort, and don't be timid about blatant self-promotion. Make a concerted effort and maximize every opportunity to establish or increase your Internet presence. As I've said before, a strong Internet awareness is both self-propagating and compounding.

As with Internet distribution, your motives are to increase awareness but since this isn't your primary distribution channel you'll need a great trailer. The object is to get it placed on as many sites a possible and then e-mail every person you know to e-mail every person they know.

I'm a big fan of doing it yourself and a fundamental understanding of HTML will go a long, long way in your quest for online media domination.

Get involved in local festivals to learn how they work and then keep an eye out for golden opportunities where you can promote your movie.

Always remember that "Advertising is what you say about yourself, Public Relations is what others say about you." An ounce of PR is worth a pound of advertising and the nice thing about PR is that it's practically free.

The popular misconception is that PR means Press Release. As annoying as these terse missives were in the early days of faxes and desktop publishing, the Internet has allowed them to breed like mosquitoes in the pixelated pool of on-line, interconnectedness. You must create a unique voice that will break through the media clutter and enhance the perceived value of your project.

Good public relations should always be based on your project's strongest points and echo its timbre and voice. Keep driving key points over and over regardless of how repetitive it feels. Actively seek out interviews about your project and line up interviews for your actors as well. Send out high-quality DVDs or the best VHS dubs you can generate (along with your one page press release) to people who write articles for film and entertainment magazines.

Your one page synopsis should contain a punchy little, scenario-driven story about some unique aspect of your movie's production or content. A cute or salacious anecdote with regard to the lead characters always seems to catch the eye of overworked staffers... and that's really what your intent is. You want someone to read something that makes them stop and go "hmmmmmm." Don't pay it off in your little one -pager either, make them contact you for the punch line.

Hopefully you've read a good deal of the leading publications so you know what the different magazines like to cover. Figure out a unique aspect of your project that fits into their editorial voice and build a little human interest or technical methodology story about it.

Keep it short and punchy; a well-constructed paragraph or two should do it. Remember that a good press release gets to the point efficiently. Your goal here is to whet their interest, not deliver a blow-by-blow report on how you did it. These people are looking for angles, unique points of view and unusual approaches. If your project doesn't have any, then you're just not (please forgive the banal expression) "thinking outside the box."

Self-aggrandizement is a touchy subject, and one that takes a good deal of craft. Self-promotion is the name of the game in the movie business, but just keep in mind that if you've got a movie to promote, the movie owns you; not the other way around. Don't spend a sentence or even a word describing yourself if it isn't in direct context of your movie. Every word you spend blithering on about yourself is a word wasted.

I realize that the main motivation for making movies is to express your inner dynamics and the development of a personal voice. Keep it to yourself. Until you've proven yourself capable of creating anything of value, no one outside of a very tight circle of family and friends has any interest in you. This is especially true of journalists and the webmeisters that are going to help you promote your movie.

If you are lucky enough to land an interview, don't spend it talking about yourself. It will never hit the page and you'll have just wasted a golden opportunity. Instead, spend the time talking about the people you work with, the actors, the story, the methodology... anything but yourself.

Believe me, the more you elevate the cast and crew of your movie, the better your movie sounds and the more ink you'll get. The more ink you get, the more awareness your project will have, the better it will do and the better your chances for survival in this highly competitive industry.

Unless you really hit one out of the ballpark, PR is going to give you the highest return on your investment.

Let's say that you've actually ended up with something that people enjoy watching and you've decided to enter it in a few festivals. Don't start with Sundance or Cannes unless you find that you are motivated by rejection. Start small and work your way up. Since there are several festivals every week, you won't need to wait long for an opportunity.

Whither goest thy film, so too shall ye goest. And when you get there, don't hesitate to buy the next round. Always drink less than half of what you're pouring down potential patrons and never stop schmoozing your ass off.

Don't get involved in relationships that aren't business-related. A lot of deals have been lost because a newbie filmmaker was busy hustling up company for some late night tryst rather than sniffing out business and promoting their film. Oh, and have fun. People see you having fun, they'll figure that you're a fun guy or gal and that you've made a really fun movie. And don't forget to put me on your guest list.

Unless you are a maestro at self-promotion, figure on spending at least 20% of your budget on promotion. Flyers, a nice press kit, DVD duplication, HD up-conversion and dubs, festival fees... this all adds up and is every bit an important part of a good budget as the camera rental.

Add to this the transportation, housing, and schmooze expenses involved with going to and hanging out at the various festivals, and you'll see why successful promotion campaigns often exceed the production costs of a small project.

13 ⠿ BYTE-SIZED CHUNKS

"The first 90% of a project takes 10% of the time.
The last 10% takes the other 90%."

Peter Marx

The Internet is not, as so many put it, "*a digital gold rush*" but rather the purest form of free enterprise in the entire history of mankind. Anyone of above room temperature IQ, who doesn't at least give mind service to some harebrained, entrepreneurial scheme is missing out on this lifetime's golden opportunity. Just about any topic, product, or service has its niche in this bitstream of humanity. And you, well you make one of its hottest commodities. Content.

You've made your movie, invested time and resources far beyond your original intention, and now you're pondering the myriad choices of distribution scenarios. Maybe you're planning on releasing your mini-blockbuster through one of the many independent film sites on the Internet.

Ahh, that's the ticket, just sit back and let them generate clamoring throngs of ardent fans. After all, movie sites are one of the fastest growing venues on the Internet. Generally all you need to do is send them a DV copy of your movie and they'll prep it, compress it, and post it for you.

While some sites deal mainly with a certain style or genre, others offer a wide spectrum of content from Flash cartoons and animations to mini theatrical releases.

Atom Films (*www.AtomFilms.com*) is one of the Internet's pioneers and offers a broad assortment of titles in a wide selection of bandwidths and players. Its founder, Mika Salmi, is well-known for his unique and well-articulated view of the industry so I asked him what he looks for in submissions from new sources.

"Quality, always! and projects that take advantage of the new mediums, such as the interactive nature of the Internet or the portable, on-demand nature of handheld devices.

Right now, everyone is focused on short-form and low-bandwidth friendly technologies, both of which are extremely important today, but there's a place for all approaches, and the live action films are quickly catching up to 'made for the web' animation technologies in popularity. All genres and lengths will eventually work in these new platforms just like they do in the rest of the media world. That doesn't mean that there won't be whole new kinds of entertainment that take advantage of the new distribution platforms — those will exist, too.

The other thing is that the Internet offers unique opportunities to build communities of artists, entertainment enthusiasts, and consumers. This means that artists have direct access to their audience and both artists and consumers can directly determine what entertainment they want to make and see. In the future, neither the artist nor the consumer will need to depend on a movie studio to accomplish their goals or have the kind of entertainment they want. This is truly revolutionary."

Gary Zeidenstein of Always Independent Films (*www.alwaysindependentfilms.com*) thinks that the leaders in streaming media will soon evolve into a unique variation of a cable channel.

"Right now we have a lot of splintering going on in media distribution. Content plays differently depending on which environment you are plugged into and the bandpass of that content stream.

Convergence is constantly pulling audiences in different directions, but as soon as the television and the computer have finished merging into their final form, it will be hard to tell the dotcoms from the conventional broadcasters. The true difference will undoubtedly be the inherent quality of the content. There is a broad pallet of opportunities for moviemakers who can adapt to these changing venues."

Not all dotcom honchos are solely vested in the Internet's growing parade of pixels. HonkWorm's (*www.HonkWorm.com*) President of Cross Media has a shelf full of the top accolades in broadcasting including numerous Emmys, Peabody Awards, and Golden Globes. Having overseen the development of such shows as *The X-Files*, *In Living Color*, and *The Simpsons* for Fox Television and then *Ally McBeal*, *Chicago Hope*, and *The Practice* for David E. Kelley Productions, Jeffrey Kramer personifies the high caliber profile of the Internet's big guns.

I asked Jeffrey what there was about this new environment that could possibly lure him away from one of the more successful careers in conventional broadcasting? *"Streaming allows an unbelievable democratization,"* he replied. *"In traditional media and broadcast, we tapped into talent pools in Los Angeles and New York and maybe Chicago. With HonkWorm, and the other online venues, creators can generate content from Martha's Vineyard or Pocatello, Idaho or The Bayou in Louisiana. We provide a platform for talents that would never have been found using the traditional approach."*

When asked what he looks for in submissions, Kramer replies simply: *"The quality of an idea. Traditional entertainment has a more laid-back style to it, you're physically sitting back to watch an hour of* The Practice *or* Sopranos. *With online entertainment, you're generally sitting there leaning into your monitor, it has a lot more urgency to it and is much more interactive. You generally can't get away with as many characters because you simply don't have the time. Maybe you're just dealing with an emotion, an ethic, a moral, a feeling, or a point of view. In some ways it's like Harry Cohn's ass, if it wiggles in the seat, it's not a good story."*

But let's say that your movie has a special nuance that these guys just didn't get. You've sent clips out to twenty or thirty of the main movie websites but nobody shares your vision. Perhaps you posted some clips at the DigitalFridge (*www.digitalfridge.com*) or your trailer's been running at TrailerVision (*www.singlereel.com*) for a couple weeks and still the phone hasn't rung.

As marvelous as your movie may seem to you, and even though your mother thinks it should be submitted for academy consideration, you've got a daunting task to generate an audience. Don't get me wrong, your audience is out there. You'd be hard pressed to create anything of any value that didn't appeal to some sort of market segment. The trick is to connect with the right market segments (audience), and connect in the right way.

THE FINAL INJUSTICE

The technology that drives Internet content more than any other is compression. All your hard work, the effort you put into salvaging and protecting your delicate signal, is now about to be crushed like an empty soda can. In fact, if we were to extend that metaphor, the compression that you are faced with would equate to reducing the soda can down to a point where it would fit nicely between these parentheses ( ).

Hopefully this isn't the final stage of your production but rather an integral step in the promotion and greater distribution of your epic flick. Let's say that you've been careful about the acquisition and management of your video signal and you've ended up with a rather respectable 601/4:2:2 signal with a clean 44 kHz, stereo sound track.

Let's assume further that you've gotten yourself some sophisticated compression software like MediaCleaner and you're now faced with rather daunting compression choices. Sorenson is the current choice of compression algorithms and MediaCleaner is the leading software processing application. Virtually every major desktop software program (Adobe Premiere and AfterEffects, Avid, Media100, Edit DV, and Final Cut Pro) is including a basic copy of MediaCleanerEZ with its application.

<<<<<   Media Cleaner's well-designed interface painlessly walks you through an otherwise daunting task.

One of the many cool things about MediaCleaner is that it conducts a unique interview that takes you through the process of compression and allows you to compile a series of intelligent choices based on the factors that are relevant to your project and market. MediaCleaner's manual alone is perhaps the singular, definitive resource for dynamic media compression. (It is one of the few software manuals that is so well-written and laid out that it warrants a cover-to-cover reading.)

The final decisions with regard to size and data rates should be based on the collective bandwidth of your prospective market. Do you compress for the relatively limited, industry average modem speed or DSL speeds? Do you make your movie into a down-loadable QuickTime or do you utilize streaming technology so it can be viewed in quasi-real time on the Web? All these questions and more are addressed as you click your way through MediaCleaner's unusually friendly WIZZARD interface. For those with a bit more confidence in their technical acumen, there is the ADVANCED SET-TINGS panel that allows you to configure your own compression battle plan.

>>>>> For those who love to tweak, Advanced Settings offer seemingly endless options.

SIMPLE MATH

Let's figure that your video is going to weigh in somewhere around 30 Megabytes per second. A CD-ROM would be able to hold less than half a minute at this rate and couldn't even come close to playing it back. The audio alone would gag all but the most robust Internet connections. Figure that the vast majority of the Internet world is still using 56.6K modems, without compression it would take them more than a week to download the 160 Gigabytes of your movie.

The key to presenting your video/movie over the Web is a subtle balance between compression and bandwidth. Just because you may or may not have big pipes is no indication of what your potential market is dealing with. If your audience does not have cable modem, ISDN, DSL or faster, virtually any methodology that you use will present your movie in a tiny window, with limited colorspace and haltingly bad synchronization.

THE HOLY TRINITY OF STREAMING

What broadcast entertainment was to the past, streaming content will be to the future.

The two most important trade shows for the technology of transmitted entertainment are NAB (National Association of Broadcasters) and Streaming Media. While NAB has traditionally represented the bastion of time honored methodology, for the fourth year in a row at NAB, virtually every other booth was showing some sort of streaming adaptation. The incredible growth in this industry segment is a cogent portent of the not-to-distant future.

If you want your movie to be accessible to the widest possible audience, you'll need to offer it in a couple of bandwidth choices on at least two of the three main player formats. A critically important factor to keep in mind is that the four leading OS/computer platforms (PC, Mac, SGI, LINUX) all have very different gamma settings. What appears well-balanced on a Windows machine is blown out on a Mac and inversely, a well-lit and balanced shot on a Mac is so dark that it is barely recognizable on a Windows machine.

Then there are the always important data rate issues. Let's figure for reference purposes that a decent 4x CD-ROM is good for a sustained data rate of around 400KBps. Really good compression management can potentially give you about 48 minutes of marginal quality 640 × 480 video. A 56.6 modem is generally good for only 4KBps and even the industrial strength T1 connection is generally only dependable for 20KBps.

You must be prepared to do battle with the compression gods. The more you understand the potential pitfalls and tricks of streaming media, the brighter your future becomes. Sure the Internet's bandwidth will increase with time, but the people who have the best compression strategies will always lead the way.

The first step in developing your particular battle plan is deciding on which player technology you want to deal with. Your main choices are QuickTime, Real, and the Windows Media Player.

>>>>> **The Plain Jane of players also packs the most versatility.**

QuickTime (*www.apple.com/quicktime*)

Apple's QuickTime software has more installed users than any other compressed video format. Initially released as part of the Macintosh operating system, QuickTime is now an integral part of most contemporary browsers. The playback is by far the smoothest of the three players listed here and its ability to translate and share data between dissimilar platforms has made it an industry standard. QuickTime's wide ranging acceptance and ease of use make this the optimum distribution mechanism for the vast majority of general Internet users. It has built-in translators that support more than 200 different file formats as is particularly well-suited to high-quality streaming.

<<<<<   Kind'a hard to figure out what does what in the RealPlayer's cluttered environment.

RealPlayer (*www.real.com*)

Originally developed as a player for the emerging web-audio market, the RealPlayer is the most popular streaming standard in the PC market and still leading the way as the codec of choice for a majority of sites. Not nearly as convenient or simple to use as the widely accepted QuickTime, Real does have a few advantages when it comes to embedding the data stream into HTML. The picture quality is quite good at high speeds but the frame rate is quite sensitive to bandpass fluctuations and has a tendency to become choppy. When it's good, it's very good.

<<<<<   While simplicity generally indicates superior engineering, the case of the Windows Media Player is an exception. With the best design and integration of user controls, the WMP is much better than it was, but still has a way to go.

Windows Media Player (*www.microsoft.com*)

This is the streamable version of the popular AVI extension and despite the fact that it comes from the world's leading software empire, the Windows Media Player had a rather disappointing introduction. Although it is available on both Mac and Windows platforms, the integration with Web browsers is still poorly initiated.

WMPs scalable window can occasionally deliver full screen video streams with near MPEG1 quality if you have the bandwidth. Key word, occasionally. On those rare occasions when the bandwidth gods are smiling down upon you, the Windows Media Player can actually deliver inherent image quality noticeably superior to either QuickTime or Real.

In their defense, it's really hard to write this kind of application without stepping on someone's intellectual property and we all know how many people are out gunning for Microsoft. These guys are long overdue for a killer app, hopefully it will be a robust Web application.

While the Media Cleaner software can create consummately optimized data packages for these and many more compression scenarios, QuickTime is perhaps the codec of choice for many content creators. Ancillary applications such as MacroMedia's Flash and Shockwave are enjoying great success on the Web and are inherently more compatible within QuickTime's comprehensive architecture.

Since Streaming video often requires a special server, hosting services have become the favored means of distribution. They'll generally cater to one of the three flavors of players and can compress your movie for you, or allow you to download it through their FTP site.

(*http://streamingmediaworld.com*) is a good road stop on your journey through the maze of ambiguity that surrounds this esoteric realm. If you've got an itch to be out on the leading edge of technogogic hipness, delve into the zippy world of Macromedia Flash to pump up the graphic artist in your soul or how about savoring the soothing richness of Java scripting.

As with all decisions in the moviemaking process, test, tinker, and try out everything before you crush your movie down to byte sized chunks.

ON THE OTHER HAND

While streaming most definitely represents the future of media delivery, it does have its drawbacks. Most importantly, it is nearly impossible to save a streamed movie to disk. The paranoid and short-sighted see this as a way to protect their precious intellectual property. The reality is that it severely limits the audience-building potential of your movie.

The Net's economy is entirely different from the corporatized democracy in which we live our physical lives. In the interconnected and reciprocating world of the Internet, the more you give away, the richer you become. When you give your QuickTime away, you're capturing attention. Every time someone e-mails your movie to an associate or shows it to a friend, you're compounding the attention that you and your project receive. To quote Kevin Kelly once more: *"The only factor becoming scarce in a world of abundance is human attention. Giving stuff away captures human attention, or mind share, which then leads to market share."*

Micro movie venues are about to cascade down from the technological heaven. They'll eventually be integrated into just about everything you can imagine. A brisk walk up the Ginza will take you past hundreds of people walking to work, shopping, or just leaning up against a building. In their hands are a wide assortment of micro-miniaturized, portable venues. Phones playing streaming video in diminutive screens, ultra-tiny LCD panels playing movies from postage stamp-sized RAM cards.

<<<<< Due to its close proximity to the observer, the relative viewing size of this PCMCIA video monitor card far exceeds the average home television's perceived size. Movies can be downloaded into the card directly from the Internet via the PCMCIA port found on most laptop computers or via the tiny RAM card which holds more than 30 minutes of Sorensen compressed, QuickTime video.

The chasm between the theatre screen and the hand-held device is a big one. Each environment requires certain production considerations, but neither can become exclusionary of the other. Kind of interesting really, how even if you're shooting a multi-million dollar movie, the original shot is seen on a tiny screen within the camera's viewfinder.

Micro-screens, head-mounted displays, and corneal refracting devices are all coming soon to a Circuit City near you. In a way, the coming trend of hand-helds is perhaps the most intimate and personal venue yet. Until the day when the first cyber-squatter jacks in to re-runs of *I Love Lucy*, we're on a one way, no-holds-barred, smack-down battle for human attention.

Compression is the key to this digital future, whether used for down-linking a data stream for theatrical release or bouncing some home-spun content off of a fan's cornea halfway around the world. Where it all ends up is a matter of conjecture, but I can promise you that it will be a most exhilarating ride.

14 ⋗ BREAKING OUT OF HOLLYWOOD

"And now for something completely different."
Monty Python

The most significant factor in the digital assault on Hollywood is not so much from the outside as from the inside. People, well established in the conventional production community, are discovering the freedom that digital technology brings, and they're doing something about it.

Empowerment it would seem, is even more consuming than the lure of power or fame.

Producers, writers, directors, actors... everyone in town seems to have been bitten by the digital bug almost simultaneously. While nearly everything in this chapter is in direct opposition to the overall theme of this book, it represents a fairly good, day-in-the-life visit with a few of my good friends and business associates. It also portends what the industry is facing.

If you travel West from the Hollywood sign and the namesake Boulevard with its big brass stars, and keep on going until you've actually driven beyond the borders of your *Map to the Homes of the Hollywood Stars*, you'll eventually arrive in PixelWood. Just as Beverly Hills was the utopic haven for the Old Hollywood, so to are the majestic flanks of the adjacent Santa Monica Mountains for its contemporary counterpart.

<<<<< Dale Launer.

DALE LAUNER

Perched on the rim of a particularly verdant canyon overlooking the Pacific Ocean, lies the sprawling manse of one of my more eccentric friends. As a card-carrying member of the WGA, Dale Launer has written movies like *My Cousin Vinny*, *Ruthless People*, *Dirty Rotten Scoundrels* and the charming Sandra Bullock entree *Love Potion Number 9*, which he also directed.

"Think of the last movie you saw," says Dale as we settle back on his sprawling deck. *"If you enjoyed the movie then the director was a genius, but if you didn't like it, then chances are that you felt that it was a bad script. Thing is, when you're writing consistently at the studio level, you don't really write bad scripts. Once a screenplay get sucked into the system, it goes through a series of changes that are made by studio executives, not filmmakers. Generally, the more interaction there is with studio executives, the worse the script becomes.*

There is of course a covert mechanism at work here. As more and more MBAs and lawyers slither their way into the rotting carapace of the old studios, they rely on the guild system to generate qualifiable investment packages rather than dynamic storytelling ventures. Craft and original thought don't transpose well into their contemporary world of highly leveraged market ventures. Deeply revealing story lines scare them, so they play it safe and resort to formulas, remakes, and sequels, recycling the same handful of 'safe' faces over and over and over again.

I remember when I turned in the first draft of My Cousin Vinny *to the studio,* Dale continues. *At the first 'creative' meeting, the studio head starts out by saying 'Great script, really funny, good work, good work. (beat) Do you think you can cut the character of Lisa out of the script?' "* (Author's note: The character of Mona Lisa Vito was played by Marisa Tomei for which she won an Academy Award.)

At first blush, Dale's experience within the conventional studio system may not seem that unusual. Another talented cinematic craftsman, distraught with how their work is violated by a clan of studio barbarians. The same story is played out daily as the growing cadre of pedantic attorneys and scholastic dilettantes who amuse themselves by making what they consider to be creative decisions.

What makes Dale's tale so inspiring is that one day he gets a wild digital hair up his bum and, like a growing number of well-entrenched, card-carrying guild members, actually does something about it. After reviewing his enviable selection of cars, Dale selected the one with the largest trunk and drove over to BandPro Video, where he plunks down his American Express and buys himself a $200,000 Sony F900-HDCAM system.

Michael Braven is the General Manager of LA's preferred arsenal for digital moviemaking notes: *"While millions of DV-wielding moviemakers are lined up at the gates trying to break into Hollywood, Dale and a growing number of established industry professionals are breaking out. As the movie industry becomes more of a formula and less of an art form, craftsmen from all aspects of the industry are taking matters into their own hands by embracing the get-up and go, do-it-yourself mentality of HD."*

"I'm very lucky to have had so many of my scripts turned into successful movies, but none of them have made it to the screen intact. It's always a battle to maintain the integrity of your screenplay. I've always thought that if I could control the means of production I could shepherd my characters and themes from script to screen," says Dale as we head to the kitchen for another round.

Now I'm not saying that we should fee sorry for guys like Dale. True, he's only had a half dozen paydays in his writing career, but they were all for several millions of dollars. We meander through his palatial digs, past his eclectic collection of art, past the Hi-Definition entertainment system, past the bank of FireWire drives constantly downloading and playing the latest MP3 throughout the hilltop enclave.

Finally arriving in the well-appointed kitchen, Dale throws open the massive refrigerator door, moves aside a sizable cluster of Dom Perigion and pulls out another round of beers. *"I sold a script to DreamWorks for three million dollars,"* he adds as he rummages around for a couple glasses, *"... and ended up doing rewrites for the past year. It was a miserable experience and it really made me want to just go off and make a movie by myself. The idea was to write something that was easy to make and could be shot quickly."*

We head outside with our beers, past the classic 289 Ford Cobra, past the über Porsche Boxter, past the... you get the idea. *"After a good many years in this industry, I've come to the realization..."* Dale gestures widely with his beer which sloshes over onto the Cobra's finish, *"...that a basic movie really costs about $150,000 to make."* He wipes the beer off with his T-shirt. *"That's it, all the rest is above the line shenanigans, producer's fees, studio shell games. Visual effects don't even pump it up all that much if you really know what you're doing."*

According to Dale's math, for about $200,000 you can get yourself a full HD camera system, a decent little lighting and grip package, and a desktop non-linear system like a CineWave. Add in the $150,00 for production and for $350,000 you've got yourself a movie. *"You don't need to spend $150,000, you could spend much more or much less,"* adds Dale. *"It's just from what I've seen, $150,000 seems like a respectable and workable number."*

Of course talent, good talent at least, doesn't come cheaply in this town. Dale's strategy harkens back to those childhood days where if one kid had a ball, another had a bat, and another had a glove... you pretty much had yourself a baseball team. *"Instead of paying people a lot up front,"* Dale says with evangelical fervor. *"Now they can participate in the real back end of the production. This is how movies should be made. If you're a crew member or an actor, you should only make a decision to make a movie if it is something that you believe in."*

THE LONE GUNMAN

Leo Grillo is a hard-working, card-carrying member of SAG. He has one of those faces you remember seeing in dozens of movies and television shows, but you just can't remember the name. There are a lot of people in this town who make a very nice living on the fringes of celebrity. Well, Leo went out and bought himself a gun. A big gun. A Sony F-900 HDCAM and a lovely set of Fujinon primes.

<<<<< Leo Grillo.

"As an actor in this town you're totally at the whim of other people," says Leo as he takes inventory on the contents of a sizable collection of Anvil cases that lay scattered before us. *"It's a tough way to make a living, especially if you've got a family to support."*

After examining the contents of his rather extensive mobile production arsenal, Leo plops himself down on the rear bumper of his Ford Econoline van and gestures widely to the pile of gear. *"The only way to have any control over your destiny is to make your own movies. So I've been working my way up, shooting documentaries, getting ready to start shooting my own feature."*

Leo continues, "I went out and bought a Bauer MovieCamSL, 35mm film camera system, but the problem with film is that the smaller the crew, the harder it is to manage. There's a critical mass with film crews. So along comes Hi-Definition and like so many others from the Hollywood community I'm intrigued by the freedom it affords. With HD, it seems as though smaller crews are actually more efficient. Now I can make stuff cheaper and faster. Heck, I've got an entire production company that fits inside this van."

As if motivated by the thought, Leo gets up and starts loading in the cases. "So now I'm an actor and a DP and a producer and a director. This is really an artist's medium, you look around this town and it is the artists that are embracing it."

I help him load a few of the larger cases, after which he reaches into a cooler, pulls out a couple sodas and tosses me one. "The first time I saw HD screened theatrically, that was really created by an artist, was at the Pacific Theatre on Hollywood Boulevard," says Leo. "It was some shots from the movie that you did with Faye Dunaway. There she is, an icon among actors, and she decides to make her own movie. She just gets herself an HD camera and some friends and just does it. And it looked absolutely spectacular. I listed my film camera for sale the next day."

The sun is getting hot as Leo arranges the cases inside the Econoline. "I'm in a perfect place at the perfect time," he says. "I've got my studio right here in my truck, I'm a well-trained actor, I know how to light and compose a good shot from my years as a professional photographer. Hey, it's movie time! I'm simply driving out into the desert, and shooting a one man show. Just me and my camera."

I make some lame joke about "Swimming to Dinner" to which Leo rises like a trout to a fly, "I'm not making Swimming to Cambodia, and I'm not making My Dinner with Andre, I'm making a real movie! Regardless of what format you shoot with, it all comes down to story. 'Ugg, Hunt, Kill, Eat.' Story was originally created to teach us how to live our lives. When we stopped having a relevant story, we stopped leading relevant lives."

As the last of the cases are lashed down, Leo sits atop the case holding his F-900 HDCAM. "As I see it, story is simply the basic elements in the human psyche. How we live is brought to the surface by story, that's why people love

Love Stories." Leo takes a long pull on his soda and climbs into the driver's seat. *"All the religions are based on a story that simply got written down. Bring it to 21st century relevance and you've got a real hot commodity. That's what I'm going to do out in the desert."*

As Leo starts his mobile production studio, I pull the sliding door shut and lean in the passenger side window to wish him luck. *"I've always felt that the Hollywood studio system got off track somewhere along the line,"* he says. *"Maybe it's the way it's organized, maybe it's the people that the studios attract. Until now, there really wasn't much anyone could do about it. That's the way it was and you learned to adapt. Then along comes HD and now you only need one person below the line to make a movie."*

Leo pulls out and drives away to make his one-man movie. I climb in my Land Cruiser and chuckle to myself... "Swimming to Dinner..." I can't believe I said that.

TIM CUTT

Pixel for pixel, pound for pound, the Hi-Definition signal from a Sony HDR-F900 will blow just about anything out there away, but there are contenders. At almost half the cost, Panasonic stepped out onto the dusty streets and started firing away at Sony's appreciable lead.

<<<<< Tim Cutt.

In addition to being a multi-award winning director, Tim Cutt is a rather energetic fixture in PixelWood. After suffering through years of making other people's mistakes, he grabbed a Panasonic AJ-HDC27 camcorder and set out to make his own. *"I chose the DVCPRO-HD because I knew I needed to get enough resolution so that I had the option to print to film if the situation arose,"* says Tim as he plays some recent footage in his beach front studio. *"When you pull a 3:2 on 24P, it gives you a very filmic look which transposes well to contemporary MOW production. The future-proof resolution and cinematic nuance are why so many major shows are going for HD."*

When asked why he chose 720P HD over 1080P HD, Tim shakes his head. *"I've been trying to figure out why television production people would use anything else. 720P gives you everything you could want in contemporary broadcast content creation. High-resolution, film-like frame rate, wide aspect, and when you pump it onto the desktop for effects or editing, it moves a whole lot faster, easier and cheaper than 1080P. As far as I'm concerned,"* he says on our way to the patio. *"1080P is really nice if you're heading for the big screen or printing out to film, but it's overkill for television."*

Having seen 720P and 1080P projected side-by-side both digitally and printed to film, I have to admit that the cinematic difference isn't all that obvious. Tim's footage has a very film-like quality to it that really does seem to enhance the perceived value. *"The thing that I like the best about HD is that it seems to be getting a lot of really unique projects off of the shelf,"* says Tim with a wry grin. *"Let's face it, pitching a project to a bunch of studio executives has become a cliché. They don't understand story, they don't understand character development, but they do understand resolution. If nothing else, HD is a qualitative commodity that tells these guys that it'll look good."*

For someone like Tim with more than a hundred national television shows under his belt, HDs ability to online for broadcast or print to film makes it a prime contender for cross-dressing production environments that need to adapt to a constantly changing industry. *"On a video monitor all formats look about the same,"* Tim adds. *"But when you compress it down for DVD or up convert and print to film, well that's a whole different story. Whether using 1080 x 1920 or 720 x 1280, HD is simply the most versatile format we have in our arsenal."*

Tim's company, It's a Secret Studios, is one of the more highly-respected DVD production houses in Hollywood. *"Like everyone else in this business we've created a lot of titles from DigiBeta masters,"* says Tim. *"Lately we've been advocating that the studios telecine to a HD 24P master for our DVD composition and the results have really been astounding."*

We hang out on the patio, watch some girls playing volleyball, drink a few beers. Eventually the game ends and the girls head off... our thoughts drift back to HD. *"After packaging major titles for almost six years,"* Tim says as we pick up the now ancient conversation. *"We've gotten to a point were we can start to introduce our own content into the distribution stream. HD gives us the capabilities we need without turning us into something we aren't."*

ALLEN DAVIAU

From deep within the hallowed bowels of ASC (American Society of Cinematographers), Allen Daviau, notably one of the industry's more respected sharpshooters, emerges with a miniDV camcorder in hand. *"Elyse Couvillion was putting together a short called* Sweet *and asked me to shoot it for her,"* says Daviau in his decidedly courtly manor. *"She didn't have the budget for HD so we used a tiny Sony VL-1000 PAL miniDV camcorder."*

<<<<< *Sweet* director,
Elyse Couvillion, checks out
the shot under the watchful
eye of cinematographer,
Allen Daviau ASC.

"Elyse asked me to accompany her to the CSI film lab the day that the first print of Sweet *came back from the Orphanage's MagicBullet process. Prior to the screening I had been somewhat skeptical of a process that made so many promises. Since resolution is a fixed commodity, and the process of converting interlace footage to progressive is generally quite degratory, I wasn't expecting to be as impressed as I was."*

Neither as long or complex as Couvillion's earlier project *Is2o* (a personal favorite of the author), *Sweet* consisted of a couple, each fantasizing about the other, he an executive, she a school teacher. In a well-orchestrated final scene they see each other at the end of the day at the apartment mailboxes and we realize that the whole movie was their fantasies of each other.

"The thing that I found interesting was that Elyse had everything so well visualized and storyboarded that you could actually see the piece before it was shot. She even had the music picked out," says Daviau. *"Since the scripting was so simple and we were shooting MOS (Mit Out Sound) we could move quickly and effectively."*

Daviau adds, "One of the things I like best about the digital cameras is the ability to get such long shots. On the set it creates a different type of atmosphere when you're not constantly worrying about how much film is left on the spool. That gets translated through the director and gives the actor a much less pressured environment in which to create and maintain their character."

Following a screening of his latest 1080P HD piece at the newly refurbished Pacific Theatre in Hollywood, Daviau screened the miniDV short which had just been printed to film. Obviously not the same resolution of the preceding Hi-Def piece, the image quality of Sweet held up amazingly well on the forty foot screen. "With film we try so hard to eliminate all of our mistakes whereas with digital acquisition we just tend to keep on rolling," says Daviau. "Sometimes it is our mistakes that become the real gems. With all digital cameras, it seems as though they work best when you try to hold some amount of detail in the highlights so that you can still see the what's going on and at least 10% above what you would consider minimum in the blacks. It is very easy, whether shooting DV or HD to fry the whites and crush the blacks. You can always go back and get that dense look, or that blown-out look in post, but if you've recorded it that way, that's all you have. You need to give yourself room to wiggle."

When asked whether his temporary indiscretion caused dissension in the ranks of the bastion of Hollywood convention, Daviau smiles. "There is so much speculation and anxiety in this town over digital cinema. Some of it warranted, some not. I constantly find myself telling people to take a deep breath and just calm down."

DAVID HAYS

It is probably safe to say that E-Film's David Hays is responsible for printing more digital video to film than anyone one else in the world. While his views are decidedly conservative and biased, his acumen and experience in this lawless, pixelated corner of the industry is unmatched. While we were waiting for some of my visual effects files to be transferred into the E-Film print que, I asked him about how he saw the difference between HD and DV.

David leans up against the kitchen counter that is familiar to so many contemporary filmmakers and twists open a bottle of Arrowhead water. "Our goal is to offer the filmmaker the ability to transpose what they've shot *digitally onto film. People often view HD as an alternative to film, much the same way that others view DV as an alternative to HD. These digital formats are simply new tools that allow filmmakers to tell their story in different ways. There are obviously different looks involved but generally people come in and look at the different choices, and they may say that their story has a gritty feel to it and that they think that the DV is going to work for them. Others come in with three- or four million dollar budgets and they want the enhanced color and clarity that HD offers."*

We headed into the I/O room to see how my transfer was coming when he added, *"We're seeing quite a few filmmakers who are actually tailoring their look through format choices. Perhaps more important to the look than format is the way they shoot their project. Movies like* The Anniversary Party *(shot on DV) end up with a bigger look simply because of the way it was shot. You work within a film like production environment, you shoot like you're shooting film using crew that are versed in film and you end up with a film look."*

Having printed nearly all of the different flavors of digital video at E-Film, I asked David for his views on creating organic looks with the various formats. *"For something that was shot on HD, getting that 'shot on film' look is a lot easier than with DV,"* he says as we head back to the kitchen. *"With DV, since you're scaling it up so large, you really can start to see the difference between the various cameras. You get so that you can tell the difference between footage shot on an Canon XL-1 or a Sony PD-150 or a Sony-500. More importantly though is the differences in the lenses. You're recording so closely to the edge with DV that seemingly insignificant variations in the quality of the optics can have a significant impact on the final image that you print to film.*

Anyone who is considering shooting digitally, especially DV, should make sure that the camera is finely tuned and that the lenses are aligned properly. It's noticeably harder to focus the lenses on these little DV cameras so focus is something that really needs to be paid attention to. More than saying that one camera is better than another, or choosing a particular brand name, people are choosing the look that they want and then use the camera that generates that look."

REFERENCE
SECTION

15 ⋮⋅ CAMERA ALIGNMENT

David Corley, DSC Laboratories

(Author's Note: I was going to massage this piece so that it was warm and friendly, but after reading it through a few times I realized that it is already perfect. Anything I could add would dilute the information and I figure that anyone who's managed to make it this far back in the book should be able to get this easily.)

<<<<<   **David Corley.**

I was flattered when Scott asked me to write something on camera alignment for his latest book. *How many words,"* I asked. *"100 to 200,"* he replied. *"No problem, Scott, the procedure is well-defined and reasonably straightforward, right?"* Pecking away at the keyboard, it soon became apparent that I would have to tiptoe through a veritable minefield of diverse opinions.

How a camera is aligned and reproduces an image depends to a large degree on personal preference. Cameras aligned by Hollywood's leading rental houses all make good pictures, but they do look different. Ask any of the technician/artisans who are the acknowledged experts — each believes that his/her procedure is correct and that the others "haven't a clue on aligning cameras." So, in the interest of self-preservation, this old turtle is going to stick his neck out only so far and discuss basic camera alignment. We will also talk about some other factors that tend to be overlooked.

The tools you need

At minimum, an accurate, calibrated Colorbar/Grayscale chart, a large well-calibrated color monitor, and a good Waveform Monitor — a Vectorscope is useful, but not mandatory and is usually built into digital scopes. Use either rear-lit or front-lit test patterns; rear-lit are generally considered to be more accurate and are typically the choice of labs and maintenance shops. The convenience of front-lit charts makes them popular for production.

However, the mobility of the Ambi illuminator and precision of CamAlign charts has blurred the issue and both are now used in either application. Front-lit charts are more economical, so the next decision for most users is:

>>>>> Colorbar/grayscale
resolution pattern
generally called
the CamAlign.

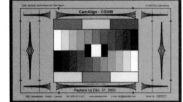

Glossy or Matte?

This should be a "no brainer." Modern high-gloss charts have a number of advantages:

a.) Higher dynamic range (white to black ratio).
b.) Consistency under different lighting conditions.
c.) Better apparent resolution.
d.) Can take a beating that would destroy a matte chart.
e.) Easy maintenance — fingerprints and dirt can be washed off.

What are the downsides?

Some would call reflections from the chart's surface a downside. But, we can argue that they're a benefit, because you can't miss them. With matte charts, the reflections are still there, but they are diffuse so we don't see them. The problem is that cameras do see them, and they affect camera alignment. Consider it a case of "better the Devil you see, than the one you can't see." Specular reflections from glossy charts are easily eliminated by tilting the chart slightly, or in the worst-case scenario (a snowstorm behind the camera), reflecting the chart into something black.

>>>>> Reflections easily
eliminated in
black velvet.

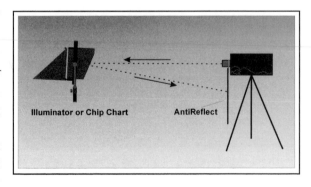

Illuminator or Chip Chart   AntiReflect

The adverse effect of matte chart flare on camera setup is significant and even more troubling, it's inconsistent. Flare not only lowers the contrast of grayscales, but also desaturates color chips.

It may be helpful to understand the physics behind the flare phenomenon. The level of flare in matte charts is typically between 3% to 6%, it can be even higher depending on lighting conditions.

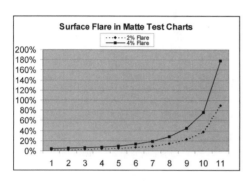

<<<<< This chart illustrates how flare increases drastically from a relatively insignificant value at the white end of a grayscale (step1) to a serious level at the dark end (step 11). Note that the flare level at step 6 (gamma), between 6% and 13%, would make it difficult to achieve accurate and consistent alignment. Add in variables such as the angle and type of lighting (spots, floods, fluorescents), and the results are, to be charitable, less than perfect picture quality.

If surface flare was consistent, a flare factor could be built into a matte chart's total reflection, but this is not possible because flare is not consistent. For more than 50 years, engineers have avoided matte chart troubles by using rear-lit test patterns.

With the advent of HD and digital cinema flare has become a much bigger issue. In addition to the inconsistency factor, matte charts are simply too low contrast. Their grayscales have the same dynamic range as early TV cameras, about 20:1 or 30dB. Modern digital cameras have a dynamic range of 3000 or 4000:1, 70-80dB. It may be overly simplistic to say: *"With that matte chart you've aligned half the camera, how about the other half?"* But you get the point.

Relative Dynamic Range in dB

72 dB Test Pattern	
Typical HD Camera	
11 step Grayscale	
9 step Grayscale	6 dB = 1 f.stop or 50% reduction in light

0   6   12   18   24   30   36   42   48   54   60   66   72 dB

<<<<< Dynamic Range Comparison Chart.

HD and even SD systems are capable of great looking images, but to use the full capability of the system we need to know what is happening in the shadows and to use every single "Bit" of data available. We stand a much better chance of doing this using a full dynamic range chart.

So how do you align a camera?
Here are some generalities, but keep in mind that opinions on alignment differ greatly, also that there are differences in the equipment — so read the camera manual first.

a.) Set up an accurate colorbar/grayscale chart and light it evenly (if front-lit, use 2 lights at 45°) — check color temperature of light source.

b.) Use test signals to check that color monitor and scope are properly adjusted.

c.) Frame chart accurately in camera viewfinder — meaningful resolution measurements require accurate framing.

d.) Follow camera manufacturers' recommended practices for basic electronic setup.

e.) Adjust camera iris so that the chart's white chips produce 700mV (100 IRE) on the Waveform Monitor.

f.) Null out any chroma in the grayscale steps — i.e. achieve equal RGB levels in mV across all steps of the grayscale from white to black.

g.) Adjust transfer function to desired gamma, 0.45 is typical and is adjusted by setting the level of the middle step using an accurate crossed grayscale chart.

h.) Align camera to desired colorimetry by adjusting color matrix. A six-vector precision color chart is a must and should have calibration data for the system you're using — HD, SD, etc. The most accurate way to adjust colorimetry is by setting color levels on a Waveform Monitor displaying colors in RGB levels. A Vectorscope is useful, but it is important to remember that it only provides Hue and Saturation data, not Brightness. Many different brightness levels of a color can all fall in the same position on a Vectorscope.

i.) Check the camera's flare levels using a high-contrast flare test pattern (black squares on a white background). Set camera iris to produce white at 700mV, and note the RGB levels of the black patches. They should all be at the same, low level. If one channel is higher than the others, dark tones and shadows will have a color cast corresponding to that channel (R, G or B).

j.) Back focus is critical in HD and is normally adjusted using a Siemens star.

k.)   Check resolution of lenses using a good multiburst or hyperbolic resolution pattern. Some of these patterns are excellent for detecting aliasing and chromatic aberration.

So much for basic alignment, but this topic opens up many other issues such as:

Modern cameras make good pictures straight out of the box; why do we need to align them?
There are at least three reasons:
a.)   All cameras are not created equal, even if the electronic paths are identical. Manufacturing tolerances in optical components, prism block, dichroics, filters, CCDs, etc. can result in significant colorimetric variations — even between cameras of the same make and model.
b.)   Unless the whole production is being shot under identical lighting conditions, camera matrices will need to be adjusted from time-to-time.
c.)   DPs who have spent more than twenty minutes in the business develop a personal preference as to how a scene should reproduce and that preference seldom matches a camera's factory presets.

Which alignment system should I use, rear-lit or front-lit?
Your choice — five years ago I would have said rear-lit, but now high-gloss charts are accurate, economical and generally more flexible. With rear-lit you are usually confined to the light box or sphere's basic illuminant; however the Ambi illuminator lets you use different sources. Front or rear-lit, pattern accuracy is the key.

>>>>>   Ambi Illuminator.

What is meant by "camera alignment goal?"
Your goal could be accurate reproduction of the scene, matching a previous set-up, or developing your own unique "look," etc. The logical starting point is technically accurate reproduction of a scene. This is simply "good engineering practice" and a sensible goal. That said, because accurate reproduction seldom makes the most pleasing pictures, I encourage people to subsequently add their own individual "look." Film has been doing this for

years and is rarely designed to reproduce a scene accurately. Kodachrome, Ektachrome, Fujichrome, and the various flavors of Eastman color all have their own larger than life characteristics.

How do I develop my own "look?"
First, use an accurate colorbar/grayscale chart to attain basic 1:1 alignment. Then shoot some everyday items, bowl of fruit, people, etc., adjusting the camera to produce what you feel is the best-looking picture — to judge image quality a good, well-aligned monitor is a must. Then re-frame your colorbar/grayscale and make notes or take digital stills of the Waveform and Vectorscope displays. You now have all the data needed to reproduce the same look, at any time in the future, on the same or any other camera.

If I align my cameras, do I need to shoot a chip chart on the set?
A well-aligned camera will give you the best images to take on to post. But, it's not always possible to have a camera perfectly aligned for every shot. Having a known reference at the head or tail can save you time (money) in postproduction.

Selecting test patterns — what features are important?
Colorbar and grayscale are essential, resolution is also useful and having the three patterns on the same chart is very handy. Framing data for different motion picture formats also on the same chart is invaluable when making transfers.

Another useful pattern is backfocus; Backfocus has become very impor-tant in HD and should be checked regularly, particularly during changes in climate.

TrueWhite white balancing cards are also invaluable on the set. White balancing to a sheet of white paper or T-shirt will virtually guarantee inconsistencies.

>>>>> BFR-XW.

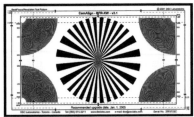

What color temperature should I use for camera alignment?
Normally the answer would be 3200 degree K, because the daylight filter in a camera is designed to convert 3200 degree to daylight. However, there are a couple of wrinkles you should consider. If you use quartz for most of your shooting, it has a typical color temperature of between 3000 and 3100 degree K and is also used for camera alignment. The downside could be that when you do shoot exteriors, the images will appear 100 degree K cool and cold blue images are not as pleasing as warm.

<<<<< White'nWarms.

Why white balance to blue cards?
From an engineering perspective, I dislike the concept even though, at the request of a client, our company originated warming cards.

CamWarm and White'nWarm image-warming sets are popular because when you white balance a camera to the selected bluish color, the pictures will have a warm rosy glow.

A little history — the blame for this nonsense falls primarily on TV set manufacturers. Since the introduction of color television, the international standard for TV colorimetry has been D65 (6500 degree K). The production side of the industry has dutifully produced programs to this standard and broadcast executives view the programs on monitors set to D65.

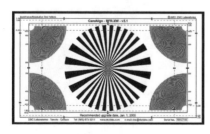

<<<<<
NTSCat709.

>>>>>
NTSCat240M.

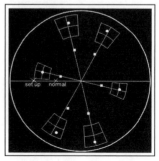

Left Vectorscope shows CamAlign colors adjusted for ITU BT-709 (SMPTE 274) colorimetry on NTSC system. When dubbing to NTSC (SMPTE 240M) colorimetry, include a few frames of the chart on the show header and use the offset shown at right.

The problem began when home color television set makers figured that they could sell more TVs if the sets had brighter pictures. The easiest way to make brighter pictures was to make the color temperature colder. So they abandoned the 6500 degree K standard and produced TV sets at a frigid looking 9000 degree K or colder.

Warming the image by white balancing to a CamWarm or White'nWarm helps to compensate. It is ironic that TV set makers are now producing sets with optional D65 settings, while many shooters and DPs, even network shows, are using CamWarms to warm their images.

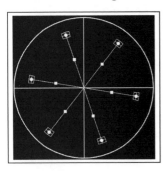

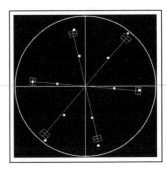

<<<<< SDat709.

>>>>> SDat240M.

Left Vectorscope shows CamAlign colors adjusted for ITU BT-709 (SMPTE 274) colorimetry on SD system. To make a dub to SD on SMPTE 240M colorimetry use offset at right.

I'm shooting for digital cinema and HDTV, but the show will also be shown on NTSC - should I have any colorimetry concerns?

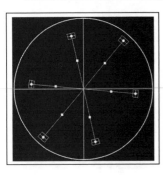

<<<<< HDat709.

>>>>> HDat240M.

Left Vectorscope shows CamAlign colors adjusted for ITU BT-709 (SMPTE 274) colorimetry on HD system. It is unlikely you would want to do it, but to make a dub to HD using SMPTE 240M colorimetry use offset at right.

Possibly, but it depends on the sophistication of the equipment used in making the transfer.

To make accurate transfers the technical problems are significant, because the derivation of luma and encoding are different in the two systems. For this reason, making an accurate NTSC copy from HD requires enormous computing power.

First HD encoding has to be stripped out and the signal reduced to RGB, then new luma values have to be applied with different encoding to produce the NTSC signal.

Calibrated Vectorscope simulations showing where 709 color signals should appear in NTSC or SD systems are available for CamAlign and Combi colorbar/grayscale patterns. The Waveform and Vectorscope simulations can be very helpful to the colorist or engineer during the transfer providing a few reference frames of the colorbar/grayscale have been recorded at the head of a show. Note the differences between Vectorscope graticules used on NTSC, SD and HD.

Should I align a camera differently when shooting for international distribution?
North America generally prefers a larger-than-life look with more saturated colors. Europeans seem to prefer a more true-to-life look. I have heard of million-dollar sales to Europe being lost because the show had too little range and too much "Zap."

Digital imaging can make great-looking pictures, but you need to use all the "digits" in the system, being careful not to drop any off the end. If you align for a full grayscale, mid-saturated picture, you will have a more flexible image to work with in post. Generally speaking, contrast and saturation can be more successfully increased than reduced.

What is the difference between a 9-step and 11-step grayscale?

>>>>> 9-step NTSCWForm.
The 9-step has a 20:1 contrast ratio with the white chip reflecting 60% of the light. The 11-step has a theoretical 50:1 contrast ratio, with the white chip reflecting 80-90%. Note, 11-step matte grayscales seldom exceed 20:1.

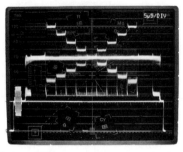

Either can be used if the operator is aware of the differences; bear in mind that the gamma curves are different. In fact, every manufacturer's 11-step chart we have measured had significant differences in the gamma curve.

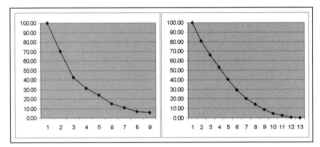

<<<<<
9-step, 11-step Prichard.
Prichard spectroradiometer readings made from two widely used grayscale charts.

Left - typical 9-step matte chart. Right - 11-step glossy CamAlign. Note the low reflectance of steps 12 and 13 on the CamAlign chart (TrueBlack and CaviBlack steps.) CamAlign's high-gloss black chips are almost as black as CaviBlack (step 13), the ultimate cavity black.

Other important chart considerations.
Few grayscale charts are truly neutral across the grayscale.
White chips are usually more yellow than the other chips.
Black ink or pigments frequently reflect a high IR level.

The importance of chart neutrality cannot be over emphasized. By aligning a camera to a chart having color bias across the grayscale will result in the camera shooting images with a corresponding, but opposite color bias. The Waveform displays below show a camera aligned to a truly neutral grayscale.

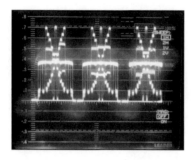

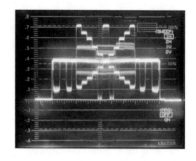

>>>>> 11-step WformRGB.   >>>>> 11-stepWformRGBCombined.

Waveform at left shows sequential RGB display of CamAlign chart from 720P camera. Right Waveform shows RGB signals superimposed and excellent color tracking of camera.

Bottom Line
Good charts are probably the best investment you will ever make. They will help you generate the best possible signal under a wide range of conditions. However, it's better to use factory presets than to risk your reputation using inaccurate charts. Final thought — test patterns do not last forever; replace them every couple of years, earlier if they have been working hard. Like the rest of us, they will change with age, and not for the better, I guarantee it!

16 ⟫ USING A LIGHT METER

by Bill Holshevnikoff

One of the more common questions that I received from the last edition of this book was with regard to using a light meter. Since I've used one almost my entire life, I took it for granted that they were self explanatory. Apparently not... so, rather than reinvent the wheel, I am including a lovely, soup-to-nuts tutorial from one of the best lighting guys in the industry.

I'll admit that setting your shot by using a high-quality monitor is both easy and fast, but all that you're seeing is the results. What happens if your monitor goes down, or you need to shoot something out on location where there isn't even electricity? There are many times when a firm grasp of essential methodology will save your ass. By learning how to expose a correct image, you start to understand lighting ratios on a fundamental level, and nothing will elevate your craft more than that.

<<<<< **Bill Holshevnikoff.**
I feel that it is appropriate that Bill gets the only formal, studio portrait in the entire book.

Bill Holshevnikoff has been lighting and shooting award-winning shots for nearly 15 years. His *Power of Lighting* seminars and video series, as well as his countless articles for magazines such as such as *American Cinematographer* and *Video Systems Magazine,* have helped many to generate far more professional-looking shots. Bill was kind enough to crank out this chapter so that anyone with the desire to create cinematic excellence, regardless of the format, now has the guidance to do so.

The use of light meters is a subject that many professional videographers are unfamiliar with. Due to the automatic exposure system designed into video cameras, it is not necessary for today's videographer to understand or use a meter for most circumstances. But a light meter is a very important tool to understand, and there are many ways that a meter can be used when working with video. More importantly, if you wish to work in film, you should have a thorough understanding of meters and the use of the gray scale. This column is designed to provide you with the basics about the use of meters with video and film.

There are two basic types of meters; an incident meter and a reflected light, or spot, meter. The two meters measure and calculate light readings in different ways, and consequently the information that each meter provides must be used properly by the camera person. Before we discuss how each meter works, we should first explain several things about the mechanics of meters, and how they can be used to work with film or video.

<<<<<   Many of the newer
light meters like this Sekonic L-508,
include both spot and incident
metering capabilities.

Light can be quantified in several different ways; f-stops, footcandles, lux, etc. The meters shown in this article are digital meters that show light readings in f-stops, which makes sense to me because cameras work in f-stops also. Some meters measure light in footcandles, which is then translated into f-stops. A footcandle is a measurement of light that theoretically equals the amount of light received from one candle at a distance of one foot. Lux is the European equivalent of footcandles. For the purpose of the article, we will use f-stops as the standard measurement of light.

There is some information that the meter must "know" before you can accurately use a meter. Let's begin with the shutter speed. If you are shooting video, you should set the meter to 1/60th of a second. The reason for this is that there are 30 frames of video per each second of tape, but there are two fields of video per each frame. Therefore, there are 60 fields of video for each second, and one field takes approximately 1/60th of a second to expose.

If you are shooting film, most often you will shoot at either 24 frames-per-second (fps) or 30 fps. If you are shooting at 30 fps, you should set the meter at 1/60th. Unlike video, the reason for this is that each of the 30 times that a frame of film is exposed, the camera shutter opens to expose the film and then closes while the film is advanced to the next frame. Half the time the shutter is open and half the time it is closed. The exposure time is actually only half the time for each of the 30 frames, so your exposure for 30 fps would 1/60th of a second. If you're shooting at 24 fps, the same logic will bring us to a shutter speed of 1/50th of a second.

Once you have set the proper shutter speed on the meter, you must then set the meter for light sensitivity. The light sensitivity rating, or ISO rating, is a numerical value that rates how sensitive the film stock is to light. Some films are very sensitive to light and require very little light to make an exposure, and some are very "slow" films which require a great deal of light. You must set the meter with the appropriate ISO rating so that the meter will "see" light the same way the film or video camera does.

If ISO numbers confuse you, think about the film we all use to shoot snap-shots at home. Most people today are using an ISO 100 or 200 film. The major difference between these films is that the ISO 200 film is twice as sensitive to light as the ISO 100 film. ISO 400 film is four times more sensitive to light than the 100 film. ISO 50 film is only half as sensitive as ISO 100 film. Generally, the size of the grain in the film affects how quickly light is absorbed. The higher speed films usually have larger films grains, so they can absorb light quicker, and we call that a faster film. These ISO numbers, which used to be referred to as ASA, are just a relative rating system for film stock light sensitivity.

So now that you've set the meter properly and are ready to shoot, you might be wondering which meter is best for what, and how to use them. As previously mentioned, there are two basic types of meters; an incident meter and a reflected light, or spot, meter.

Incident Meter: An incident light meter is used to measure the amount of light falling on the subject area. Incident light is light coming from the source before it strikes a subject or surface. When placed in front of the subject, with the dome of the meter facing the main light source and/or the camera, an incident meter will measure the amount of light striking the subject area by averaging light and shadow values.

>>>>> The GOSSEN DigiSix incident light meter is a
vicious new competitor for the "tiny available light"
segment of meters. At a street price under $100,
your list of excuses just ran out.

If you set your aperture (iris) at the f-stop reading that the meter shows, the diffused value (true tone) of the subject should be accurately reproduced onto film or tape. All other shadow and highlight values that fall within the same main light area also will be accurately reproduced. It's as if there were a hypothetical gray scale in the meter. If you do what the meter tells you to do, any middle gray tone in the scene will be exposed as middle gray, white will be white, and black will expose properly as black.

The incident meter is used primarily to meter subject areas. Whether you're shooting film or tape, this meter can be useful to check consistency on a set, such as check the light levels at each chair on a news set or talk show. An incident meter also can be used to check light levels on a drama or comedy set, such as checking a crossing area for an actor. The meter will accurately show you relative light levels anywhere on a set or stage, or outdoors. But what if you need to meter a window behind an actor, or the brightness of a cloud in the sky?

Reflected Light (spot) Meter: Reflected light is light after it has bounced off of a subject or surface. Because so many surfaces reflect and absorb light differently, a reflected light, or spot, meter is a very useful tool to measure light returning from any surface, near or far. Used from camera position, you simply look through the meter's eyepiece, much like a 35mm camera, and select the area that you wish to measure.

<<<<< The Minolta LS-100 Spot Meter
has a very small circle (one-degree angle of acceptance)
in the eyepiece for targeting your light measurement,
thus the name spot meter. It is also equipped with
2-WAY RS232 Communication making it easy
to log exposure data to your computer. Toys, toys, toys...

These meters measure the amount of light reflecting off of any area in the scene, or even the brightness of a light source (candle, lighted sign, etc.), and they should be used right next to the camera lens. That way your meter will see any reflected light exactly as the camera sees it. But, like the incident meter, the spot meter is unable to determine the tone of the surface that you're metering. It doesn't know what you're pointing at. Therefore, this meter "assumes" that the surface measured will reflect 18% of the incident light. In other words, if you set your aperture (iris) at the reading that the spot meter shows, that surface will reproduce on film or tape at an 18% (middle gray) tone. Regardless if the surface is black, white, or any color, a reflective meter will provide you with a reading that will reproduce that tone at an 18% midtone. Using that reading, it is then your job to determine at what tonal value the surface should be placed for accurate reproduction onto film or tape.

Confused?! Once you have taken your meter reading off of a white wall or cloud, for instance, you then need to figure out how much you need to open up your aperture from what the meter tells you, to achieve a white surface on film. The meter will tell you how to make that white surface a middle gray, so you need to then open your iris maybe 2 full f-stops from the meter reading to end up with a white wall or cloud on film. If the wall were black, the meter would tell you how to make the wall gray on film, so you need to check the gray scale and close down your aperture maybe 2-1/2 to 3 f-stops to achieve black on film.

Another example might be metering a Caucasian face. The spot meter will tell you how to make the skin tone a middle gray, but you want the skin to read about one-stop brighter than 18% gray (in most cases). Take the reading off of the skin (i.e., f-5.6), then open up one stop from where the reading says (to f-4.0). If, by chance, the area you were metering was an 18% gray tone (tone, not color), then you would just set the camera aperture where the meter indicated to get an accurate middle gray tone on film. Many shooters just hold an 18% gray card in any area to meter the light, and they then just set the camera to what the meter says. No calculations necessary. The spot meter is a bit more complex to understand, but is can also be a much more valuable tool for the serious filmmaker. The gray scale provided here is just a reference. Use a proper gray scale as an accurate reference when using a meter.

Okay, back now to the ISO question: what if you are shooting video? What ISO rating do you use to set the meter to match your video camera sensitivity? An easy way to determine an ISO rating for your camera is to set up a chip chart or gray scale and illuminate the chart with light as you normally would. It's best to use a Waveform Monitor for a proper setup. Once you've achieved a proper exposure of the chart, mark the iris setting on your camera and lock the iris. We'll say it was f-2.8. Now meter the middle gray area on the chart with your spot meter, and keep changing the ISO setting on your meter until the meter reads the same f-stop as your camera is reading. Once the f-stop on the meter matches the camera, you have found the ISO rating for your camera. Many of the new ENG camcorders rate at either ISO 320 or 400, which is very light sensitive.

<<<<< With its bright yellow case you can see this high-end cine meter coming from a distance. Designed especially for cinematographers, the Spectra P-2000EL-A reads both incident and reflected light, measures foot-candles and lux, and reads out in both Frames per Second and Shutter Speeds.

A word of caution: At times I have metered for video and the camera's internal auto-iris system does not agree with my meter. With video, I use an incident meter most often to check relative values, such as the chairs at a news desk. What is most important is that the areas in your set are consistent. If the video iris setting turns out to be slightly different than my meter reading, that's okay, and I go with what looks best on the scopes and on the monitors.

Finally, if you're completely confused after reading this, read it many more times, and then you need to run some tests on film. But who has an extra 35mm or 16mm film camera laying around, with a bunch of money for film, processing, and transfers to video tape. Bad excuse! Film is film, for the most part, so take your 35mm still camera, a roll or two of slide film and your meters, and start learning. Bring a note pad and take detailed notes as to each meter reading and how you shot each frame.

Don't shoot print film, because your local one-hour lab will fix all of your mistakes and you'll think you're a genius your first time out. With slide film, what you shoot is what you'll see, and making mistakes is an important part of learning to use a meter. You just don't want to make mistakes on your client's projects. Also, ask that the slide mounts be marked with frame numbers, or just don't have the slide film mounted. You'll end up with a long roll of images, and you then can check the frame numbers with your notes. If you don't have a meter, you can rent one from a photo shop for a reasonable rate. And if you think you might never have a reason to use a meter, at least now you know what those black things do that the camera person uses. Good Luck!

17 ⋗ HI-DEFINITION GUIDEBOOK

I've been pestering my friend Sean to write his own book on Hi-Definition production for several years, but like so many people who should be writing books, he's just too busy shooting. As I mentioned previously, Sean and I quite often end up on the same projects where one or both of us is shooting or engineering, or some combination thereof.

<<<<< Your basic
Sean Fairburn SOC.

Over the course of several years, I've managed to wrangle a good deal of hard data from Sean. He is always quick to point out that he in turn wrangled it from people like Jeff Cree, who is Sony's official HD guru, and Harry Mathias, who is a Director of Photography and author of *Electronic Cinematography*, and Steve Lucas, who is the chief engineer at Wexler and has held many of our hands as we ventured off into the esoteric world of HD.

So, with a "Top O'The Howdy" to Sean Fairburn and a tip of the hat to Jeff Cree, Harry Mathias, Charles Caillouet, Pete Fasciano, Steve Lucas, Dave Canning, Barry Rebo, Marc Shubin and all the HD pioneers, here is my best attempt to render down what should be a book in itself.

HD PRODUCTION
1.) Shoot 23.98P not 24P or you will have difficulty down converting and keeping sound in sync.
2.) You don't need to off-line in HD. Down convert your footage to DigiBeta or Beta SP and off-line conventionally.
3.) Running time of HD Tape is 50 minutes @ 23.98 even though the box will say 40 minutes (40 & 22 minute tapes are available for field use).
4.) The average cost of one HDCAM tape is $80.00. They come in a case of 10.
5.) Record the master sound on the HD tape in addition to external recording devices (which should be running at 29.97 NDF).

6.) By shooting this way, you will save money by skipping timing and syncing of dailies. This step is replaced with down-converting.
7.) Editing of dissolves, CGI, Slow motion effects and titling can all be done in the final HD online session to create the final HD master.
8.) HD camera packages will be more expensive to rent than film packages. The savings is in HD tape vs. the purchase, processing and transfer of rolls of film. One HD tape equals 5,000 feet of film run time.
9.) Transfer only your final edited HD show to film. This step may cost around $60,000 for an entire feature.
10.) The money savings is in the production medium and post, not in personnel.

HD PRIMER FOR THE DIRECTOR OF PHOTOGRAPHY
1.) HD exposes like color reversal film (slide film rather than negative)
2.) HD has less latitude than film (4.5 under and 1.5-ish over).
3.) HD has much more bottom end in the blacks than top end in the highlights, so it's better to underexpose than overexpose.
4.) You can time your image in camera, which will give you more range than had you done nothing to the image. *The best way to get to a good image is to start with one.*
5.) You can do a digital color-correction session after the picture is locked, then again after it gets filmed out, but you lose colorspace every time.
6.) HD is tungsten-balanced, so ND and color-correction filters are built into the camera, as are ND.6, ND1.2 and ND2.4, and also an 85B and 81B.
7.) The electronic shutter set to ON at 1/48th is equal to a 180° shutter. Shutter OFF increases blur in motion equal to 24 fps at 1/24th.
8.) Like any new film stock, <u>TEST</u> to determine how your lighting style looks with this medium.
9.) Make sure your First ACs and operators know how to properly set the back focus, or your images will be soft. *Check back focus before every setup.*
10.) Shoot Record-Run-Time code, even if you use multiple cameras. Cameras do not need to match TC for post to sync it up, but it creates more problems than its worth to shoot Free Running TC.

HD PRIMER FOR THE SOUND DEPARTMENT
1.) Record master sound on the HD Camera. This will create a permanent synced source of CD quality sound for down converts and off-line.
2.) Always record sound separately as well.

3.)   Always listen to the sound coming from the HD deck, You'll need a five-pin XLR for discrete Ch-1 and Ch-2 return.

4.)   Whether you chose to record on Nagra, DAT, DA88, or DEVA, use 29.97 NDF (Non Drop Frame).

5.)   Use of a time code slate is helpful, with the time code being YOURS, not the cameras. In addition, have Second ACs clap the sticks as always.

6.)   Also very helpful is feeding your time code into an available channel of audio on the camera with a Deneke Brain (Is this the right term? Couldn't find any references to it…). It's wireless and provides a permanent source of sync for the external sound recording device.

While this is not a complete and bullet-proof list, it will keep you from screwing up too badly on your first venture into HD.

SETTING YOUR BACK FOCUS
Back focus is a vital step in the effective setup and operation of the lens. Poor back focus alignment is also the most common mistake that people new to HD make. Ive seen several movies that were shot entirely without attention to back focus calibration that had to be abandoned in Post.

The essential purpose of the back focus is to align the rear element of the lens so that it focuses the image on the faces of the CCDs. In principal, this is similar to adjusting the flange focal depth for a film camera; in practice it is much easier and faster.

The First AC and the Camera Operator should ideally perform a back focus:
- With every lens as part of the prep.
- At the start of each day.
- Every time you change a lens, especially to a wide-angle zoom.
- Any time the camera or lens undergoes a significant temperature change (e.g. moving from a lit set to a night exterior). Wait until the camera has had a chance to stabilize at the new temperature.
- After transporting a camera with the lens attached.

Here's How:
1.)   Remove all diffusion and filtration.

2.)   Set the back focus chart flat to the film plane beyond minimum focus at eight feet out. For wide-angle lenses, move the chart to four feet, and for long lenses, ten feet.

3.)   Open the iris wide and use shutter to darken if the target blows out.

4.)   Zoom in if you are using a zoom and focus on the chart till it is crisp.

5.)   To help you see the focus, turn both the Peaking knob and the Contrast on the viewfinder UP and turn the Brightness down.

6.)   Zoom out and look at the target. It should still look crisp. If it looks soft, loosen the locking screw and turn the back focus ring back and forth, passing in and out of focus to find the place where it is most crisp. Then tighten the locking screw back down.

7.)   Zoom back in and check the whole range of the zoom. If it's soft at the wide, repeat steps three and four. When the back focus looks crisp through the entire range of the zoom, you are good to go. If not, ensure the lens is seated properly and the retaining ring is tight, then repeat steps.

8.)   Reset the Viewfinder back to normal.

Prime Lenses should be adjusted as well by running a tape measure out from the witness mark, one inch behind the lens, and setting focus on the barrel to that distance. Then adjust the back focus to get the chart crisp.

RATING YOUR CAMERAS ASA

HD cameras using ENG video style lenses will generally have a feature that allows you to automatically expose the frame. While this auto system is far better than the systems found in consumer MiniDV camcorders, it is still a video tool, and the object here is to develop a cinematic methodology.

Turn it off!

Professionals use manual exposure and with cine-style lenses, auto-exposure is not even an option. While the use of an on-set or on-location monitor is a great tool for composing and setting a shot, proper exposure is best evaluated using a light meter or Waveform Monitor.

NECESSARY TOOLS INCLUDE:
Camera with shooting lens.
Light meters (spot and Incident).
18% Gray Card.
DSC Labs chart with 11-step chip.
HD Waveform Monitor.
HD monitor (properly tweaked).
Down-converter and all monitors (HD or NTSC) going into the field.
A large, even light source positioned close to camera (flat light).
A person possessing good skin tone (preferably leading lady).
Common sense and gut instinct on how things should look.

Once you have all your elements:
Set the camera up using No Gain, No ND, DCC or Auto Knee OFF in Tungsten light with no internal or external filter.
Turn shutter OFF (even though you will be using the camera with it on).
Frame up the gray card at full frame (but not at the end of the lens).
Focus up and set the stop to f4.
Set your light meter to 500 ASA at 24 FPS or 1/50th of a second (actually 1/48th but many meters cannot display it).
Light the gray card to f4.

Your Waveform Monitor should now display a flat, fuzzy line. Looking at the HD monitor, open or close the iris stop until the gray card is at the basic level you want it. The line on the WFM should be hovering between 40 and 45, or whatever you want to call proper exposure.

Look at the f-stop on the lens barrel and adjust the ASA on your meter so that the f-stop matches from meter to lens. You have just rated the camera to properly expose light consistently. For me, it generally comes in around 350 ASA.

Frame up on the DSC chart and look at the crossover point on the WFM. The black chips on the chart should be at the bottom, crossover in the middle and highlights at the top.

Pan over to your live person. Does your subject look like you want? If not, put the exposure where it looks good. Look at the stop once again, make a note of it in relation to the gray card level and pan back to the chip and the gray and see how they hold up. Make note of any deviations and adjust your ASA so the f-stop matches the stop on the lens.

Proper shutter speed should be set at whatever you want to call normal, in most cases shooting 24P "Normal" is equal to 180° shutter angle or 1/48.

Based on a 23.98 or 24Psf Base

1/24th	=360°	Wide Open	+1
1/30th	=315°	Qtr Stop	+3/4
1/36th	=270°	Half Stop	+1/2
1/42nd	=225°	Qtr Stop	+1/4
1/48th	=180°	One Stop	BASE
1/72th	=135°	Half Stop	-1/2
1/96th	= 90°	One Stop	-1
1/144th	=57.5°	Half Stop	-1.5
1/192th	=45°	One Stop	-2
1/288th	=33.75°	Half Stop	-2.5
1/384th	=22.5°	One Stop	-3
1/576th	=17°	Half Stop	-3.5
1/768th	=11°	One Stop	-4
1/1152th	=8.25°	Half Stop	-4.5
1/1536th	=5.5°	One Stop	-5
1/2304th	=2.75°	Half Stop	-5.5

Changing your shutter angle from 180° to 90° reduces motion blur and cuts the amount of light by one stop. If your ASA was 500 it is now 250.

Have your model move around and look from side to side and bring some hand movements into frame. Turn ON the shutter and decide what shutter speed/shutter angle you want to shoot at.

Once you've determined your baseline ASA, build a label with gaffer tape and a Sharpie, and stick it to the smart side of your cameras. An average baseline may look something like this:

250 ASA Base Tungsten 180° shutter or 1/48th Sec, No Gain, No ND.

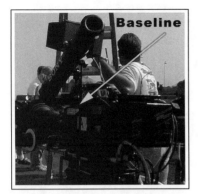

<<<<< The smart side of an HDCAM with the baseline tape marking.

You should re-rate your cameras every time you modify or change your look.

Once you have established your baseline, shoot an exposure test three stops over and three to five stops under your ASA rating. This will help you become more familiar with the HD medium and its limitations, as well as developing a comfort zone as to how far off road you can go before the beast comes back to bite you.

In the end, the final look that you decide upon should be chosen using your eye, light meter, Waveform, and HD monitor, and don't forget to down-convert it and view it on more commercial monitors as well.

Film Directing: Shot by Shot
Visualizing from Concept to Screen

Steven D. Katz

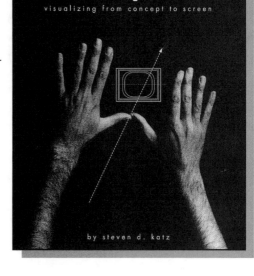

An instant classic since its debut in 1991, "Film Directing: Shot by Shot" and its famous blue cover is one of the most well-known books on directing in the business, and is a favorite of professional directors as an on-set quick reference guide. This international bestseller is packed with visual techniques for filmmakers and screenwriters to expand their stylistic knowledge.

Contains in-depth information on shot composition, staging sequences, previsualization, depth of frame, camera techniques, and much more.

Contains over 750 storyboards and illustrations, including never before published storyboards from Steven Spielberg's *Empire of the Sun*, Orson Welles' *Citizen Kane*, and Alfred Hitchcock's *The Birds*.

> "(To become a director) you have to teach yourself what makes movies good and what makes them bad. John Singleton has been my mentor...he's the one who told me what movies to watch and to read the book Shot by Shot."
> **Ice Cube**, Rap artist, actor and filmmaker
> Quoted in *The New York Times*, April 16, 1998

Doubleday Stage & Screen Book Club Selection
Movie Entertainment Book Club Selection

$27.95, ISBN: 0-941188-10-8
370 pages, 7 x 10, 750+ illus.
Order # 7RLS

Both Katz books only $44

THE WRITER'S JOURNEY
2nd Edition
Mythic Structure for Writers

Christopher Vogler

Over 100,000 units sold!

See why this book has become an international bestseller and a true classic. *The Writer's Journey* explores the powerful relationship between mythology and storytelling in a clear, concise style that's made it required reading for movie executives, screenwriters, playwrights, scholars, and fans of pop culture all over the world.

Both fiction and nonfiction writers will discover a set of useful myth-inspired storytelling paradigms (i.e., "The Hero's Journey") and step-by-step guidelines to plot and character development. Based on the work of Joseph Campbell, *The Writer's Journey* is a must for all writers interested in further developing their craft.

The updated and revised second edition provides new insights and observations from Vogler's ongoing work on mythology's influence on stories, movies, and man himself.

"This book is like having the smartest person in the story meeting come home with you and whisper what to do in your ear as you write a screenplay. Insight for insight, step for step, Chris Vogler takes us through the process of connecting theme to story and making a script come alive."
> — Lynda Obst, Producer
> *Sleepless in Seattle, Contact, Someone Like You*
> Author, *Hello, He Lied*

Christopher Vogler, a top Hollywood story consultant and development executive, has worked on such high-grossing feature films as *The Lion King* and conducts writing workshops around the globe.

$24.95, 325 pages
Order #98RLS
ISBN: 0-941188-70-1

SETTING UP YOUR SHOTS
Great Camera Moves Every Filmmaker Should Know

Jeremy Vineyard

Written in straightforward, non-technical language and laid out in a nonlinear format with self-contained chapters for quick, on-the-set reference, *Setting Up Your Shots* is like a Swiss army knife for filmmakers! Using examples from over 140 popular films, this book provides detailed descriptions of more than 100 camera setups, angles, and techniques — in an easy-to-use horizontal "wide-screen" format.

Setting Up Your Shots is an excellent primer for beginning filmmakers and students of film theory, as well as a handy guide for working filmmakers. If you are a director, a storyboard artist, or an animator, use this book. It is the culmination of hundreds of hours of research.

Contains 150 references to the great shots from your favorite films, including *2001: A Space Odyssey*, *Blue Velvet*, *The Matrix*, *The Usual Suspects*, and *Vertigo*.

"Perfect for any film enthusiast looking for the secrets behind creating film. Because of its simplicity of design and straightforward storyboards, *Setting Up Your Shots* is destined to be mandatory reading at film schools throughout the world."
— Ross Otterman, *Directed By Magazine*

Jeremy Vineyard is a director and screenwriter who moved to Los Angeles in 1997 to pursue a feature filmmaking career. He has several spec scripts in development.

$19.95, 132 pages
Order # 8RLS
ISBN: 0-941188-73-6

Directing Actors
Creating Memorable Performances for Film & Television

Judith Weston

The most crucial relationship on a movie set is between the director responsible for the telling of a story and the actors entrusted with bringing that story's characters to life. Good communication between actor and director can mean the difference between a great film and a missed opportunity.

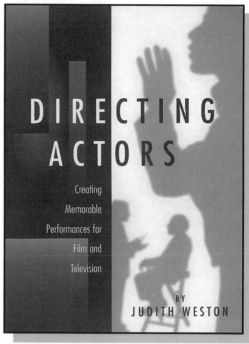

Directing Actors is a method for establishing creative, collaborative relationships between actors and directors that takes the reader on a journey through the complexities of the creative process itself. Using simple, practical tools that both directors and actors can use immediately, this book shows you how to get the most out of rehearsals, troubleshoot poor performances, and give directions that are clear, succinct and easy to follow.

"This is everything a director should know about working with actors."
Steven Charles Jaffe, Executive Producer, *Ghost*; producer, *Star Trek VI*, *Strange Days*

"I think that if Judith's book were mandatory reading for all directors, the quality of the director-actor process would be transformed, and better drama would result."
John Patterson, Director, *The Sopranos, The Practice, Law and Order, Hill Street Blues, Rockford Files*

"Judith's course is probably the single best thing you could do for yourself as a director. I was able to use the

techniques the very next day on the set. Judith has made a difference in my career."
Brian Roberts, Director, *Everybody Loves Raymond, The Drew Carey Show, King of Queens, The Hughleys*

Doubleday Stage & Screen Book Club Selection

JUDITH WESTON draws on 20 years of experience as an actress and teacher of acting. With her seminars, workshops and private consultations, she has helped thousands of actors refine their craft and nearly as many directors clarify their directing and casting choices.

$26.95, ISBN 0-941118-24-8
300 pages, 6 x 9
Order # 4RLS

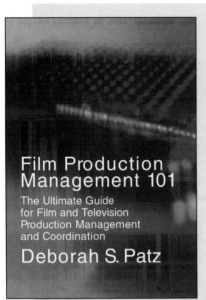

Film Production
Management 101
The Ultimate Guide
for Film and Television
Production Management
and Coordination

Deborah S. Patz

FILM PRODUCTION MANAGEMENT 101
The Ultimate Guide to Film and Television Production Management and Coordination

Deborah S. Patz

Two books in one, *Film Production Management 101* is a detailed insider's guide for managing a film or television production, covered from both the Production Manager's and the Production Coordinator's points of view.

In this greatly expanded second edition of *Surviving Production*, Deborah Patz taps into her eighteen years of independent production and studio experience to advise you from before the first day of preproduction through production and wrap, all the way into postproduction. Deborah shares detailed insights and tells it like it is. She delivers the nuts and bolts of the business in 35 in-depth chapters and 70 additional pages of essential forms (also downloadable from the Web).

Includes: how to get hired; budgeting and breakdowns; setting up the production office; how to hire crew; workspace organization; production scheduling; daily production reports; location management; production insurance and completion bonds; cast contracts; script format and revisions; customs & immigration; cost reporting; postproduction; audits; and much more.

This book is not only for production managers and production coordinators. It will also inform executive producers, producers, assistant directors, production assistants, film students, and anyone interested in knowing the true details of the business of filmmaking.

Deborah S. Patz is a filmmaker with experience in both film and television: from children's programming to science fiction extravaganzas, from video to IMAX 3D, from studio shoots to international co-productions. Deborah has arranged shoots around the world.

$39.95, 478 pages | Over 50 Production Forms, Lay Flat Binding for easy use
Order # 103RLS
ISBN: 0-941188-45-0 | **Available September 2002**

SCRIPT PARTNERS
What Makes Film and TV Writing Teams Work

Claudia Johnson & Matt Stevens

Foreword by Marshall Brickman

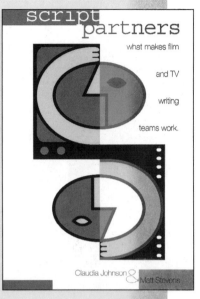

Many of the most important and successful films
and television shows of the past and the present
have been written by script partners, from Billy
Wilder's legendary collaborations with Charles
Brackett and I.A.L. Diamond to the Coen Brothers'
collaboration today; yet, no serious study exists of
this unique and important process. Of the more
than two hundred books about screenplay and
television writing available today, not one focuses
on collaborative writing.

This book brings together the experience, knowledge, techniques, and
wisdom of many of our most successful writing teams for film and television.
It examines the role and the importance of collaboration, then illuminates the
process of collaborative screenwriting itself: its unique assets, from the partners'
complementary strengths to the mysterious but often-mentioned "third voice"
that occurs during collaborative writing; why and how they choose each
other; the myriad ways that different teams work; how teams create their
ideas, choose projects, develop character, story, and structure, write scenes,
dialogue, draft the screenplay, rewrite, and how they manage and maintain
their creative relationship. At its deepest level, that's what collaborative
screenwriting is about: human relationships.

Includes interviews with such successful collaborators as Andrew Reich &
Ted Cohen (*Friends*), Jim Taylor (*Election, About Schmidt*), Marshall Brickman
(*Annie Hall, Manhattan*), Scott Alexander & Larry Karaszewski (*The People vs.
Larry Flynt, Ed Wood*), and Larry Gelbart (*M*A*S*H*).

Claudia Johnson is the author of *Stifled Laughter*, nominated for the Pulitzer
Prize, and *Crafting Short Screenplays That Connect*. Matt Stevens is a Los
Angeles-based writer/producer who has sold both fiction and documentary
projects. Two of their co-written scripts were recent finalists for the
Sundance Screenwriters Lab.

$22.95, 300 pages
Order # 104RLS | ISBN: 0-941188-75-2 | **Available February 2003**

FILM DIRECTING: CINEMATIC MOTION
A Workshop for Staging Scenes

Steven D. Katz

With this practical guide to common production problems encountered when staging and blocking film scenes directors can better develop a sense of what is the right solution for any given situation. Includes discussions of scheduling, staging without dialogue, staging in confined spaces, actor and camera choreography, sequence shots, and much more — with hundreds of storyboards and diagrams.

Some of the staging examples are technically simple, others require substantial choreography. The underlying assumption for all is that the filmmaker wants to explore the dramatic potential of the camera to the fullest, within the day's shooting schedule.

Contains illuminating interviews with these well-known professionals, commenting on the practical aspects of production: director John Sayles (*Eight Men Out*, *Lone Star*), cinematographer Allen Daviau (*ET*, *Hearts of Atlantis*), visual effects expert Van Ling (*Doctor Doolittle*, *Not Another Teen Movie*), art director Harold Michelson (*Catch-22*, *Terms of Endearment*), producer Ralph Singleton (*Clear and Present Danger*, *Juwanna Mann*), and key grip Dusty Smith (*Rounders*, *Cop Land*).

"The art of staging movies scenes hasn't been written about very extensively, so the best way to learn is by watching others at work. *Film Directing: Cinematic Motion* provides a better idea with complete illustrated staging techniques and storyboards."
— *Millimeter Magazine*

Steven D. Katz is a writer/filmmaker. His work has appeared on *Saturday Night Live*, in feature films, and in numerous film festivals around the world. He is also the author of *Film Directing: Shot by Shot*.

$24.95, 294 pages
Order # 6RLS | ISBN: 0-941188-14-0

DIGITAL FILMMAKING 101

An Essential Guide to Producing Low-Budget Movies

Dale Newton and John Gaspard

DIGITAL FILMMAKING 101
An Essential Guide to Producing Low-Budget Movies

Dale Newton and John Gaspard

The Butch Cassidy and the Sundance Kid of do-it-yourself filmmaking are back! Filmmakers Dale Newton and John Gaspard, co-authors of the classic how-to independent filmmaking manual *Persistence of Vision*, have written a new handbook for the digital age. *Digital Filmmaking 101* is your all-bases-covered guide to producing and shooting your own digital video films. It covers both technical and creative advice, from keys to writing a good script, to casting and location-securing, to lighting and low-budget visual effects. Also includes detailed information about how to shoot with digital cameras and how to use this new technology to your full advantage.

As indie veterans who have produced and directed successful independent films, Gaspard and Newton are masters at achieving high-quality results for amazingly low production costs. They'll show you how to turn financial constraints into your creative advantage — and how to get the maximum mileage out of your production budget. You'll be amazed at the ways you can save money —and even get some things for free — without sacrificing any of your final product's quality.

"These guys don't seem to have missed a thing when it comes to how to make a digital movie for peanuts. It's a helpful and funny guide for beginners and professionals alike."
> — Jonathan Demme
> Academy Award-Winning Director
> *Silence of the Lambs*

Dale Newton and John Gaspard, who hail from Minneapolis, Minnesota, have produced three ultra-low-budget, feature-length movies and have lived to tell the tales.

$24.95, 283 pages
Order # 17RLS | ISBN: 0-941188-33-7

ORDER FORM

MICHAEL WIESE PRODUCTIONS
11288 VENTURA BLVD., # 621
STUDIO CITY, CA 91604
E-MAIL: MWPSALES@MWP.COM
WEB SITE: WWW.MWP.COM

WRITE OR FAX FOR A FREE CATALOG

PLEASE SEND ME THE FOLLOWING BOOKS:

TITLE	ORDER NUMBER (#RLS _____)	AMOUNT
_____	_____	_____
_____	_____	_____
_____	_____	_____
_____	_____	_____
_____	_____	_____
	SHIPPING	_____
	CALIFORNIA TAX (8.00%)	_____
	TOTAL ENCLOSED	_____

PLEASE MAKE CHECK OR MONEY ORDER PAYABLE TO:

MICHAEL WIESE PRODUCTIONS

(CHECK ONE) ____ MASTERCARD ____VISA ____AMEX

CREDIT CARD NUMBER _____

EXPIRATION DATE _____

CARDHOLDER'S NAME _____

CARDHOLDER'S SIGNATURE _____

SHIP TO:

NAME _____

ADDRESS _____

CITY _____ STATE _____ ZIP _____

COUNTRY _____ TELEPHONE _____